SUBSTANCE ABUSE PREVENTION HANDBOOK

SUBSTANCE ABUSE PREVENTION HANDBOOK

Dr. William L. Callison
Professor of Educational Administration
California State University at Fullerton

Dr. Nancy R. Colocino
Director of Guidance Resources
Irvine Unified School District, Irvine, California

Ms. Diva Abel Vasquez
Walnut Valley Unified School District, Walnut, California

TECHNOMIC
PUBLISHING CO., INC

LANCASTER · BASEL

Substance Abuse Prevention Handbook
a **TECHNOMIC** publication

Published in the Western Hemisphere by
Technomic Publishing Company, Inc.
851 New Holland Avenue, Box 3535
Lancaster, Pennsylvania 17604 U.S.A.

Distributed in the Rest of the World by
Technomic Publishing AG
Missionsstrasse 44
CH-4055 Basel, Switzerland

Printed in the United States of America
10 9 8 7 6 5 4 3 2 1

Main entry under title:
  Substance Abuse Prevention Handbook

A Technomic Publishing Company book
Bibliography: p. 367
Includes index p. 377

Library of Congress Catalog Card No. 95-60050
ISBN No. 1-56676-238-3

To all those school staff who spend time each day working with students who are or who may become substance abusers

Contents

10. ALCOHOL AND OTHER DRUG PREVENTION PROGRAM COMPONENTS   161

11. ASSESSING PRESENT PROGRAMS FOR REDUCTION OF ABUSE   181

This book will change behavior. Designed to reach, ultimately, the behavior of students, it must first reach the minds of teachers and administrators. Whether your school is beginning an attack on substance abuse and dropouts or is in the middle of the struggle, this book will give you guidance and stir up your courage and confidence.

How does one combine into a single highly readable book the undergirding of scientific research with an awareness of the daily, hands-on problems of running a school? Well, it isn't easy. Callison, Colocino, and Vasquez, in their *Substance Abuse Prevention Handbook*, have succeeded. They have been in the struggle for many years, both in research and in face-to-face relationships with students, and have produced a book of good practice based upon sound theory.

Hardly a person in America does not believe that the schools should "do something" about substance abuse. Although conceding that this problem transcends the classroom, most people want the schools to act and, in many communities, are willing to foot the bill. Turning their conviction into action, however, brings them up short. But the problem is not intractable. Solutions have been found, and there have been successes. At this point, I invite the reader to turn to the table of contents, with its concise previews of the material to be treated; here, the scope, depth, and general usefulness of this work will be apparent at once.

It is not my purpose in this foreword to summarize or restate what is so effectively set forth in these pages, but to urge you to begin reading at once. No one who reads this book will return to the classroom or office unchanged.

DR. CLYDE BRESEE
Former Director of Guidance
Athens Township High School
Athens, Pennsylvania
and
Part-time Faculty in Counseling
Cornell University
Ithaca, New York

A previous book by Callison and Colocino, titled *Substance Abuse, Dropout and Gang Prevention Strategies*, published by Students-at-Risk, Inc., in 1991, was written to give school districts information about how to establish programs in all three areas of concern. It contains information about substance abuse prevention and, throughout the book, information about how to utilize technology to carry out many of the tasks connected to helping at-risk students.

The first book in this series is by Callison and is titled *Dropout Prevention Handbook: Apprenticeships and Other Solutions*, also published by Technomic Publishing Company, Inc., in 1994. It contains more than 400 pages and is filled with detail for those interested in in-depth coverage. A third book by Callison and Galvan, *Gang Prevention Handbook*, to be published by Technomic, is in progress.

This book adds a strong component of detailed information about how to plan and implement substance abuse prevention, including many interventions that have been evaluated carefully and shown to work. Evaluation is a key factor in improving programs for students at risk, and our software, which uses self-report forms, makes evaluation much easier and more economical than has been true in the past. A "before" and "after" comparison is available each year. Many interventions from around the country and, especially, from Irvine Unified School District, Irvine, California, are described. We know from firsthand experience that the interventions from Irvine dramatically limit what could be, without them, a serious substance abuse problem.

Acknowledgements

Our co-author, Nancy Richards-Colocino, is Director of Guidance Resources, Irvine Unified School District, Irvine, California. She has guided the design of some of the finest substance abuse prevention models we know about. The Guidance Resources Office has been recognized by funding agencies as a key innovator in this field. Nancy's contributions are part of Chapter 2, the Review of the Literature; Chapter 4, A System of Staff Responsibility for Student Assistance; part of Chapter 5, Placing Students in Interventions; Chapter 8, School Policies, Laws, and Programs That Reduce Alcohol and Other Drug Use; Chapter 9, A District Plan for Reducing Alcohol and Other Drug Use; Chapter 10, Alcohol and Other Drug Prevention Program Components; Chapter 11, Assessing Present Programs for Reduction of Abuse; Chapter 12, The Effective Use of Paraprofessionals in School-Based Alcohol and Other Drug Prevention Programs; and Chapter 14, Developing Cultural Competence.

Diva Vasquez is an administrator in the Walnut Valley Unified School District in Walnut, California. She has worked extensively on problems connected to hard drug use by parents which affect their children. In this book she has written Chapter 19, The Cocaine Problem; Chapter 20, Drug-Exposed Babies; and Chapter 21, Drug-Exposed Children in Elementary School.

Nancy wishes especially to acknowledge the outstanding work of her colleagues at IUSD who greatly contributed to the development and implementation of the innovative Guidance Resources programs described in her chapters. Special thanks to Dr. Bruce Givner, William Benn, Christine Honeyman, Debra Krumpholz, Marion Zenoff, Judi Confrey, Ida Lennard, and many others for their excellent writing, design, training, and implementation skills.

Chapter 1

INTRODUCTION

This book is intended to offer a clear statement of the problems schools face in helping students at risk of substance abuse and to assist them in finding solutions that have worked in many school districts.

PURPOSES OF THIS BOOK

This book is written to give school districts information about how to establish programs to prevent substance abuse and, throughout the book, information about how to utilize technology and other strategies to carry out many of the tasks connected to helping at-risk students. There is a strong component of detailed information about how to plan and implement substance abuse prevention, including many interventions that have been evaluated carefully and shown to work. Evaluation is a key factor in improving programs for students at risk, and our software, which uses self-report Scantron forms, makes evaluation much easier and more economical than has been true in the past. A "before" and "after" comparison is available each year.

We have written the book to provide schools and other interested professionals with some of the latest research and programming strategies that are being shown to be effective in reducing the use of substances among our youth. The book suggests a sequence of steps to be taken in developing strategies for reducing substance abuse. These begin with the third chapter, which deals with creating a student information system, and continues through a sequence of chapters that many districts refer to as they add detail to their prevention planning.

The Comprehensive Risk Assessment system helps districts identify students likely to abuse substances or drop out and, in the process, creates a very useful data base of problem students, which can be used by school staff in setting priorities for the allocation of time and resources within a school. This process has been simplified by the introduction of Scantron forms, which allow self-report information from students to be automatically entered into the software. This typically follows a referral from the teacher to the principal. Another innovation in the past year is the capability to automatically place students into interventions based on their characteristics. For example, a student whose family is not particularly against her use of drugs or a student who expresses anger in a disruptive manner in the classroom is scheduled for interventions that deal directly with those problems.

At-Risk Model

(*1*) Use a technology that identifies and places at-risk students in interventions using Macintosh and IBM compatible computers and Scantron scanners.

(*2*) Implement the technology so it is very easy for the principal — at a low cost.

(*3*) Train administrators to understand how to identify at-risk students, place them in appropriate interventions, and pre/postevaluate the interventions to see if they work using a scanner.

(*4*) Give an annual award, recognition, or incentive to top implementors.

Perhaps the most important step is number 4. If principals are not motivated, nothing will happen. This strategy works pretty well, as long as the benefits outweigh any additional work for present staff, which should be minimal, as step 2 indicates.

COMBINING EFFORTS TO REDUCE DROPOUT AND SUBSTANCE ABUSE AND OTHER PROBLEM BEHAVIORS

Dropout and substance abuse together are the key factors preventing students "at risk" from completing high school. There are many other situations that place students at risk, of course, such as pregnancy and child abuse, as well as emotional, learning, and social problems. Many districts are now working to integrate their established efforts for dealing with students likely to drop out with the "new" efforts in substance abuse and prevention of problem behaviors. As the research in Chapter 2 indicates, two thirds of the substance abusers drop out, so there is good reason to integrate these activities (Skager and Frith, 1989). It is important that the individuals responsible for substance abuse and dropout prevention report to the same senior administrator in order to assure sound coordination of the two efforts. As the reader will note in reading about dropout and abuse interventions later in the book, there is a considerable overlap in the behaviors of the dropout and the abuser, such as poor attendance, low grades, and poor self-image, and, consequently, both types of students will be placed in interventions that address these problems in a well-run system.

SUBSTANCE ABUSE

Students report pressure from peers to use drugs and alcohol in elementary school as early as fourth grade. These young people are at risk not only because of pressure from peers but because substance abuse has been shown by research to be a symptom of socioeconomic deprivation, parental abuse or neglect, inadequate health care, and cultural alienation (Goplerud, 1990).

It is important for educators to understand that our best hope for success with young people with a tendency toward substance abuse and other problem behaviors is to intervene early. This requires us to identify potential abusers through indicators such as disruptive behaviors, defiance of rules, hyperactivity, nervousness, talk about drugs, avoidance of contact with others, depression, and irritability, to name some predictors. Characteristics such as frequent drunkenness; friends who use alcohol, marijuana, and other drugs; drug sale offenses; pick-ups by police; and sales of drugs have been used by some districts to identify abusers.

To identify students as early as possible, the model we use for substance abuse prevention is adapted, in part, from a model used for dropout prediction developed by Sappington (1979). One can predict potential dropout at the fourth, sixth, and ninth grades with an accuracy rate of 79% or better. Student characteristics used are all available in the student's cumulative file. They include absences, grades, reading scores, mobility, citizenship, juvenile delinquency, special education history, physical disability, and grade retention. In order to save money and staff time, students self-report this information on a Scantron form, which then places the data in the comprehensive risk assessment software automatically, beginning at grade 3.

Our substance abuse prevention model is also based on Hawkins and Catalano's model of risk and protective factors (1989), which is detailed further in Chapter 2. To identify abusers as early as grade 3, we have software that uses factors such as family use of alcohol and drugs, friends use of alcohol and drugs, level of parental information about student whereabouts after school, frequency of anger, family attitude toward use of drugs, school suspensions/expulsions, and arrest record (Callison et al., 1990).

In addition to efforts to identify at-risk students, the risk and protective factor model is used to design interventions that increase protective factors and/or decrease risk factors in the important domains of individual, peer, family, school, and community. An example of these interventions is listed next with more complete descriptions found in Chapter 5 and other chapters.

TYPES OF SUBSTANCE ABUSE PREVENTION PROGRAMS

Peer Risk	Peer Interventions
Association with friends who use alcohol and other drugs	Increase bonding to positive peers and decrease bonding to negative influences, e.g., peer assistance programs, support groups, and drug-free clubs

These interventions can be found in programs such as Peer Assistance Leadership and Conflict Resolution. The barriers to achievement that lead to abuse may be attitudes, and attitudes can be changed by peers who have skill in communication and sensitivity. In Chapter 17, we describe the Peer Assistance Leadership (PAL) program, which is built around peer counseling and facilitation, and the peer assistant software, which is designed to help students help each other become aware of the consequences of drug use.

Family Risk	Family Interventions
Unclear messages by parents about their children's drug and alcohol use and lack of supervision	Parent training on norm setting, communication, and family management

These interventions can be found in programs such as Counseling, Neighborhoods in Action, Preparing for the Drug-Free Years, and Active Parenting of Teens. Descriptions of parent programs can be found in Chapter 9.

School Risk	School Interventions
Academic failure and lack of attachment to school	Tutoring, student study team, computer-assisted learning, portfolios, work experience, community service, teaching social and emotional skills (e.g., STAR and STAGES)

These interventions can be found described in Chapters 4 through 9.

We need to focus not only on substance abuse and dropout prediction much earlier in the student's school career, but look as well at the type and amount of contact students have with their teachers. In many school districts, our elementary and middle/junior high schools have become large and, often, impersonal. This is especially true for students who don't do well in the typical school environment.

Many districts like to place their initial thrust at the middle school level because 1) the problem behaviors are quite visible at this age, unlike the elementary level, and 2) substantial success can be achieved in these grades, whereas there is less payoff in later years. The following set of general educational recommendations are aimed at middle school students at risk, but they certainly would benefit all students at risk (Report of the Superintendent's Middle Grade Task Force, 1987).

Middle School Task Force Recommendations for Students At Risk

(*1*) Local school boards should mandate at least one extended time block daily in two or more of the core curriculum subjects during the middle grades to ensure that
  • Every middle grade student is known personally and well by one or more teachers.
  • Individual monitoring of student progress takes place systematically so that teachers and counselors can quickly identify learning difficulties and take corrective measures.

- Cooperative learning strategies are implemented as a means of building strong, positive peer group relationships and reinforcing essential educational values and goals.

(2) Superintendents should give leadership in helping principals devise means for reducing the pressure of large, complex schools, which leaves many students with a sense of anonymity and isolation. Particular attention should be given to organizational and scheduling concepts that are student-centered and that maximize opportunities for strong personal bonds among smaller numbers of students and teachers throughout the full span of the middle grade years.

(3) Local school boards should authorize and fund peer, cross-age, and/or adult tutorial and mentor programs in the middle grades as a proven response to the needs of many at-risk students.

(4) The state department of education and local district curriculum departments should assist teachers in devising instructional strategies that allow students with basic skills deficiencies to engage in learning experiences that develop higher order thinking skills; these strategies should correspond with core curriculum goals and should enable students to learn in regular classrooms. Learning experiences should be consistent with the maturity and interest levels of young adolescents.

(5) Principals should give leadership in creating cultural support systems for students—particularly those with limited English-proficiency—whose self-identify is threatened through the loss and implicit devaluing of their native language; teachers and counselors should understand the psychological trauma involved in the transition from one language to another and the bearing that this phenomenon has on the negative attitudes and values of some categories of at-risk students.

(6) Teachers, counselors, and principals should continuously model behavior that affirms their commitment to the basic mission of those who work in the middle grades: to enjoy young adolescents and to create conditions for academic success and educational commitment for every student (Report of the Superintendent's Middle Grade Task Force, 1987).

As we consider students at risk, we need to think of those involved in substance abuse, as well as those prone to drop out. A list of characteristics of students who have become involved in substance abuse was

Catching up on Skill Deficiencies.

mentioned above, as were the characteristics of dropouts. Our efforts to identify students with these characteristics will pay off handsomely if we can provide them with opportunities that have meaning for them in our school programs.

PREVIEW OF THE BALANCE OF THE BOOK

We turn now to Chapter 2, a literature review where we will discuss research relevant to the needs of students at risk. Chapter 3 discusses means for setting up a student information system, a key step in improving attendance and identifying at-risk students. Chapter 4 describes staff responsibilities for student assistance using the student study team model. Chapter 5 illustrates a seamless system for identification and placement of at-risk students in interventions. Chapter 6 presents the use of computer-assisted instruction as a teaching strategy for at-risk students. Chapter 7 expands the repertoire of instructional strategies to include work experience. Chapter 8 further demonstrates the use of portfolios to measure progress of at-risk students. Chapter 9 summarizes the relevant school policies, laws, and programs that are used for drug prevention. Chapter 10 speaks of assessing the needs of students at risk and gives sample tables of the kinds of data one school district uses to locate and work with substance abusers.

Chapter 11 is a specific district's plan for reducing substance abuse, and Chapter 12 describes the substance abuse program components used. Chapter 13 deals with the effective use of paraprofessional counselors in school-based alcohol and other drug programs. Chapter 14 presents an urban school district's drug prevention staff development program. Chapter 15 focuses upon needed knowledge to deliver a culturally competent AOD program. Chapter 16 features evaluation approaches useful to assess effectiveness of programs for students at risk. Chapter 17 highlights the effective use of peer assistants in a prevention program, and Chapter 18 offers suggestions and a model for writing proposals to obtain external funding for substance abuse efforts.

Chapter 19 offers some suggestions for using volunteers and foundations to supplement limited district resources for working with students at risk. Chapter 20 investigates the problems that cocaine has brought to our society and schools. Chapter 21 focuses on the research and knowledge known about cocaine babies, and Chapter 22 concludes this focus and the book by describing effective strategies for meeting the needs of drug exposed children in the public schools. Extensive appendices are included with relevant information on creating safe and drug-free schools, using computer-assisted instruction, and recommendations for educators working with children who are drug-exposed or have attention deficit disorder.

Chapter 2

REVIEW OF THE LITERATURE

The research literature on substance abuse prevention has grown substantially over the years as the federal government has recognized the problem and funded efforts to combat it. This review of the literature focuses on youth and risk factors and protective factors that relate to substance use.

RESEARCH BASIS FOR PREVENTION AND INTERVENTION PROGRAMS

Research on youth most at risk for alcohol and other drug abuse has consistently demonstrated the importance of risk and resiliency factors in the development of drug abuse problems (e.g., Block et al., 1988; Newcomb et al., 1986; Jessor and Jessor, 1977). If risk factors such as antisocial behavior, association with drug-using peers, family management practices, and academic failure can be assessed along with resiliency factors, such as involvement in church activities and strong attachment to parents and school, appropriate programmatic interventions can follow. Resiliency factors are important even if they only represent the opposite end of the risk factor continuum, because resiliency factors buffer the effects of risk indicators (Hawkins and Catalano, 1989). A list of these important risk and protective factors follow.

Risk Factors

(*1*) Laws and norms favorable toward behavior
(2) Availability of drugs and alcohol

(*3*) Extreme economic deprivation

(*4*) Neighborhood disorganization

(*5*) Physiological factors

(*6*) Early and persistent problem behaviors (i.e., aggression, conduct, hyperactivity)

(*7*) Family history of alcoholism and parental drug use

(*8*) Poor and inconsistent family management practices

(*9*) Family conflict

(*10*) Low bonding to family

(*11*) Academic failure

(*12*) Low degree of commitment to school

(*13*) Peer rejection in elementary grades

(*14*) Association with drug-using peers

(*15*) Alienation and rebelliousness

(*16*) Attitudes favorable to drugs

(*17*) Early onset of drug use

Protective Factors

(*1*) Small family with low conflict, a high IQ, and being a firstborn child

(*2*) Strong attachment to parents

(*3*) Commitment to schooling

(*4*) Regular involvement in church activities

(*5*) Belief in the generalized expectations, norms, and values of society

(*6*) Low affiliation, autonomy, exhibition, impulsivity, and play

(*7*) High achievement, cognitive structure, and harm avoidance

Research on risk indicators over the years has identified that many paths lead to drug abuse (Oetting and Beauvais, 1987) and that having more risk factors increases the chances of drug abuse (Newcomb et al., 1986). Following is a summary of the findings on risk factor research.

STUDENT RISK FACTORS

Antisocial, Problem Behaviors, and Drug Use Risk Factors

Research reveals that there is a direct, high correlation between antisocial behaviors, delinquency, and illicit drug use among adolescents

(Jessor and Jessor, 1977; Elliott et al., 1982). Early signs of delinquency and antisocial behaviors are predictable from kindergarten on, through acting out, defiance, impulsivity, negativity, temper tantrums, or even shyness (Spivack, 1983). It is therefore critical that the initial screening for high-risk adolescents include a review of their records of maladaptive behaviors such as aggressiveness, passivity, hyperactivity, and acting out, along with teachers' current assessments of the student's behavior.

The youth's attitudes and behavior related to drug use are very predictive of later abuse of alcohol and other drugs. Kandel (1978) found that values favorable to drug use preceded initiation. She also found that the earlier the age of onset of use, the greater is the involvement with other, more dangerous drugs. Other studies identify smoking and drinking as "gateway" drugs leading to harder substances. Youth who report smoking cigarettes frequently (Robinson et al., 1987) and experiencing intoxication frequently (Kovach and Glickman, 1986) are clearly statistical candidates for drug abuse.

Peer Risk Factors

Association with drug-using peers has been among the strongest predictors of adolescent drug use (Swaim et al., 1989). Drug experimentation, according to Hawkins et al. (1985), may be viewed as a peer-supported phenomenon reflecting the importance of peers during adolescence. Peer-related risk factors include peers as a source of drug information, the number of peers who use or are perceived to use, and the perceived level of resistance to peer pressure (Newcomb et al., 1986; Kovack and Glickman, 1986).

The link between peer rejection and substance abuse is unclear; however, low acceptance by peers does put youth at risk for school problems and criminality (Parker and Asher, 1987), which are also risk factors for drug abuse (Hawkins and Catalano, 1989). Whether personality creates rejection and subsequent problems or rejection limits the child's positive opportunities also remains unclear.

Family Risk Factors

The family role in preventing drug use among adolescent youth has been well documented. The importance of family socialization includes the adult role as a model for the youth of the family. Kandel (1982) found that three factors help predict youth initiation into drugs: parent drug use, parent attitudes about drugs, and parent and child interactions.

Parental "use" seems to act as an impetus to experimentation, according to most findings (Rachal et al., 1980, 1982). Parents are quietly molding the child's behavior.

Early in life, children's antisocial behavior begins (i.e., temper tantrums or aggressiveness) and often continues into adulthood. Patterson (1989) and others have found that the path to chronic delinquency unfolds very predictably, an action-reaction sequence. Likewise, there is evidence in their findings that antisocial children frequently have harsh and inconsistent disciplinary parents; these parents have poor parenting skills and give little positive reinforcement. The most successful intervention for these children appears to be parent-training interventions where family management and communication practices are offered (Baramarindi, 1985; Patterson, 1989).

The correlation between living in a single-parent family and using drugs remains unclear. Although parental discord may lead to family breakup, conflict among family members is a better predictor of drug abuse (Simcha-Fagan et al., 1986) than "broken homes" themselves.

School Risk Factors

Poor school performance, though not always leading to drug use, is a common antecedent of drug initiation (Jessor and Jessor, 1977; Kandel et al., 1978). Robins (1980) noted that drug users are noticeably "underachievers." Spivack (1983) further concluded that academic failure in the late elementary grades does exacerbate the effects of early antisocial behavior. Hawkins et al. (1985), previously cited, found that such factors as how much students like school, time spent on homework, and perception of the relevance of coursework are also related to levels of drug use, confirming a negative relationship between commitment to education and drug use, at least for adolescents in junior or senior high.

Physical and Emotional Health Risk Factors

Adolescence is an appropriate time to learn how to tolerate pain due to physical or emotional problems (Jones and Battjes, 1985). However, the research shows that some adolescents learn early to retreat into regressive patterns, some life-threatening (i.e., anorexia), rather than experience stress or pain. Adolescents may become phobic and even self-medicated in an attempt to alleviate suffering.

Personality Risk Factors

Many at-risk children suffer from poor coping skills and low self-esteem. Kaplan et al. (1982) noted that persons who fail to interact with peers become self-critical and lose self-esteem. Likewise, if behaviors associated with traditional society have failed, deviant behaviors are tried, in an effort to improve one's self-image. These behaviors include drug use, which serves as a mechanism for improving self-esteem among new peers when the old self-image has not worked. Research cited earlier by Botvin (1986) suggests strongly that such students need training in social and communication skills and some cognitive strategies to increase their self-worth and to interact confidently in resisting peer pressures to use substances.

One common personality characteristic found in at-risk students is chronic anger. Swaim (1989) compared the effect of five emotional distress variables, including anger, self-esteem, depression, blame-alienation, and anxiety. Only anger was found to be directly related to drug abuse and serves as a mediator of other emotional distresses.

Environmental Risk Factors

A number of environmental risk factors has also been identified. For example, economic deprivation can be a factor in drug abuse. However, Hawkins and Catalano (1989) conclude, after reviewing the literature, that only when poverty is extreme and occurs in conjunction with childhood behavior problems is it a predictive factor.

Studies have shown that laws, norms, and alcohol distribution policies can predict use levels, according to Hawkins and Catalano (1989). Drinking levels vary by community, depending on the legal drinking age, the acceptance of drinking by others, and the number of outlets selling alcohol. Skager and Frith (1986) found that perceived availability of drugs is also a factor, that is, the more youth or adults an adolescent knows who can supply him or her, the more likely they are to use.

The effect that neighborhood disorganization has on drug abuse remains unclear, according to Hawkins and Catalano (1989). However, some risk factors, such as neighborhood disorganization, extreme poverty, psychological predisposing factors, and a family history of alcoholism, though not necessarily modifiable, can be useful to target high-risk groups.

PROTECTIVE FACTORS AGAINST DRUG ABUSE

Protective factors serve to increase resiliency or inhibit the development of drug abuse problems. These factors have been inconsistently defined; however, they are generally viewed as opposites of risk factors (Hawkins and Catalano, 1989). For example, the effect of religious attachment has been frequently studied as a protective factor. In a recent study by Newcomb et al. (1986), low religiosity correlated .13 with drug use, ranking seventh out of ten variables studied.

Block et al. (1988) studied a number of factors longitudinally and found that drug use at age fourteen was related to concurrent and preschool personality characteristics, an absence of ego-resiliency, ego undercontrol, and, in boys, lower IQ. Conversely, being raised in small families with low conflict, having a high IQ, and being a firstborn child buffers the effects of other risk factors, as found by Werner and Smith (1982). Research concerning protective factors usually occurs in the context of research on risk factors, such as attachment versus estrangement from parents, school, and peers.

Interest in the role of resiliency concepts vis-à-vis risk factors has recently appeared in many writings. Robert Linqunati (1992), from the Western Regional Center for Drug Free Schools and communities, concludes, "A growing body of research suggests that development of particular attributes in kids by promoting and enhancing protective factors in their environments is as important, necessary, and effective for their healthy development as reducing the risk factors threatening their future."

Bonnie Bernard (1991), a noted resiliency expert, has synthesized the literature to find three important protective factors that adults can impact for at-risk children:

(*1*) Having a caring and supportive relationship with at least one person

(*2*) Communicating consistently clear, high expectations to the child

(*3*) Providing ample opportunities for the child to participate in and contribute meaningfully to his or her social environment

These protective factors help foster the growth of a resilient child who is socially competent and has problem-solving skills and a sense of autonomy, purpose, and future. The factors are closely related to Hawkins and Catalano's (1989) social development theory and are based on Hirschi's (1969) social control theory and Bandura's (1977) social learning theory. Therefore, being socially bonded to school, family, and/or society can reduce the effect of risk factors, like extreme poverty, which may not be directly modifiable, especially in the school setting.

Perhaps it provides comfort to program implementors to know that the researchers are really in agreement on what children need in this area. In fact, there is evidence that protective factors do counteract the impact of risk factors in the lives of students if they impact at an equally powerful level (Benson, 1990; Blyth, 1992). As Wolin and Wolin (1993), authors of *The Resilient Self*, believe, survivors of troubled families can emerge and thrive by developing seven strengths: insight, independence, relationships, initiative, creativity, humanity, and morality.

Sometimes a shift is required for prevention program operators, from a "fix-it" focus with youth as objects or recipients to one that views youth as resources, who, given opportunities, will develop competencies to meet their own needs to contribute and be connected to the community (Gardner, 1992; Lofquist, 1989; Pittman, 1991).

NEED FOR SCHOOL-BASED ASSESSMENT

There is a clear need to identify and intervene early in the development of addictive behavior and other problem behaviors. Settings like schools and local agencies have the opportunity to be successful with early intervention by focusing on decreasing individual risks, such as the inability to resist peer pressure and lack of attachment to family and school.

Schools play a major role in the implementation of an effective prevention program in at least two distinct ways. The school provides a reference point with credibility for initiating and ensuring community interest and, in its primary education role, allows educators to provide students with appropriate prevention materials (curriculum, videos, handouts) and activities (e.g., "Red Ribbon Week"). Likewise, support staffs who recognize the risk factors can intervene rapidly and effectively make referrals for services outside the school.

In its role as an institution of learning, the school has an excellent opportunity to infuse prevention materials into regular classroom courses (i.e., health, social studies). To emphasize wellness as a choice requires health courses that teach the need for building both healthy bodies and attitudes; students are also taught the detrimental aspects of drug use. However, health courses and lectures alone do not produce significant results. Research studies by Botvin (1986) and

Baumarind (1985) verify that cognitive (i.e., appeal to health) and the social skills training (i.e., assertion training), when combined, form the most effective basis for a strong prevention program for students at risk. Baumarind adds that, through health and social skills, an effort can be made to persuade adolescents that their personal attributes that they "value" are impaired by substance use.

Research indicates that teachers observe school adjustment problems in 23% to 31% of all kindergarten through third grade students. These early adjustment difficulties often predict future maladjustment, including emotional problems, antisocial tendencies, and drug abuse (Cowen, 1966; Rubin and Balow, 1978). Assessment of risk factors can also help identify the one out of four children who come from families of substance abusers—a need that is often ignored, according to Battjes and Jones (1985). Educators who are trained in screening and assessment of specific risk factors in young children are in an excellent position to effectively intervene to decrease at-risk behaviors through prevention, early intervention, and referral for treatment.

Most research on risk factors continues to be gleaned from anonymous surveys with large samples (Battjes and Jones, 1985). What is needed is a way to identify an *individual* student's level of use, along with associated risk factors to determine his or her individual risk level baseline.

We Need to Identify Risk Factors by Grade 3.

If schools can identify at-risk students as early as possible in their chronological and drug experience age, fewer resources will be needed to decrease the identified risk factors, and the interventions will be more successful.

NEED FOR PARENT AND COMMUNITY INVOLVEMENT

A primary reason for parent and community involvement in prevention is found in the research on the effectiveness of school prevention curricula. The reasons youth use alcohol and other drugs are so varied that any school curriculum can only produce a small decrease in use rates (Moskowitz, 1989). For example, businessmen and parents need to recognize that advertising and promotion of alcohol by role models (i.e., sports or rock stars) creates the wrong impression within the minds of vulnerable youth. Consequently, the community as a whole, backed by local law enforcement, must work together to change the attitudes and behaviors of youth and adult citizens, as well.

Research shows that parents are in denial about the possibility of their children using drugs. Parents need to become better informed on the current information about drugs, their prevalence, and signs of drug use. Finally, parents' greatest impact is in the creation of positive family functioning and relationships and attachments that appear to discourage the initial experimentation with gateway drugs (Jessor and Jessor, 1977).

SUMMARY

A review of the research literature shows that much is known about why some youth are prone to use alcohol and other drugs, separate from their need to experiment and rebel. Most significantly related to drug use and abuse are antisocial and problem behaviors; previous drug use experience; predisposing personality characteristics, such as chronic anger and low ego control; association with peers who use; parental conflict; economic deprivation; and low academic interest and achievement.

Conversely, resilient youths may be exposed to risk factors but may be protected by high self-esteem or attachment to family or religion. These positive attachments compete with risk factors to guide youth in their decisions not to use, as described by social development theory.

Thus, the research literature on risk factors has evolved into a more cohesive understanding than in the past.

The school setting has become the obvious arena for prevention and intervention. Educators are advised to develop comprehensive programs with consistent community involvement (Pentz, 1986).

Chapter 3

DEVELOPMENT OF A STUDENT INFORMATION SYSTEM

This chapter describes alternatives for a substance abuse prediction system using four options easily implemented in the schools. The systems described have been developed and proven to predict at-risk behavior leading to substance abuse (Richards-Colocino, 1991) and are based on research of the most predictive risk factor variables (Hawkins and Catalano, 1989). However, the holistic risk factor approach used can also be used to predict other at-risk behavior, including dropping out and emotional problems. For example, Skager and Frith (1989) found that dropouts were also identified in two-thirds of the students identified as at a high risk for substance abuse.

OPTION 1

Risk Assessment Survey—Paper and Pencil Short Form

Description and Purpose

The Risk Assessment Survey – Paper and Pencil Short Form is an eighteen-item questionnaire designed for school-based prevention and early intervention programs to assess risk factors for drug abuse in youth in grades 6 – 12. The Risk Assessment Survey – Paper and Pencil Short Form contains the most significant items found in the validation and reliability studies at Pomona, California, an urban, high minority area (Callison et al., 1990), and Irvine, California, a suburban middle class community (Richards-Colocino,1991). The Risk Assessment Survey (RAS) correctly identified 82% of drug users through their risk scores on the nondrug items.

Confidentiality

Parent permission is needed to conduct the Risk Assessment Survey since it asks personal questions regarding behavior and drug use. Research has shown that most students will give accurate information if they feel giving the information will benefit them and that the information will be handled sensitively (Harrell, 1985). It is important to explain how the information will be used and what you plan to share with teachers. Please note that parents do have a right to see student records. Legal opinion indicates that, to prevent parental access of any data, it must be summarized for sharing and destroyed or kept as personal notes that are not shared with anyone else. In reality, most parents do not insist on their rights to access information at the expense of their child's privacy. (If you want to decrease the sensitivity of this form of Option 1, remove the four drug use questions: #'s 6, 8, 16, and 18. It is still valid.)

Use (Follow-up)

The survey can be used to determine the level of risk and the specific interventions needed, which are useful for planning school-based prevention and intervention services. The determination of "user" status can be helpful in assessing the level of intervention for drug use needed, i.e., drug education, insight group, or referral for assessment or treatment. Counselors may find that Option 1 may be of therapeutic value to bring an adolescent out of denial by having him/her complete and score it by him/herself. The survey is also helpful in evaluation for tracking students to measure the effectiveness of interventions.

Scoring

After scoring the RAS short form, students' scores will place them at low, medium, or high risk, and their "user" status can be determined as nonuser or user. In addition, their risk factors usually reveal patterns of problems and intervention needs.

Contact/Costs

Permission is given by the author, Nancy Richards-Colocino, for Risk Assessment Seminar participants to reproduce the survey (Figure 3.1)

RISK ASSESSMENT SURVEY

Short Form

Project # or Name _____   School _____

Gender _____   Age _____   Grade _____

Just as there are risk factors for heart disease, there are also risk factors for drug abuse. Please answer the following questions honestly, so we can best assist you in reducing your risk from developing problems due to addiction or abuse. *Your answers will be kept confidential* and the survey will not affect your grade or anything else in school. You may skip any questions that make you feel uncomfortable or that you cannot answer honestly.

1. How important is it to you to get good grades in school?
   ____ Not important (3)   ____ Somewhat important (2)
   ____ Important (1)   ____ Very important (0)

2. Do you ever argue with teachers?
   ____ Not at all (0)   ____ Sometimes (1)
   ____ Often (2)   ____ Very often (3)

3. Are you absent from school when you are not sick? How many days?
   ____ Never (0)   ____ 0 to 3 days (1)
   ____ 4 to 6 days (2)   ____ More than 7 days (3)

4. Have you ever been suspended or expelled from school?
   ____ No (0)   ____ Yes (1)

5. What do you learn from school prevention activities such as STAR, DARE, Health class, or assemblies on drug prevention?
   ____ Nothing (3)   ____ A little (2)
   ____ Some things (1)   ____ A lot (0)

6. How many times in the last year have you taken amphetamines (uppers), barbiturates (downers), or other prescription drug without a doctor telling you to take them?
   ____ None   ____ 1 or 2 times
   ____ 3 to 6 times   ____ More than 6 times

7. How many of your close friends use alcohol or drugs?
   ____ None (0)   ____ 1 or 2 (1)
   ____ 3 or 4 (2)   ____ 5 or more (3)

8. How many times have you used marijuana (hashish; MJ; weed) in the past year?
   ____ Never   ____ 1 or 2 times

Figure 3.1 Option 1 (copyright © 1990 by N. Richards).

8. (continued)

____ 3 to 6 times   ____ Over 6 times; not once a

____ Once a week for past   week

     3 months

9. What would you do if a friend gave you some marijuana and dared you to try it?

____I would not try it (0)   ____ I am not sure (1)

____ I would try it (2)

10. How often do you feel angry?

____ Never (0)   ____ Sometimes (1)

____ Often (2)   ____ Very often (3)

11. How often do you argue or fight with members of your family?

____ Not at all (0)   ____ Sometimes (1)

____ Often (2)   ____ Very often (3)

12. How much do you think your parents are against your using alcohol and other drugs?

____ Not at all (3)   ____ Mildly (2)

____ Somewhat (1)   ____ Very much (0)

13. How much do adults you are close to have problems with their use of alcohol or other drugs (such as, getting into arguments or breaking promises at work or home)?

____ Not at all (0)   ____ Sometimes (1)

____ Often (2)   ____ Very often (3)

14. How often do you smoke cigarettes?

____ Never (0)   ____ Sometimes (1)

____ 1 to 2 a day (2)   ____ More than 2 a day (3)

15. Have you ever been arrested?

____ No (0)   ____ Yes (2)

16. How often did you drink alcohol in the last year?

____ Never   ____ Once a month

____ Once a week   ____ Every day

17. In your free time from home, does your mother or father know where you are?

____ Always (0)   ____ Usually (1)

____ Seldom (2)   ____ Never (3)

18. How many times in the last year have you tried inhalants (glue, etc.) or an illegal drug (such as cocaine, crack, PCP, angel dust, LSD, heroin, etc.)?

____ None   ____ 1 or 2 times

Figure 3.1 (continued) Option 1 (copyright © 1990 by N. Richards).

and use it within these guidelines. The author also requests information and feedback on its use.

Scoring for Risk Assessment Survey (Option 1)

Section I: Drug Use in the Last Year

- #6 illegal, or misuse of legal pills—any answer except none = user status
- #8 marijuana—either over six times or once a week = user status
- #16 alcohol—either once a week or everyday = user status
- #18 Inhalants—any answer except none = user status

Classification as a drug user from any of the above questions means one definitely is at risk for later abuse problems.

Section II: Other Risk Factors

Total the scores for Questions 1−18 and compare below:
- low risk = 0−7
- medium risk = 8−13
- high risk = 14−38

OPTION 2

Computerized School Record Data

Description

Computerized school record data can be used to identify students at risk for drug use and/or dropping out. This data has the advantage of being more readily available than survey data. Developing a computerized at-risk list does require programming expertise on a district's mainframe and collection of additional information from school site teams.

Purpose

A computerized at-risk list has two uses: first, as an alternative to surveying students and, second, as a screening tool that helps identify students to be surveyed for more specific intervention needs. The second use is preferable because more specific information is gathered on a student's needs through the survey. The computerized at-risk system in Irvine correctly identified 76% of drug users, compared to 82% being correctly identified by the Risk Assessment Survey (Richards-Colocino, 1991).

Confidentiality

Since the information contained in school records is public, parent permission is not needed to collect this information, according to recent legal opinion. Of course, access to the information must be limited and kept confidential to avoid labeling and other problems. For example, it may be helpful to identify principals as the only personnel with access to on-line information or to be sent at-risk printouts.

Use (Follow-up)

This information can prevent schools from overlooking students before school problems become insurmountable. There is also some accountability built in for schools when both the district and the school know which students need extra help. Finally, students may appear who are already receiving appropriate services, thereby creating a check on the use of valuable support staff time.

Scoring

The most effective factor found in predicting risk factors from school records was the number of D's and F's, with a correlation of .36 to user level. The second most predictive factor was the weighted risk factor score, with a correlation of .29 to user level. The weighted risk factor score is a compilation of grades; achievement; absences; and documented incidents of retention, discipline, juvenile record, mobility, economic hardship, physical disability, suicide ideation, and substance abuse (Figure 3.2).

Contact

Information on this model to identify students at risk for drug use and dropping out is available from Guidance Resources, Irvine Unified School District. This computerized at-risk model is an adaptation of Jack Sappington's model to identify dropouts, which is available through

```
CTBS: reading, language, math
Absences
Grades
Retention
Discipline
Juvenile record
Mobility
Economic hardship
Physical disabilities
Suicide ideation
Substance abuse
```

Figure 3.2 *Option 2: School Record Data.*

Students-at-Risk, Inc.: contact William Callison, President, Students-at-Risk, Inc., 1260 Brangwyn Way, Laguna Beach, CA 92651.

OPTION 3

Expanded Risk Assessment Survey

Description

The Expanded Risk Assessment Survey (Figure 3.3) has three components that provide a valid measure of risk factors in students. This form is to be used with a standard fill-in-circle answer sheet. The components measure the youth's self-esteem (self-concept), peer relations, and risk factors described in research (e.g., anger management, arrest and absentee record, perceived parental attitudes and involvement, etc.). Drug access, perceptions, and demographic information are also gathered. The forty-three-question instrument takes approximately one-half hour to administer to fluent English-speaking students.

Purpose

The purpose of this instrument is to provide detailed information concerning the individual child, thereby supporting the school's ability to tailor interventions to specifically meet that child's needs. When pre/post-information is gathered with this survey, a summative evaluation of the success of the interventions may be made.

Directions

Please, read the questions and pick the answer that best fits what you think or feel. Find the question number on your answer sheet and fill in the proper circle for your answer. Be sure to:

1. Use soft (Number 2) pencil. Do not use ball-point or felt-tip pen. If you do not have a Number 2 pencil, please raise your hand.
2. Pick the one answer that best fits what you think or feel.
3. Fill in the circles with heavy, black marks. These kinds of markings will not work: ⊘ ⊘ ◖ ⊛

Your answers will remain confidential, and specific item information will not be shared with your teachers and parents. If you have any questions please ask them now. When you have finished answering all the questions please wait quietly until everyone has finished. Thank you for your help in this important survey.

Please write your first and last name in the right hand corner of side 1 of the Scantron sheet.

1. = Grade Level

   A = 6th Grade   E = 10th Grade
   B = 7th Grade   A & B = 11th Grade
   C = 8th Grade   A & C = 12th Grade
   D = 9th Grade

2. = Age

   A = 11 years   E = 15 years
   B = 12 years   A & B = 16 years
   C = 13 years   A & C = 17 years
   D = 14 years   A & D = 18 years

3. = Sex

   A = Male   B = Female

4. = With whom do you live?

   A = Both parents   C = 1 parent
   B = 1 parent and step parent   D = other

Questions

When answering these questions, respond how you *currently* think or feel.

5. Currently, the friends I usually hang out with are mostly:

   A. 2 or more years older than me.   D. About a year younger than me.
   B. About a year older than me.   E. 2 or more years younger than me.

Figure 3.3 Irvine Risk Assessment Survey.

6. How many of the kids in your grade at school do you think use alcohol or other drugs?
   A. None
   B. A few
   C. More than half
   D. Most

7. How many times in the last six months have you been offered alcohol or other drugs?
   A. Not at all
   B. Once
   C. Sometimes
   D. Very often

8. Where do most kids at this school who use drugs get them? (Fill in only one answer.)

   A. At home (parents, brothers/ sisters)
   B. At school (friends, dealers)
   C. At parties, social events outside school
   D. Hanging out with friends outside of school or parties
   E. Directly from dealers

9. What is the strongest reason kids use alcohol or other drugs? (Fill in only one answer.)

   A. To experiment, to see what it's like
   B. To relax or relieve tension
   C. To feel good or get high
   D. To have fun with friends or fit into a group
   E. To get away from problems or troubles

10. The best reason for not using alcohol or other drugs is that you . . . (Fill in only one answer.)

    A. Might become an addict or alcoholic
    B. Could get into trouble with the police or school
    C. Might lose close friends who do not like alcohol or drugs
    D. Your parents or other adults who care about you would be angry and sad
    E. Would not be the kind of person you want to be

11. I am satisfied that I can turn to my friends for help when something is troubling me.
    A. Almost always   B. Some of the time   C. Hardly ever

12. I am satisfied with the way my friends talk over things with me and share problems with me.
    A. Almost always   B. Some of the time   C. Hardly ever

13. I am satisfied that my friends accept and support my wishes to take on new activities or directions.
    A. Almost always   B. Some of the time   C. Hardly ever

Figure 3.3 (continued) *Irvine Risk Assessment Survey.*

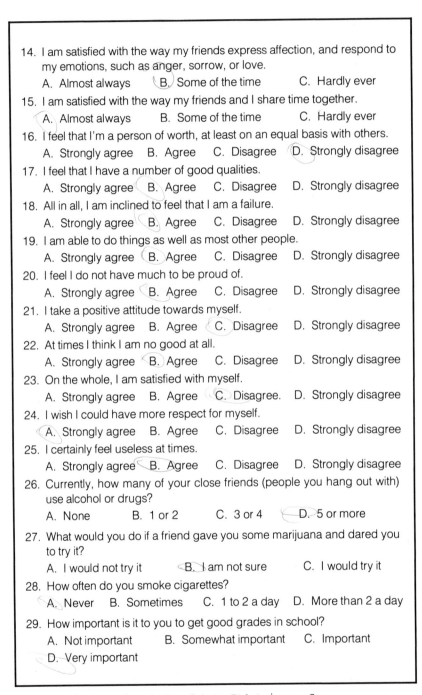

14. I am satisfied with the way my friends express affection, and respond to my emotions, such as anger, sorrow, or love.
    A. Almost always   B. Some of the time   C. Hardly ever
15. I am satisfied with the way my friends and I share time together.
    A. Almost always   B. Some of the time   C. Hardly ever
16. I feel that I'm a person of worth, at least on an equal basis with others.
    A. Strongly agree   B. Agree   C. Disagree   D. Strongly disagree
17. I feel that I have a number of good qualities.
    A. Strongly agree   B. Agree   C. Disagree   D. Strongly disagree
18. All in all, I am inclined to feel that I am a failure.
    A. Strongly agree   B. Agree   C. Disagree   D. Strongly disagree
19. I am able to do things as well as most other people.
    A. Strongly agree   B. Agree   C. Disagree   D. Strongly disagree
20. I feel I do not have much to be proud of.
    A. Strongly agree   B. Agree   C. Disagree   D. Strongly disagree
21. I take a positive attitude towards myself.
    A. Strongly agree   B. Agree   C. Disagree   D. Strongly disagree
22. At times I think I am no good at all.
    A. Strongly agree   B. Agree   C. Disagree   D. Strongly disagree
23. On the whole, I am satisfied with myself.
    A. Strongly agree   B. Agree   C. Disagree.   D. Strongly disagree
24. I wish I could have more respect for myself.
    A. Strongly agree   B. Agree   C. Disagree   D. Strongly disagree
25. I certainly feel useless at times.
    A. Strongly agree   B. Agree   C. Disagree   D. Strongly disagree
26. Currently, how many of your close friends (people you hang out with) use alcohol or drugs?
    A. None   B. 1 or 2   C. 3 or 4   D. 5 or more
27. What would you do if a friend gave you some marijuana and dared you to try it?
    A. I would not try it   B. I am not sure   C. I would try it
28. How often do you smoke cigarettes?
    A. Never   B. Sometimes   C. 1 to 2 a day   D. More than 2 a day
29. How important is it to you to get good grades in school?
    A. Not important   B. Somewhat important   C. Important
    D. Very important

Figure 3.3 (continued) Irvine Risk Assessment Survey.

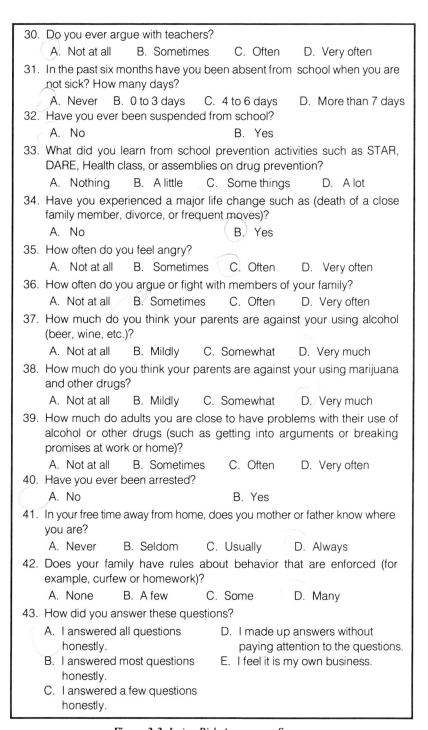

30. Do you ever argue with teachers?

    A. Not at all   B. Sometimes   C. Often   D. Very often

31. In the past six months have you been absent from school when you are not sick? How many days?

    A. Never   B. 0 to 3 days   C. 4 to 6 days   D. More than 7 days

32. Have you ever been suspended from school?

    A. No   B. Yes

33. What did you learn from school prevention activities such as STAR, DARE, Health class, or assemblies on drug prevention?

    A. Nothing   B. A little   C. Some things   D. A lot

34. Have you experienced a major life change such as (death of a close family member, divorce, or frequent moves)?

    A. No   B. Yes

35. How often do you feel angry?

    A. Not at all   B. Sometimes   C. Often   D. Very often

36. How often do you argue or fight with members of your family?

    A. Not at all   B. Sometimes   C. Often   D. Very often

37. How much do you think your parents are against your using alcohol (beer, wine, etc.)?

    A. Not at all   B. Mildly   C. Somewhat   D. Very much

38. How much do you think your parents are against your using marijuana and other drugs?

    A. Not at all   B. Mildly   C. Somewhat   D. Very much

39. How much do adults you are close to have problems with their use of alcohol or other drugs (such as getting into arguments or breaking promises at work or home)?

    A. Not at all   B. Sometimes   C. Often   D. Very often

40. Have you ever been arrested?

    A. No   B. Yes

41. In your free time away from home, does you mother or father know where you are?

    A. Never   B. Seldom   C. Usually   D. Always

42. Does your family have rules about behavior that are enforced (for example, curfew or homework)?

    A. None   B. A few   C. Some   D. Many

43. How did you answer these questions?

    A. I answered all questions honestly.
    B. I answered most questions honestly.
    C. I answered a few questions honestly.
    D. I made up answers without paying attention to the questions.
    E. I feel it is my own business.

Figure 3.3 Irvine Risk Assessment Survey.

Confidentiality

Maintaining the confidentiality of the information gleaned from this survey is a critical component of its use. The students are informed of the use of the information and where the information does and does not go. This information is kept in a secure area, and access is limited to a "need to know" basis. An adjunct survey that asks directly about drug and alcohol use patterns is an anonymous instrument. A student number described by the student themselves is on a cover sheet of the survey. No name is attached to this survey, thereby keeping it completely anonymous. Students are taught the difference between confidential and anonymous and are allowed to ask questions until they indicate that they are comfortable with the information.

Use (Follow-up)

After the information has been transferred to a spreadsheet format, a review of each student's answers is performed. This provides valuable information on the three global areas of resiliency and risk factors and, with more in-depth study, offers identification of more specific areas of weaknesses that can then be addressed with interventions that research has shown to be effective.

Scoring

Scoring may be done by hand, but it is recommended, for larger number of responses, that the use of a Scantron or some other type of automatic scoring service is used. This information can than be converted to a spreadsheet format that provides usable data to involved support people.

Contact and Cost

Please contact the Irvine Unified School District's Guidance Resources Office at (714) 552-4882 for more information.

Interpretations for Risk Assessment Survey Data (Option 3)

The following information aids in the interpretation and use of the Risk Assessment Survey data. Risk factors, self-esteem, and peer relations are each scored separately.

(1) Risk Factors: Total score maximum = 44 (the higher the score, the higher the risk)

Low Risk	Medium Risk	High Risk
0−11	12−18	19−44

(2) Self-Esteem: Total score maximum = 30 (the higher the score, the stronger the self-esteem)

Low Self-Esteem
0−16

(3) Peer Relations: Total score maximum = 10 (the higher the score, the more positive the peer relations)

Poor Peer Relations
0−5

OPTION 4

Comprehensive Risk Assessment Software

Description

The Comprehensive Risk Assessment (CRA) package offers software using an expert system (Figure 3.4). An expert system is a kind of artificial intelligence program that mimics human logic within a specific area of expertise, in this case, the characteristics of at-risk students. The CRA approach uses Scantron forms, where students self-report the needed data, which is then put through the scanner. The data is then automatically entered into the software, and identified students are scheduled into appropriate interventions.

Purpose

Students-at-Risk, Inc. is a software company that has developed its reputation by working with school districts to identify potential dropouts and substance abusers and place them in appropriate interventions using Scantron forms filled out by students themselves. Students are automatically placed in interventions that will help them in the areas where they are most at risk.

Research Base for Questions

We have utilized research on risk factors for both substance abusers and dropouts to develop software for identification. For substance abuse we use the factors identified by J. David Hawkins (1985) and validated by Richards-Colocino (1991). For dropouts we use variables identified by Sappington (1979). The Scantron forms we use are available for Elementary and Secondary levels in both English and Spanish. If you need them in additional languages we can develop them upon request.

Substance Abuse Questions (in the Comprehensive Risk Assessment Software)

1. How old is the student?
2. How many times have you been high or drunk?
   a) never
   b) once or twice
   c) 3 to 5 times
   d) 6 or more times
3. Have you ever been SUSPENDED or EXPELLED from school?
   a) yes
   b) no
4. How many of your FRIENDS or ASSOCIATES do you believe use alcohol or drugs?
   a) none
   b) 1 or 2
   c) 3 or 4
   d) 5 or more
5. How many D's and/or F's did you receive last semester? (maximum 6) _____
6. If a friend gave you marijuana and said that you're chicken if you don't try it would you:
   a) not try it
   b) not sure what I would do
   c) try it
7. How many ADULTS do you know well that are frequent users of alcohol or drugs?
   a) none
   b) 1 to 4
   c) 5 to 9
   d) more than 9
8. How frequently are you ANGRY?
   a) never
   b) sometimes
   c) frequently
   d) very frequently
9. To what extent do you feel your family is AGAINST drugs:
   a) very much against
   b) quite a bit against
   c) a little against
   d) not against

Figure 3.4 Comprehensive Risk Assessment Package.

10. When you are away from home, after school and evenings, how often do your parents know where you are?
   a) always
   c) seldom
   b) usually
   d) never
11. Have you ever been ARRESTED?
   a) yes
   b) no
12. How many times have you been ARRESTED ?
   a) 1 to 2
   c) more than 5
   b) 3 to 5

We provide a list of the substance abuse prediction items as well as the dropout items. The reader then sees a printout from our Comprehensive Risk Assessment software, which can not only identify potential abusers and dropouts but, also, schedule them into interventions.

Dropout Questions

1. How many times last semester were you absent? _____
2. How many D's and F's did you receive last semester? (maximum 6) _____
3. Number of months above or below grade level in reading score? _____
4. How many times have you moved or changed schools in the previous year? (maximum 6) _____
5. Do you have a juvenile delinquency record ?
   a) true
   b) false
6. Do you have a certifiable disability ?
   a) true
   b) false

In this model we use an expert system software (Comprehensive Risk Assessment) to connect the identification of at-risk students with one or more of the interventions now available in your school. Student numbers are assigned for processing the student risk data. Only school staff who have direct responsibility for student advisement have lists of student names and ID numbers, so they can identify students and connect them to their risk profiles.

Intervention Completion

Information about the extent to which staff are implementing interventions comes from the Completion of Intervention Form from the Comprehensive Risk Assessment (CRA) System. A Level of Intervention Completion for

Figure 3.4 (continued) Comprehensive Risk Assessment Package.

Intervention Completion (continued)
each CRA item is filled in by the school staff member responsible. When a Pre-Post comparison of scores is made at the end of the testing period the staff member can then check the level of Intervention Completion Forms to see if areas of no improvement resulted from staff not completing the interventions they agreed to implement.

COMPLETION OF INTERVENTIONS FORM

1. How often are you angry?

   (0) never   (2) frequently

   (1) sometimes   (3) very frequently

   Level of Completion of Intervention

   High (3); Moderate (2); Low (1); and None (0)

2. How many ADULTS do you know well that often drink alcohol?

   (0) none   (2) 5 to 9

   (1) 1 to 4   (3) more than 9

   High (3); Moderate (2); Low (1); and None (0)

3. How often are you afraid to express your anger to people?

   (0) never   (2) frequently

   (1) sometimes   (3) always

   High (3); Moderate (2); Low (1); and None (0)

4. How much do you feel your family is against drugs?

   (0) very much against   (2) a little against

   (1) quite a bit against   (3) not against

   High (3); Moderate (2); Low (1); and None (0)

5. When you are away from home or after school, how often do your parents/guardians know where you are?

   (0) always   (2) seldom

   (1) usually   (3) never

   High (3); Moderate (2); Low (1); and None (0)

6. How often do you feel all alone?

   (3) always   (1) seldom

   (2) usually   (0) never

   High (3); Moderate (2); Low (1); and None (0)

Figure 3.4 (continued) Comprehensive Risk Assessment Package.

7. Do your parents/guardians listen to you and attempt to understand your problems?

    (0) always   (2) seldom

    (1) usually   (3) never

    High (3); Moderate (2); Low (1); and None (0)

8. If a friend offered you a drug or alcohol and said that you're chicken if you don't try it, would you:

    (0) not try it   (2) try it

    (1) not sure

    High (3); Moderate (2); Low (1); and None (0)

9. Have you ever been sent to the Principal's Office for a behavior problem?

    (1) yes   (0) no

    High (3); Moderate (2); Low (1); and None (0)

10. How may D's and F's did you receive last semester/quarter?

    1   2   3   4   5

    High (3); Moderate (2); Low (1); and None (0)

11. Have you ever been SUSPENDED or EXPELLED from school?

    (1) yes   (0) no

    High (3); Moderate (2); Low (1); and None (0)

12. Have you ever been disciplined for a behavior problem?

    (1) yes   (0) no

    High (3); Moderate (2); Low (1); and None (0)

13. How many times last semester were you absent?

    Responses will vary from 0 to 99

    High (3); Moderate (2); Low (1); and None (0)

14. How many times have you moved or changed schools in the previous year?

    1   2   3   4   5

    High (3); Moderate (2); Low (1); and None (0)

Figure 3.4 (continued) Comprehensive Risk Assessment Package.

Confidentiality

Students fill out the Scantron forms and use a school identification number on their form; a school staff member keeps a confidential master list to match names and ID numbers to protect student privacy.

Use (Follow-up)

School staff use the recommended interventions as a guide and place students into appropriate interventions. Individual students are monitored as needed, and participating students fill out Scantron forms once each semester to provide staff with data on student improvement.

Scoring

Students receive a batting average type score (.356) for likelihood of substance abuse and dropout. They are then scheduled into interventions for areas of great need, for example, anger control.

Contact/Costs

Students-at-Risk, Inc., 1260 Brangwyn Way, Laguna Beach, CA 92651, phone (714) 773-3368. We provide the Scantron forms that you administer and mail to us for processing at a cost of $1.00 per form. We send you a report that lists each student by number and his/her recommended interventions.

Use at the School and District Levels

The Comprehensive Risk Assessment software can be used in the following ways:

(*1*) At the school level to
- predict who will drop out
- predict who will be a substance abuser
- schedule them into needed activities
- track their progress
- evaluate the success of the interventions students are placed in

(2) At the district level to
- identify schools with dropout/abuse problems

- identify students at lower levels who may drop out/abuse later
- identify interventions that fit needs identified
- evaluate interventions
- generate funds through improved attendance

Chapter 4 gives a sample student report from the Comprehensive Risk Assessment software and explains the scheduling of interventions.

DEVELOPMENT OF A STUDENT ASSISTANCE SYSTEM

The development of a student information and assistance system is multi-faceted. The system must be able to react quickly and competently for students as their needs are identified by staff, parents, and the students themselves. The system must also be proactive in providing information for prevention and early intervention of students before they slip to real trouble of school failure.

In order to be reactive, schools must have a way to respond that is efficient and helpful to a variety of needs. The following are procedures that are used in response.

ALTERNATIVES FOR DEALING WITH AT-RISK STUDENTS

There are a variety of strategies that administrators can use in order to work with students who are showing signs of being unable to be successful in the school environment, usually becoming more complex as the problem dictates.

The teacher/student conference is often the first step in identifying a problem. Staff can be trained to implement a system to respond to at-risk behavior, which is called Carevention, which was developed by the Johnson Institute as part of their student assistance program. This technique involves a teacher or counselor confronting a student with their behavior using a five-step process:

- I care . . . (express concern for the student): ''I care about you and I want you to be successful in my class.''
- I see . . . (name the specific behavior that needs to be changed): ''I see that you haven't turned in your homework for the last week.''

- I feel . . . (give the student an opening to talk): "I feel like you might just want a chance to talk to someone."
- I want . . . (list expectations): "I want you to make up the work you missed by next week and not to miss any more assignments for two weeks."
- I will . . . (offer support): "I will offer support by extending the due date for the missing work, and I can be available before school if you need help to stay current."

The Irvine Unified School District adaptation of this model includes simple tracking forms to remind staff to follow up with students and to let others know about their contact. In the busy school day, it is easy for our good intentions to give a message to students that no one cares or that they can work the system. At the teacher and school level, it is important to communicate that we do care and we will follow up to resolve the issues leading to at-risk behavior. A centrally located counselor, specialist, or at-risk committee can then determine if the student's problems are isolated or repeated with other teachers, with little extra effort. Carevention takes practice; however, many teachers are already doing it. Carevention helps the staff to focus on the behavior and refer bigger problems appropriately. It also helps staff not to ask why, enable the behavior, judge or label, own the person's behavior, and expect to save everyone. With Carevention or a similarly effective front-line system in place, many problems will never proceed to higher levels.

Some schools prefer to treat alcohol and other drug risk behaviors separately from other at-risk behaviors, and others prefer to follow a generic procedure for all at-risk behavior. Sometimes the responsibility falls to a counselor, a contracted specialist, a school committee, or a school/community committee (Aguirre, Int., 1992). When someone at the school focuses on alcohol and other drug (AOD) behavior, the steps include referral process, preassessment collection of high-risk and resilient behaviors, evaluation of the need, and involving the parents. The strategies usually involve referral and often include onsite support services and follow-up.

Because of schools' primary focus on academic achievement, the student study team is sometimes used to focus on at-risk problem students. A description of this strategy follows.

THE STUDENT STUDY TEAM

The student study team (SST) concept has been in use for several years in California schools and has been supported by the state department of education. Each student is analyzed as a whole or totality, rather than in terms of special needs such as special education or bilingual education. Hence, the staff concerned with students who are predicted to be at risk of substance abuse participate in a student study team, rather than treating the student as though many other staff have not already been working to help him or her. This is easy to discuss and hard to implement, as is any strategy that requires extensive cooperation and communication. Using the student study team for at-risk students with AOD problems also requires intensive training in substance abuse prevention for the team members.

Implementation of a student study team, or the equivalent, requires the creation of a group that may include the student, the parent, administration, district support personnel, classroom teachers, and special program personnel. The principal, or her/his designee, typically appoints the members and chairs the team.

The team is a function of the regular academic program. It uses a systematic problem-solving approach to assist students who are not progressing at a satisfactory rate. The SSR clarifies problems and concerns, develops strategies, organizes resources, and provides a system for accountability (Radius and Lesniak, 1986).

Team members should include people with a variety of competencies and skills. Some members should have the authority to provide support for implementing decisions the SST makes. The SST will be more effective if the potential implementors of SST decisions are also members.

SST at Work.

The SST is not a special education function and is not, therefore, subject to the various restrictions associated with special education. On the other hand, the SST certainly can and should help with mainstreaming strategies for special education students.

Some typical services of an SST include the following:

(1) Clarify the problem(s) a student has, including a definition that leads toward realistic solutions.

(2) Gather data on student performance.

(3) Analyze information on student performance and helps classroom teachers involved design strategies to work with the student.

(4) Assist with the implementation of these strategies by providing curriculum materials, consultation, monitoring, and moral support.

(5) Provide assurance that, when a student is referred for special education, the referral is well considered, based on clearly identified need, and that less restrictive alternatives have been attempted.

(6) Provide training to teachers who need preparation to implement some of the SST's strategies.

SST benefits include efficiency in bringing together all of the resources needed to help a student, elimination of numerous site meetings about the same student, involvement of the parent in problem solving rather than just discipline, an expression of the school's concern for the student, and the creation of a team that raises the morale of members, as well as helping the school to improve its service to students and the effectiveness of its instruction.

Frequently, two days of training help prepare staff to implement the SST approach. The training includes current ideas about parent involvement, strategies for running group meetings effectively, procedures for assigning responsibilities among team members and specific approaches to providing teacher support in the implementation process. The district staff must be committed to the SST approach and, through annual evaluations, see that principals work to make SSTs effective.

Most districts have found that a minimum of lecture/discussion and a maximum of practice using real cases are the best way to train teams. Roles are clarified (see Figure 4.1) (Butler and Gilmartin, 1986), especially for the student, parent, and referring teacher, none of whom may be familiar with the approach. Group memory is used to emphasize student strengths,

Facilitator/Chairperson	Recorder	Team Member
During Meeting Coordinate logistics before and after meeting. Notify team members of meeting, time, place, and students scheduled. Insure parent and student are prepared. Know available resources and how to access them. Assume ultimate responsibility for group decisions.	Listen carefully for the key words and ideas to be recorded. Write the input on the student study team summary. Organize the information in the appropriate columns. Don't change the meaning of what was said. Ask for clarification; get accurate information on the summary. Capture basic ideas. Make corrections nondefensively.	Respect and listen to other individuals. Do not cut other people off or put words in their mouths. Question any statement you feel is not accurate. Help recorder remain neutral and make sure ideas are being recorded accrately. Use facilitative behaviors as needed. Focus energy on content of the student summary.

Figure 4.1 Defined Roles for Team Members—Facilitator and Chairperson May or May Not Be the Same Person.

Facilitator/Chairperson	Recorder	Team Member
During Meeting Primary role is to facilitate, not to present information Stand in front of group. Account for time; appoint timekeeper. Help recorder take accurate notes. Check for meaning/understanding. Encourage input from all team members by asking "Any additions, any questions?" Keep group focused on task. Ask for specifics, not generalities. Be positive, compliment group. Be nonjudgmental, encourage others to be nonjudgmental. Diffuse emotionally charged statements. See that team prioritizes concerns and actions. Help team find win/win solutions for teacher, student, and parents. Expect accountability for group decisions.	Write legibly and quickly. Shorten words, abbreviate. Don't be afraid to misspell. Use colors as a visual aid. Use circles and arrows to connect related information.	Help group stay on task. Serve as timekeeper or observer as needed. Come prepared with information on student. Avoid side conversations. Look for similarities/discrepancies in the information Account for agreed-upon actions. Do not make commitments for people who are not present at the meeting. Copy SST summary on a small sheet.

Figure 4.1 (continued) *Defined Roles for Team Members — Facilitator and Chairperson May or May Not Be the Same Person.*

as is problem identification prior to recommendations for helping strategies, and to keep the team focused and accountable (see Figure 4.2).

One person should play the role of parent specialist and recruit parents as team members. Students, if at the junior or senior high school level, should be involved, and the team should have information about the student from the student referral information sheet (see Figure 4.3). The team is responsible for setting up their own procedures, such as when to meet and how to provide in-service for staff. Team members need to be taught skills in group facilitation, time management, and conducting effective meetings for the team to be effective.

Elements of the SST model include use of the SST summary sheets, parent and student participation, and carefully defined roles for team members. The summary is placed on butcher paper in the team meeting room and allows members to see their work as they progress. Parent involvement is critical and, unfortunately, hard to achieve with parents of students who are predicted to drop out.

Referral of students must be done with care, because too many referrals will overload the staff and cause the system to break down. The procedure for student referral should include evaluation of the student by appropriate teachers, a parent conference, a weekly progress check, and a conference with a dean in order to ensure that the time of the SST is used for students with the greatest need for help.

Once the decision is made to refer a student, the teacher evaluations should be given to the SST chairperson, and contact should be made with the parents and the student (if secondary level) to set up a meeting. Other SST members are notified, and the meeting is held. During the meeting, the student's strengths are discussed, as well as areas of concern. Actions recommended should be based on both concerns and strengths and should be prioritized to facilitate immediate, practical implementation by teachers involved. Recommendations should be behavioral in format so teachers understand clearly what is being suggested. The parents should be asked to play an active part in the actions recommended, and a plan for monitoring the recommendations should be one result of the meeting. At the close of the meeting, a follow-up meeting should be scheduled. The SST should create a plan for evaluating the effectiveness of the SST's operations.

One member of the SST should summarize the group's discussion and recommendations and enter the data into a computer in some kind of organized format. Form design software will allow computer access to

TEACHER _____ SCHOOL _____ TEAM _____

STUDENT _____ PRIMARY LANG. _____ GR. ____ BIRTH _____ PARENTS _____

M _____ F _____

Strengths	Known Information	Modifications	Concerns Prioritized	Questions	Strategies Brainstorm	Prioritized	Persons Responsible	
							Who	When
Academic Social Physical What student likes Incentives	School background Family composition Health Performance levels	Changes in program Reading specialist Tutoring Counseling Repeating grade	Academic Social/emotional Physical Attendance	Questions that can't be answered at this time	Team brainstorms multiple creative strategies to address top concerns	Two to three actions chosen from strategies brainstormed	Any team member, including the parent and student	Specific dates
							Follow-up date: (3–6 weeks)	

Figure 4.2 Use of SSR Summary Sheet—Typical Column Topics.

ATTENTION: On request, this form will be shown to the parent, guardian, or pupil over 18 years old.

Student's Name: _____ Birthdate: _____ Sex: _____ Date: _____

School: _____ Teacher: _____ Grade: _____

Referral Initiator(s): _____

(Parent, Teacher, Principal, etc.)

REASON FOR STUDENT STUDY REQUEST: Briefly describe why student is being referred to student study team.

ACADEMIC FUNCTIONING: At approximately what grade level is pupil functioning?

Math _____ Reading _____ Language Arts _____

BEHAVIOR: Describe behavior in and out of classroom.

ATTENDANCE: Days Present _____ Days Absent _____ Total Days This Covers _____

Figure 4.3 Sample Student Referral Information Sheet (Source: Mt. Diablo Unified School District, Concord, CA).

BACKGROUND INFORMATION: What languages other than English are spoken in the home?

_____ Number of Siblings _____

Has student ever repeated a grade? Yes _____ No _____ If yes, what grade? _____

List any school support service the student is receiving (reading specialist, speech and language therapist, etc.).

List any prior special education service.

List social agency involvement.

HEALTH DATA:
Vision
Date of test _____ Within normal limits _____ Not within normal limits _____
Hearing
Date of test _____ Within normal limits _____ Not within normal limits _____
List any significant health problems.

ADDITIONAL COMMENTS (special strengths, skills, aptitudes, etc.): Please use objective, specific terms. Reference should be made to cumulative folder factors such as number of transfers, groups testing summary, and dramatic change in academic performance (approximate date).

Figure 4.3 (continued) Sample Student Referral Information Sheet (Source: Mt. Diablo Unified School District, Concord, CA).

'HEALTHY KIDS ~ HEALTHY DUARTE"
INDIVIDUAL INTERVENTION PLAN
CONFIDENTIAL

Name			Birthday
Callison, William			
PRINT	Last	First	

Address	Telephone
	714 497-13

Parents Name

Language	Home Language

Spec Prog: Spec Ed	Spec Prog: GATE	Spec Prog: Other

School	Teacher	Grade

School Status: Enrolled	School Status: Moved	School Status: Re-entered

Interviewer	Date

Assessment Survey Questions: (Circle) 1 2 3 4 5 6 7 8 9 10 11 12 13 14

Assessment Survey Questions: (Check)

Substance Abuse: Low Risk: ____Pre ____Post   Medium Risk: ____Pre ____Post   High Risk: ____Pre ____]
Dropout: Low Risk: ____Pre ____Post   Medium Risk: ____Pre ____Post   High Risk: ____Pre ____

Level 1 Interview (After topics are discussed, summarize student responses)

Recommendation:
____No Further Intervention ____Level II ____Level III

Study Team Recommendation:
____No Further Intervention ____Level II ____Level III

Figure 4.4 Screen One.

49

Level II Interventions

Date	Parent Conference		Date	Positive Activities Assigned to:
Date	Interest Analyzer		Date	1.
Date	SST (Site) Attach Plan		Date	2.
Date	SIT District		Date	3.
Date	Student-Parent-School Contract		Date	4.
Date	Academic Assistance (Tutor)		Date	DCP Parent Classes SCH. ___ ENG. ___ SP. ___
	Days and Time		Date	Operation School Bell
Date	Program/Class/School Change		Date	Psychological Testing
Date	Being Useful Project		Date	School Nurse
Date	Other		Date	Monrovia Health Clinic
Date	Community Council Services		Date	Outside Health Provider (Agency)

Quarterly Progress Report: (Include dates of Parent Teacher contacts)

Date	Progress Report I

Date	Progress Report II

Date	Progress Report III

Date	Progress Report IV

Figure 4.5 Screen Two.

END-OF-THE-YEAR RECOMMENDATION

COUNSELOR		DATE

Level III Interventions

Date		Date	
	Parent Conference		SARB
Date	Counseling-Group/Individual	Date	GAPP
	Days and Time	Date	Child Protective Services
	Counselor	Date	Juvenile Justice

LIFE SKILLS: (STAR & STAGES)

Date		Date	
	Coping Skills		Nutrition
Date	Stress Management	Date	Big Sisters/Brothers
Date	Social Skills	Date	ESL Classes
Date	Decision Making	Date	Family Counseling
Date	"Latch Key"	Date	AAA/AL-ANON-ALATEEN
Date	Resistance Skills	Date	Substance Abuse Treatment Program Agency
Date	Self Esteem Fundamental	Date	County Social Human Services Specify
Date	Special Placement	Date	County Mental Health
Date	SB 65 Outreach Consultant Attendance _____ Academic _____	Date	Outside Mental Health Provider Agency
Date	Special Friend (Peer) Name	Date	Other
Date	Church Minister		
Date	Community Service Council		

Figure 4.6 Screen Three, First Part.

Quarterly Progress Report: (Include dates of Parent Teacher contacts)

Date	Progress Report I

Date	Progress Report II

Date	Progress Report III

Date	Progress Report IV

END-OF-THE-YEAR RECOMMENDATION

Counselor

S.I.T. RECOMMENDATION	DATE

N.F.I.	LEVEL II	LEVEL III	DATE

Figure 4.6 (continued) Screen Three, Second Part.

1. With whom do you live? (any other answer than two parents)
   - Interview student to determine any associated problems.
   - If indicated, teach coping skills for major change, i.e., STAGES (Irvine Unified School District, 1987) lessons.
   - If indicated, provide parent support group or refer for counseling.
2. How important is it to you to get good grades in school? (not important)
   - Interview student to determine reason.
   - Check school records for grades and achievement.
   - If indicated, refer for special education screening.
   - If indicated, teach study skills.
   - If indicated, conduct activities to increase student's bonding to school, i.e., opportunities for recognition.
3. Do you ever argue with teachers? (often or very often)
   - Interview to determine reason.
   - If indicated, train in (STAR) assertive communication, (GOAL) accountability, or (PLUS) problem-solving skills.
   - Train teacher(s) in cooperative discipline.
4. Are you absent from school when you are not sick? (4 – 7 days)
   - Interview to determine reason.
   - If indicated, implement school-bonding activities, i.e., assign to a staff mentor.
   - Monitor and/or contract for school attendance.
5. Have you ever been suspended or expelled from school? (yes)
   - Interview for dates and specifics.
   - If indicated, monitor student behavior and/or increase school bonding.
6. What do you learn from school prevention activities? (nothing or a little)
   - Interview for reason.
   - If student is high-risk (has several risk factors), provide secondary drug prevention activities, i.e., more intense drug education/counseling in small group.
7. How many times have you used a prescription drug without a doctor? (2 – 6 or more times)
   - Provide specialized drug education/counseling in small group.
8. Where did you learn most of what you know about drugs? (other than school or parents)
   - If indicated, provide correct drug education information.
   - Train parents how to talk to youth about drugs.

Figure 4.7 Risk Factor Interventions.

9. How many of your close friends use alcohol or drugs? (3 – 5 or more)
   - Compare to student's own level of use.
   - If indicated, teach (STAR) peer refusal skills.
   - Provide opportunities for interaction with nonusing peers.
10. How many times have you used marijuana? (6 – once a week for past 3 mo.)
   - Provide specialized drug education/counseling in small group.
11. What would you do if a friend asked you to use marijuana? (I'm not sure or I would try it)
   - Interview for reason.
   - If indicated, teach (STAR) refusal skills.
12. How often do you feel angry? (often or very often)
   - Interview for reason.
   - Provide opportunity for counseling.
   - If indicated, teach (STAGES) coping and anger management skills.
   - If indicated, teach (STAR or PLUS) relaxation skills.
13. How often do you argue with your family? (often or very often)
   - Interview for reason.
   - If indicated, refer for family counseling.
   - If indicated, refer parents for education on family communication.
14. How much are your parents against your use of drugs? (not at all or mildly)
   - Interview for reason.
   - If indicated, refer parents for education on clarifying/communicating values.
   - If indicated, counsel student on being responsible for self.
15. How much do adults you are close to use drugs? (often or very often)
   - Interview to determine relationship (parents, sibs, or other) and impact.
   - If indicated, provide student counseling support for family member's use.
   - If indicated, counsel student on being responsible for self.
16. How often do you smoke cigarettes? (1 – 2 or more a day)
   - Educate about risk factors for drug abuse.
17. Have you ever been arrested? (yes)
18. How old were you the first time you were arrested? (any answer)
   - Interview for reason and date.
   - If indicated, monitor for antisocial tendencies.
   - Create opportunities for prosocial behavior.
   - If indicated, teach (GOAL or PLUS) self-control skills.

Figure 4.7 (continued) *Risk Factor Interventions.*

19. How old were you when you had your first alcoholic drink (more than a sip)? (under 15 years)
    • Educate about risk factors for drug abuse.
20. How often did you drink last year? (once a week or every day)
    • Educate about risk factors for drug abuse.
21. How many times have you been drunk or high? (3 – 6 or more times)
    • Provide drug education and counseling.
    • If indicated, provide opportunities for alternative high experiences.
22. When you are away from home, after school and evenings, how often do your parents know where you are? (seldom or never)
    • Interview for specifics.
    • If indicated, refer parents for education on limit setting.
23. If you had a personal problem, with whom would you talk? (not mother or father)
    • Interview for extent and balance in student's support system.
    • If indicated, refer parents and youth to improve communication skills.
24. Does your family have rules and are they enforced? (none or a few)
    • Interview for outcomes of rule enforcement.
    • If indicated, refer parents for education on limit setting.
    • If indicated, counsel student on self-discipline skills.
25. How many times have you tried illegal drugs? (3 – 6 or more times)

Figure 4.7 (continued) *Risk Factor Interventions.*

the data base. We show screens from Informed Designer and Informed Manager, software from Shana Corporation (see Figure 4.4, 4.5, and 4.6), which automatically creates a data base as you design your forms. The form we show is for use in Healthy Start, a program that links schools and community agencies in order to prevent duplication of agency efforts in serving low-income students and their families. These forms are used in Duarte Unified School District, Duarte, California. Healthy Start runs on the Macintosh SE or the Macintosh II. We recommend that our Comprehensive Risk Assessment software, which is described in Chapter 6, be used to identify students who are at such high levels or risk that they need to be assisted by an SST or the equivalent.

Figures 4.7 and 4.8 are examples of student risk factor interventions that you can adapt for your district over a period of years. They will be addressed in more detail in the next chapter.

The appropriateness of interventions with possible modifications for specific age groups will be noted by these symbols: (E), (M), (H); (E) = Elementary, (M) = Middle School, (H) = High School. This partial list of interventions is included as a sample of some possible activities to be used to address specific risk factors.

1. Peer Relationships:

    A. Building Good Communications with Friends
        • Learning to make ''I'' statements (E,H,M)
        • Role-playing situations (M,H)
        • Modeling (E,M,H)
        • Teaching good listening skills (E,M,H)
        • Awareness of consequences of poor listening and communication (E,M,H)
        • Elementary STAR—listening and communication lessons (E)
        • STAR—listening and communication lessons (M)
        • High school STAR—listening and communication lessons (H)

    B. Sharing Time Together (e.g., deciding what to do, what not to do, etc.);
        • Learning about positive and negative consequences of actions (E,M,H)
        • Learning to use the brainstorming techniques to make decisions with your friends (M,H)
        • Getting in touch with your values (M,H)
        • Community activities with friends (e.g., Youth to Youth conferences, sports, community service, etc.) (E,M,H)
        • STAR curriculum on decision making and problem solving (E,M,H)

    C. Peer Pressure
        • Popcorn game—One person doesn't get popcorn. That person gets a piece of paper that says they need to resist offers of popcorn. Others receive paper telling them to pressure student to accept popcorn. (E,M)
        • Descant making role-play (M,H)
        • Developing a plan of action before actual event occurs (M,H)
        • Brainstorm alternative actions that may happen—take a time out before acting (M,H)
        • STAR curriculum—decision making, handling criticism skills, etc.
        • Group and individual counseling

2. Self-Esteem:

    A. Improving Self-Concept
        • Peer assistance or peer tutoring (E,M,H)
        • ''Who am I'' college (E,M,H)

Figure 4.8 Additional Interventions Based on Identified Risk Factors.

- Modeling (E,M,H)
- Defining feelings (E,M,H)
- STAR curriculum (E,M,H) personality styles
- STAGES curriculum

B. Positive Self-Talk
- Negative thought blocking (E,M,H)
- Tape recording and videotaping activities (E,M,H)
- Positive statements in a can game (E,M,H)
- Keep positive journal (M,H)
- Practice thinking of three positive experiences they have had that day; practice in group (E,M,H)
- Contract to self-monitor positive self talk. They mark every time they give themselves a positive stroke. Set goals for how many times they will do it during the week. Set reward. (E,M)
- STAR, STAGE—stress management curriculum (E,M,H)

C. Feeling Useful
- Group leader for the day (E,M,H)
- Peer assistance or tutoring (E,M,H)
- Setting reasonable expectations and goals (M,H)
- Participating in decision making (E,M,H)
- Games that have a new leader each time

3. Risk Factors:
A. Anger Management
- Journaling (E,M,H)
- Feeling list—label feelings, clarification, etc. (E,M,H)
- Brainstorm options for expressing anger (E,M,H)
- Develop communication skills (E,M,H)
- Use playdough or crayons to express anger (E,M)
- Educate—how to handle appropriately (E,M,H)
- STAR curriculum (E,M,H)

B. Communication with Parents
- Role-play in groups (M,H)
- Role reversal—children become parents (E,M,H)
- Write letters to parents about your feelings (E,M,H)
- Develop communication skills (E,M,H)

C. Absent When Not Sick
- Behavior contract addressing absences (E,M)
- Involve student in school activities such as student clubs, decorating for dances, special helper for teachers and administrators, peer tutoring, etc. (E,M,H)
- Parent contact (again!) (E,M,H)
- Individual counseling (E,M,H)

Figure 4.8 (continued) Additional Interventions Based on Identified Risk Factors.

D. What would you do if a friend gave you some marijuana and dared
   you to try it?
   • See Peer Pressure interventions above.
E. Major Life Changes
   • Stages I and II curriculum (E,M,H)
   • Group Counseling (E,M,H)
   • Art—keep a folder of the student's art and "look back" with
     student at regular intervals.
F. Good Grades
   • Career guidance (M,H)
   • Peer tutoring (E,M,H)
   • Recognition of improvement (certificates, bulletin boards, notes
     home, etc.) (E)
G. Suspended or Arrested
   • Group counseling (M,H)
   • Individual counseling (M,H)
   • Outside referrals (E,M,H)
   • Parent contact (E,M,H)
   • Site visitations to appropriate places (job sites, college
     campuses, juvenile hall, etc.) (M,H)
H. Smoking
   • Health information (E,M,H)
   • Economic information (M,H)
   • Smoking cessation programs (peer facilitated, in school) (M,H)
   • Peer pressure interventions (E,M,H)

Figure 4.8 (continued) Additional Interventions Based on Identified Risk Factors.

POLICY RECOMMENDATION

In order to deal systematically with potential at-risk students, each
school should invest resources in the development of some type of
student assistance system that offers individual services known to correct
the problem.

Chapter 5

PLACING STUDENTS IN INTERVENTIONS

This chapter presents a model for using the Comprehensive Risk Assessment system to place students into appropriate interventions. Each district needs a procedure for placing students into interventions. Since most districts have more at-risk students than existing staff can work with successfully, it is important to have a "scientific," easily defensible means for prioritizing student needs. Districts can create their own approach or adapt the comprehensive risk assessment approach to their existing situation.

INTRODUCTION

In the first district represented here, each school does somewhat different activities from the other schools for dropout prevention. There is no "district approach," and principals can pursue whatever strategies make sense to them and their staff. To utilize the comprehensive risk assessment approach, we began with one of the high schools that has a dropout rate of about 20%. The dropout prevention effort the principal wanted to build the risk assessment system around was called Alternative to Suspension. Students could choose to work in a school for the physically handicapped rather than be suspended for a given period of time. Figure 5.1 is a sample Student Report and a description of the procedure for assignment of students into interventions for the secondary level.

(*1*) The first information to note is *032367* or some similar number. Each student will receive a number and will be identified by this number. (You will need access to the confidential key which links the number to the *name* of the student.) Note whether you are (a)

Student# 032367   **Version—Secondary**

This student scored *0.19 on the substance abuse risk* assessment test, which predicts a *medium* risk for substance abuse and scored *0.39 on the dropout risk* assessment, which predicts a *high* risk for school dropout.

1. How often angry?—very frequently
   Use Level I, Level II, and Level III interventions.
2. Friends who use alcohol or drugs?—5 or more
   Use Level I and Level II interventions.
3. Close adults who use alcohol or drugs frequently?—none
4. Times high or drunk?—once or twice
5. Family against drugs?—very much against
6. Parents know whereabouts?—always
7. Use if a friend dared you?—not sure what I would do
   Use Level I and Level II interventions.
8. Times arrested?—1 to 2
   Use Level I and Level II interventions.
9. Ever suspended or expelled?—yes
   Use Level I, Level II, and Level III interventions.
10. Number of D's or F's?—3
11. Ever arrested?—yes
12. Juvenile delinquency record?—true
    Use Level I, Level II, and Level III interventions
13. Certified disability?—false
14. Times absent last semester?—10
15. Times moved or changed schools last year?—3
    Use Level I, Level II, and Level III interventions

Figure 5.1 Sample Comprehensive Risk Assessment Report.

working with elementary or secondary students (secondary, in this case) and (b) working first with the substance abuse or the dropout prediction. Only areas of moderate or high risk are to receive interventions.

(2) Next, you will note that when you come to an area of moderate or high risk, *intervention is recommended.* Proceed to the next line to determine the area of risk.

(3) In this case, the *subject* of intervention is *anger.* Anger is the risk factor identified by the student and the area of concern, and so you should arrange for interventions that are appropriate for an anger

problem. See "The Questionnaire and Suggested Interventions, Question 1" later in this chapter.

(*4*) An interview with the student is suggested. The level tells you what Level of Intervention may be beneficial. In this case, Level I is recommended. There are three levels of suggested interventions, identified by Level l, Level II, or Level III.

EXPLANATION OF THE LEVELS OF INTERVENTION

(*1*) The interventions suggested are in order of intensity, Level I requiring the least intensive intervention, and Level III the most intensive.

(*2*) Teachers, counselors, or administrators could provide most Level I or Level II responses as a part of their usual and expected interactions with students and parents. Level III interventions may include specialized programs and outside agencies.

(*3*) In every instance that the student's response to the Risk Assessment Questionnaire has triggered a suggested intervention, it is strongly recommended that you make at least a Level I response, which typically means a one-to-one interview with the student.

(*4*) Level I interventions will suggest an individual meeting or interview with the student to gather more information. Suggestions for discussion will be offered. The Level I interview will help to ascertain whether Level II or Level III interventions will be most beneficial.

(*5*) Level II interventions may suggest ongoing support by a teacher, counselor, or mentor to monitor the student's situation. Ideas for skill building through particular programs may be noted, as well as possible referral to outside agencies for family counseling.

(*6*) Level III interventions may be more immediate and acute. Specialized skills will be noted with interventions provided by school counselors or outside agencies, depending on the need and resources available at your site.

In schools with counselors, Level III interventions might typically be provided by them, However, with special programs, training, and support, interventions could also be provided by teachers. For example, many schools already have programs in place to provide drug and alcohol education, as well as programs to foster self-esteem and communication skills.

If a suggested Level III intervention does *not* seem to fall within any program you presently have, you may be able to use the intervention description to design your own intervention or to refer the student/family to an outside agency.

It is highly suggested that educators consult with others before undertaking Level III responses. Depending upon your school situation, you might consult with another teacher, with an appropriate administrator, with the school counselor and/or psychologist, or with the student study team.

(7) *Note:* Since it is the student who decides how to respond to each question, it is also helpful for educators to use their knowledge and experience in interpreting the responses. For example, Question 1 asks: How often are you angry? The responses include: "never," "sometimes," "frequently," and "very frequently." What one student considers *frequently* may seem to peers and teachers to be *very frequently* or, on the other hand, to be only *sometimes*. It all depends on the student's frame of reference. In deciding what level of intervention is necessary, it is helpful to look at what you know of—and can learn about—the student, in addition to the student's responses to the questionnaire.

GUIDELINES FOR COMPLETING THE INTERVENTION COMPLETION QUESTIONNAIRE

Areas requiring interventions are the only questions to be completed. The list of required interventions is on the student pre-test questionnaire, and there are four degrees of implementation: high, moderate, low, and none. To receive a rating of *high*, the student/family must have

- participated in the appropriate number of levels of intervention; that is, if Levels I, II and III are required, all three were received
- completed all of the needed intervention activities; for example, in the suggested interventions under Level I, all of the suggestions would have been implemented

To receive a rating of *moderate*, the student/family must have

- participated in the appropriate number of levels of intervention; that is, if Levels I, II, and III are required, all three were received

Student# 032367   Version—Secondary

This student scored *0.20 on the substance abuse risk* assessment test, which predicts a *medium* risk for substance abuse and scored *0.11 on the dropout risk* assessment, which predicts a *low* risk for school dropout. Write the level of intervention completion (0 = none, low =1, moderate =2, high =3) under the recommended level.

1. How often angry?—very frequently
   Use Level I, Level II, and Level III interventions.
      2   3   1
2. Friends who use alcohol or drugs?—3 or 4
   Use Level I and Level II interventions.
      2   0
3. Close adults who use alcohol or drugs frequently?—1 or 4
4. Times high or drunk?—3 to 5 times
5. Family against drugs?—a little against
6. Parents know whereabouts?—seldom
7. Use if a friend dared you?—not sure what I would do
8. Times arrested?—1 to 2
   Use Level I and Level II interventions.
      2   2
9. Ever suspended or expelled?— yes
10. Number of D's or F's?—1
11. Ever arrested?—no
12. Juvenile delinquency record?— false
13. Certified disability?— true
14. Times absent last semester?— 00
15. Times moved or changed schools last year?— 2

Figure 5.2 *Sample Completion of Intervention Report.*

- completed *many* of the needed intervention activities; for example, in the suggested interventions below under Level I, many of the suggestions would have been implemented

To receive a rating of *low*, the student/family must have

- participated in *some* of the appropriate number of levels of intervention; that is, if Levels I, II, and III are required, at least one was received

- completed some of the needed intervention activities; for example, in the suggested interventions below under Level I, some of the suggestions would have been implemented

To receive a rating of *none*, the student/family must have

- participated in none of the appropriate number of levels of intervention; that is, if Levels I, II, and III are required, none were received
- completed none of the needed intervention activities; for example, in the suggested interventions below under Level I, none of the suggestions would have been implemented

The completion of intervention form is shown in Figure 5.2.

THE QUESTIONNAIRE AND SUGGESTED INTERVENTIONS

Question 1

The first question students respond to is: How often are you angry? If the student responds with a 2 score or higher, you will be directed to one of the following interventions, as will be noted on the computerized score.

1. How often are you angry? (0) never, (1) sometimes, (2) frequently, (3) very frequently

Level of Completion of Intervention: High (3), Moderate (2), Low (1), and None (0)

Level I

Interview the student for reasons, in order to select the appropriate interventions.

First, establish a caring and helpful environment/relationship with the student so that the student will trust you to give you information.

You may share some information about yourself, that you care about students, that you work on special programs, that you experienced some challenging times growing up, etc. (whatever may be *appropriate*).

Suggestions for discussion topics include: Tell me about your day. Is there a particular time of the day you notice anger? Is there a particular situation/person (teacher, peer, parent, important relationship, etc.) that triggers anger for you? Have you gone through any family or relationship changes in the last few years?

This initial interview may show you what additional interventions, if any, are needed. For example, if the student's anger is a result of inadequate social skills, identifying and teaching particular skills may be helpful. If the anger is due to a family crisis, other responses will be more appropriate (see examples below).

Level II

If indicated by the computer recommendation or information gathered in the interview, assign the student to a mentor, counselor, or peer assistant who can provide ongoing support and monitoring of the student's situation. If your school does not have a mentoring program in place, this may be done informally. The mentor needs to have regularly scheduled contact with the student and provide ''evidence'' that there is someone who cares. This might involve help with schoolwork or other problems, sending a birthday card and other little notes, and occasional activities together.

Level II interventions may also include informal discussion and brainstorming of alternative behaviors and teaching of social skills or self-esteem fundamentals.

If no mentors are available at your site, consider referral to an outside group that offers mentors. (Sample programs may include Big Sisters/Brothers, College or Business Mentoring Programs, etc.)

Level III

Level III interventions will vary according to the reasons for the student's anger. Possible interventions are as follows:

(*1*) If the student's anger is due to a crisis in her/his personal life—birth of a sibling, divorce, serious illness or death in the family, etc.— teach coping skills, such as recognizing feelings of anger, control issues, and depression; coming to terms with problems; and learning to hope. (Sample programs may include student individual or group counseling, STAGES, etc.)

(*2*) Teaching stress management skills may also be helpful. (Sample programs may include STAR, STAGES, etc.)

(*3*) If the student's anger is due to lack of social skills, teach communication skills, skills for making friends, etc., as appropriate. (Sample programs include STAR, etc.)

(4) If the student's anger is due to deep-seated family or social problems, consider referral for individual and/or family counseling.

Question 2

The second question on the questionnaire is: How many adults do you know well that often drink alcohol? If the student's response is (1) or higher, the following interventions may be recommended on your computer readout. Please note that, with this question, a Level I response is necessary with a (1) response rather than a (2). It only takes *one* adult in the family who drinks alcohol often to put a child at risk.

2. How many ADULTS do you know well that often drink alcohol? (0) none, (1) 1 to 4, (2) 5 to 9, (3) more than 9

Level I

Interview the student for reasons, in order to select the appropriate intervention(s). First, establish a caring and helpful environment/relationship with the student so that the student will trust you to give you information. You may share some information about yourself, that you care about students, that you work on special programs, that you experienced some challenging times growing up, etc. (whatever may be *appropriate*).

Suggestions for discussion topics include: Tell me about your day. What is it that you have noticed about alcohol? Who do you know that drinks often? How do you feel about that? What do you think about that? How does (that person's) drinking affect you/your family/your school work? What happens when this person drinks? (Be sure to reassure the student you are there to help and that there is someone who cares.) Have you or your family gone through any changes in the last few years? (The information in this interview may be critical, to check for child abuse.

This initial interview may show you what additional interventions, if any, are needed.

Discovering what role the adults who drink often play in the student's life will determine what level of intervention to implement. If parents or other important figures are substance abusers, Level III responses will almost surely be needed. If the student's relationship to substance-abusing adults is not very significant, Level II responses may be sufficient.

Level II

If indicated by the computer recommendation or information gathered in the interview, assign the student to a mentor or counselor who can provide ongoing support and monitoring of the student's situation. If your school does not have a mentoring program in place, this may be done informally. The mentor needs to have regularly scheduled contact with the student and provide "evidence" that there is someone who cares. This might involve help with schoolwork or other problems, sending a birthday card and other little notes, and occasional activities together.

You may consider assigning the student to drug and alcohol education programs that provide information about the requirements of a healthy body, the physical and social effects of drug abuse, the symptoms of drug abuse, and learning to say "No." (Sample programs may include STAR, QUEST, OSS, DARE, PAL, etc.)

Level III

Consider referring student and/or family to outside social agencies for family counseling and/or drug/alcohol programs. (Sample programs may include AA, specialized community hospital programs, county programs, Child Protective Services, etc.)

If needed, refer student for special programs for the children of substance abusers, which can help the student to understand that s/he is not responsible for the behavior of substance-abusing adults and which can provide coping skills. (Sample programs may include STAGES, CHILDREN ARE PEOPLE TOO, and BABES, as well as city and county programs.)

If appropriate, arrange for teaching "Latch-Key" skills for the child whose parents are not able to care adequately for him/her. (Sample programs may include checking with your County Office of Education, City Programs, etc.)

If the exposure to drug-abusing adults is so serious that a referral to Child Protective Services (CPS) is indicated, keep contact with the student as he/she proceeds through this process. (Children often feel abandoned and "at fault" when CPS is involved.) Reassure the child that s/he is courageous and that telling the truth is important: they are not responsible for the substance or other abuse! Involve administrators and other appropriate and available personnel in this decision. If there is evidence for such a referral from your initial interview with the student, you need to proceed directly to this level of intervention after the interview.

Question 3

The third question is: How often are you afraid to express your anger to people? If the student's response is 2 or higher, the following interventions may be recommended on your computer readout.

3. How often are you afraid to express your anger to people? (0) never, (1) sometimes, (2) frequently, (3) always

If the student's response is 2 or higher, the following interventions are recommended.

Level I

Interview the student for reasons, in order to select the appropriate intervention(s).

First, establish a caring and helpful environment/relationship with the student so that the student will trust you to give you information. You may share some information about yourself, that you care about students, that you work on special programs, that you experienced some challenging times growing up, etc. (whatever may be *appropriate*).

Suggestions for discussion topics include: Tell me about your day. What situations bring about anger for you? What do people do that really bothers you? How do you think people usually experience anger? What do you think about anger? What happens when people get angry? What is the worst thing you can think of that might happen to a person who expresses anger? What else? Who would be the most difficult person to show your anger to? What might happen? What do people do when they are really upset? Have you gone through any family changes the last few years? What changes has your family experienced?

This initial interview may show you what additional interventions, if any, are needed.

Level II

If student's inability to express anger seems to be primarily a function of confusion about this often misunderstood emotion, inadequate modeling, and/or information, provide education on appropriate and inappropriate expressions of anger. Explain that anger is a natural emotion, brainstorm healthy ways of both expressing and managing anger, model appropriate angry behavior, etc. Infuse such modeling and discussion into the daily life of the classroom, monitoring the student's progress informally. (Sample programs may include STAGES.)

You may want to consider the appropriateness of a simple behavior modification program for the student, such as a system of "rewards" for appropriate expressions of anger. (Remember that an elaborate program need not be designed—the system may be as simple as an agreement between you and the student that you will send her/him a private signal of congratulations when she expresses anger appropriately.)

Level III

If the student needs to learn to communicate thoughts and feelings assertively, use a communication skills program to teach these skills. (Sample programs may include STAR, YES, PAL, etc.)

If the student's fear of expressing anger is appropriate, as in the case of an abusive parent, refer to appropriate personnel and agencies—school administration, counselor and/or psychologist, or Child Protective Services, etc., keeping in contact with the student as s/he goes through this often confusing process. Reassure the child that s/he is not at fault and is a courageous person for sharing the truth with you. Let the child know you will not abandon him/her.

Question 4

The fourth question on the questionnaire is: How much do you feel your family is against drugs? If the student's response is 2 or higher, the following interventions may be recommended on your computer readout.

4. How much do you feel your family is against drugs? (0) very much against, (1) quite a bit against, (2) a little against, (3) not against

If the student's response is 2 or higher, the following interventions are recommended.

Level I

Interview the student for reasons, in order to select the appropriate intervention(s).

First, establish a caring and helpful environment/relationship with the student so that the student will trust you to give you information. You may share some information about yourself, that you care about students, that you work on special programs, that you experienced some challenging times growing up, etc. (whatever may be *appropriate*).

Suggestions for discussion topics include: Is s/he simply unaware of family's attitude because the topic isn't discussed? Are the parents articulately in favor of drug use, etc.? How can you tell people in your family feel that way? What have you been told about drugs? What have you seen happen when people use drugs? Do you know anyone who might think drugs are OK?

The responses will tell you what additional response, if any, is required.

Level II

Counsel with parents about the need for values clarification. Would parent education be appropriate and acceptable? (Sample programs may include district and/or police department parent education programs, Neighborhoods in Action, Active Parenting, etc.)

Consider assigning the student to drug and alcohol education programs that provide information about the requirements of a healthy body, the physical and social effects of drug abuse, the symptoms of drug abuse, and learning to say "No." (Sample programs may include STAR, QUEST, OSS, DARE, PAL, etc.)

Level III

If you note a crisis situation, consider referring student and/or family to outside social agencies for family counseling and/or drug/alcohol programs. (Sample programs may include AA, specialized hospital programs, city and county programs, etc.) Also, listen for signs of child abuse and make the appropriate reports, if necessary (including Child

Protective Services), reassuring the child as they go through the process.

If indicated, refer student for special programs for the children of substance abusers, which can help the student to understand that s/he is not responsible for the behavior of substance-abusing adults and which can provide coping skills. (Sample programs may include STAGES, CHILDREN ARE PEOPLE TOO, BABES, and other city and county programs.)

If appropriate, arrange for teaching "Latch-Key" skills for the child whose parents are not able to care adequately for him/her. (For sample programs check with city/county/district programs to best fit student's needs.)

Question 5

The fifth question is: When you are away from home or after school, how often do your parents/guardians know where you are? If the student's response is 2 or higher, the following interventions may be recommended on your computer readout.

5. When you are away from home or after school, how often do your parents/guardians know where you are? (0) always, (1) usually, (2) seldom, (3) never

If the student's response is 2 or higher, the following interventions are recommended.

Level I

Interview the student for reasons, in order to select the appropriate intervention(s).

First, establish a caring and helpful environment/relationship with the student so that the student will trust you to give you information. You may share some information about yourself, that you care about students, that you work on special programs, that you experienced some challenging times growing up, etc. (whatever may be *appropriate*).

Topics for discussion may include: Does the family have a child-care problem? Have the parents indicated that they don't care where the student is? Is there evidence that the parents feel they can't control the student, etc.? What would happen if your parents did know what you are doing? Has your family gone through any major changes in the last few years? How do people in your family feel? What do people in your family think about? What would happen if something happened to you while you were out? How does your family feel about your friends? At what age do you think kids can take care of themselves? How do you know that?

The responses will tell you what additional response, if any, is required.

Level II

Interview parents. The family may need referral to after-school-care programs such as latch-key programs operated by the YMCA/YWCA or local colleges or the district, Girls' Club/Boys' Club, etc. Parents may need referral to district or outside programs for parent effectiveness training — need for setting limits, communicating with children, etc.

If indicated by the computer recommendation or information gathered in the interview, assign the student to a mentor, counselor, or peer assistant who can provide ongoing support and monitoring of the student's situation. If your school does not have a mentoring program in place, this may be done informally. The mentor needs to have regularly scheduled contact with the student and provide "evidence" that there is someone who cares. This might involve help with schoolwork or other problems, sending a birthday card and other little notes, and occasional activities together.

Level III

Lack of supervision may be so serious that a referral to Child Protective Services is indicated because of neglect. Involve administrators and other appropriate and available personnel in this decision. If there is evidence for such a referral from your initial interview with the student, you need to proceed directly to this level of intervention after the interview.

Student may need close monitoring at school, having someone to "check in" with several times a day. The mentor would show care and concern in a benevolent manner.

Question 6

The sixth question on the questionnaire is: How often do you feel all alone? If the student's response is 2 or higher, the following interventions may be recommended on your computer readout (note that the numbering is different on this question).

6. How often do you feel all alone? *(3) always, (2) usually, (1) seldom, (0) never*

If the student's response is 2 or higher, the following interventions are recommended.

Level I

Interview the student for reasons, in order to select the appropriate interventions.

First, establish a caring and helpful environment/relationship with the student so that the student will trust you to give you information. You may share some information about yourself, that you care about students, that you work on special programs, that you experienced some challenging times growing up, etc. (whatever may be *appropriate*).

Topics for discussion may include: Tell me about your day. (Is the student lonely due to problems making friends? If that is the problem, is it shyness, being new, or the fact that something about the student's behavior causes his peers to reject him?) Has your family gone through any changes in the last few years? How does it feel for you to be alone? What do you think about? What happens when you get home from school? What do you and your family do after school/in the evening/on the weekend? What kinds of things make people sad? What happens when people feel sad? etc. (If you sense the student may be depressed, check with counselors, school psychologists, etc. for intervention on Level III.)

Choose appropriate Level II and/or Level III interventions according to the results of this interview.

Level II

If indicated by the computer recommendation or information gathered in the interview, assign the student to a mentor, counselor, or peer assistant who can provide ongoing support and monitoring of the student's situation. If your school does not have a mentoring program in place, this may be done informally. The mentor needs to have regularly scheduled contact with the student and provide ''evidence'' that there is someone who cares. This might involve help with schoolwork or other problems, sending a birthday card and other little notes, and occasional activities together.

It may also be helpful to assign a "special friend" to the student. Your school may have a mechanism for doing this: leadership team, peer assistance team, PAL, etc. If not, make use of your contact with and knowledge of the other students to find students who would enjoy doing this and who would also be in contact with you or other mentors, so that the peer does not feel responsible for the identified student's behavior.

Level III

If the student has been through family changes and is feeling sad, s/he may not understand this natural emotion. (Sample programs may include STAGES to help children manage reactions to changes.) The need may be in the area of social skills. (Sample programs may include STAR, HERE'S LOOKING AT YOU 2000, etc., that can help a student learn assertive social skills to reach out to peers.)

If the student seems depressed, referral of student to school/community counseling services may be necessary. Family referral to outside agencies may also be helpful. If the family has been through a major change, parenting resources through STAGES or other grief, adjustment, or loss programs may be helpful.

Question 7

The seventh question is: Do your parents/guardians listen to you and attempt to understand your problems? If the student's response is 2 or higher, the following interventions may be recommended on your comuter readout.

7. Do your parents/guardians listen to you and attempt to understand your problems? (0) always, (1) usually, (2) seldom, (3) never

If the student's response is 2 or higher, the following interventions are recommended.

Level I

Interview the student for reasons, in order to select the appropriate interventions.

First, establish a caring and helpful environment/relationship with the student so that the student will trust you to give you information. You may share some information about yourself, that you care about students, that you work on special programs, that you experienced some challenging times growing up, etc. (whatever may be *appropriate*).

Topics for discussion may include: Whom do you share your thoughts and feelings with at school/home? What happens when you get home from school/in the evening/weekends? When do people in your family talk? What happens when people in your family talk together? How do you feel during the day? (Check to see if parents' hectic work scheduling makes it difficult to provide support.) Has your family been through any big changes in the last few years? (Is there evidence that parents are unaware of the importance of listening to their children?)

The student's responses to these questions will suggest what level of intervention would be beneficial, if any.

Level II

It may be helpful to conduct a parent conference. The content will be a function of the results of the student interview and the responses the parent makes during this conference. It may be that the family is experiencing a crisis or has many demands and needs referral to outside agencies. The parent may need/desire parent education. This education may simply take the form of the communication that occurs at this conference—the parent becomes aware of the student's feelings and understands the significance of her/his responsiveness. If more education is needed, it might be provided by the school counselor or psychologist or by a district parenting class (Sample programs may include STAGES for parents, ACTIVE PARENTING, city and county programs, etc.)

Teaching the student social skills to express thoughts and feelings may be beneficial. Modeling sharing and teaching social conversation and listening skills may be needed.

(Sample programs may include STAR, HERE'S LOOKING AT YOU 2000, etc.)

Level III

The student may be experiencing some kind of life crisis—birth of a sibling, serious illness or death of a family member or other significant person, family financial crisis, divorce, etc. If so, provide support and instruction in coping skills, such as recognizing feelings of anger, control issues and depression; coming to terms with problems; and learning to hope. (Sample programs may include student counseling groups, STAGES, grief and loss information, etc.)

Referral to counseling – If the student is angry or depressed, it may be helpful to spend time with the school counselor or psychologist for additional support. It may also be important to refer student and/or family for individual and/or family counseling or district/city/county programs.

Question 8

The eighth question is: If a friend offered you a drug or alcohol and said that you're chicken if you don't try it, would you. . . . If the student's response is 1 or higher, the following interventions may be recommended on your computer readout.

8. If a friend offered you a drug or alcohol and said that you're chicken if you don't try it, would you: (0) not try it, (1) not sure, (2) try it

If the student's response is (1) or higher, the following interventions are recommended.

Level I

Interview the student for reasons, in order to select the appropriate intervention(s).

First, establish a caring and helpful environment/relationship with the student so that the student will trust you to give you information. You may share some information about yourself, that you care about students, that you work on special programs, that you experienced some challenging times growing up, etc. (whatever may be *appropriate*).

Topics for discussion may include: How many friends do you have? What do friends do together? What happens if a person does not have any friends? What does being a ''friend'' mean to you? Do you know what peer pressure is? How do most people handle peer pressure? Why do you think people have a hard time saying ''No''? Have you and/or your family gone through any big changes in the last few years?

The responses will suggest what additional interventions, if any, are needed.

How Many Friends Do You Have?

Level II

If indicated by the computer recommendation or information gathered in the interview, assign the student to a mentor, counselor, or peer assistant who can provide ongoing support and monitoring of the student's situation. If your school does not have a mentoring program in place, this may be done informally. The mentor needs to have regularly scheduled contact with the student and provide ''evidence'' that there is someone who cares. This might involve help with school-work or other problems, sending a birthday card and other little notes, and occasional activities together.

Consider assigning the student to drug and alcohol education programs that provide information about the requirements of a healthy body, the physical and social effects of drug abuse, the symptoms of drug abuse, and learning to say '' No.'' (Sample programs may include STAR, QUEST, OSS, DARE, PAL, etc.)

Level III

Consider training the student in refusal and assertiveness skills beyond those offered in standard drug education programs. (Sample programs may include STAR and individual counseling.)

If the student's response is 3, that s/he would "try it," proceed with all of the interventions suggested above, and consider these additional responses.

Assign the student to a school counseling group focused upon special problems and/or substance abuse. If this is unavailable, consider individual counseling at school and/or individual or group counseling at an outside facility.

Conduct a parent conference, if you suspect the student already is (or may soon become) involved with drugs. The conference may reveal a need for parent education programs. (Sample programs may include district or police department programs for parents about drug abuse, Neighborhoods in Action, District Tough Love Programs, Active Parenting, etc.)

If the student is experiencing a life crisis, consider teaching skills for coping: recognizing feelings of anger, control issues, and depression; coming to terms with problems; and learning to hope. (Sample programs may include STAGES, city and county programs, etc.)

Consider referral to outside programs or agencies aimed at student users or near users, such as those offered by some police and probation departments.

Question 9

The ninth question on the questionnaire is: Have you ever been sent to the principal's office for a behavior problem? If the student's response is 1, the following interventions may be recommended on your computer readout.

9. Have you ever been sent to the principal's office for a behavior problem? (1) yes, (0) no

If student's response is 1, yes, the following interventions are recommended.

Level I

Interview the student for reasons, in order to select the appropriate intervention(s).

First, establish a caring and helpful environment/relationship with the student so that the student will trust you to give you information. You may share some information about yourself, that you care about students, that you work on special programs, that you experienced some challenging times growing up, etc. (whatever may be *appropriate*).

Topics for discussion may include: How many times have you been sent to the principal's office? What is your version of what happened (choose one or more occasions)? Tell me about the kids at school. What happens during your day/after school/evenings/weekends? Have you and/or your family gone through any big changes in the last few years? What kinds of things make you angry? How do people usually express anger? What happens to them? How are you doing in class? What do you think about your teacher? What does your teacher think about you? What subject(s) do you like/not like? What consequences do you have at school/home for seeing the principal?

The responses will guide your choice of any additional interventions.

Level II

If indicated by the computer recommendation or information gathered in the interview, assign the student to a mentor, counselor, or peer assistant who can provide ongoing support and monitoring of the student's situation. If your school does not have a mentoring program in place, this may be done informally. The mentor needs to have regularly scheduled contact with the student and provide "evidence" that there is someone who cares. This might involve help with schoolwork or other problems, sending a birthday card and other little notes, and occasional activities together.

Consider referral to school counselor, if available. Consider a behavior modification program focused on reducing number of incidents of misbehavior and/or referrals, rewarding the student for appropriate behavior, etc.

Hold a parent conference. Is behavior the same at home? If not, what does the parent think is wrong at school? If behavior is the same at home, offer help. If appropriate, discuss some of the options described below, as possible steps the family might take. (Sample programs may include STAGES for parents, Active Parenting, and district/city/county programs.)

Provide new responsibilities as alternative activities to replace the patterns that have gotten the student into trouble. Provide opportunities for involvement in clubs, scouts, etc. Give the student a special responsibility (something active) at school and provide recognition for completion.

Provide academic assistance if behavior problems are related to academic problems. (Sample programs may include tutoring, peer tutoring, ESL, changing student's program, referral to the student study team, or help for parents on how to work with the child at home.)

Level III

Provide instruction in social skills if student's misbehavior reflects lack of knowledge in interpersonal communication and/or lack of social skills that lead to aggressive responses. Consider special instruction in these areas: understanding own personality style, making friends, being a friend, communicating needs (Sample programs may include STAR, PAL, etc.)

If the behaviors seem connected to a lack of interpersonal skills and relationships with peers, consider assigning a student "special friend" to give the student recognition and extra attention. (Sample programs may include peer assistance programs and PAL.)

Consider referral for individual and/or group counseling for the student and family counseling within the district/city/county if the student's behavior is due to deep-seated family or social problems.

Monitor frequency and severity of referrals to the principal to see if problems persist.

Question 10

The tenth question on the questionnaire is: How many D's and F's did you receive last semester/quarter? If the student's response is 2 or higher, the following interventions may be recommended on your computer readout.

10. How many D's and F's did you receive last semester/quarter? 1, 2, 3, 4, 5, 6

If student's response is 2 or more, the following interventions are recommended.

Level I

Interview the student for reasons, in order to select the appropriate intervention(s).

First, establish a caring and helpful environment/relationship with the student so that the student will trust you to give you information. You may share some information about yourself, that you care about students, that you work on special programs, that you experienced some challenging times growing up, etc. (whatever may be *appropriate*).

Topics for discussion may include: What do you think of/feel about school? What do you think of your teacher? What is your favorite subject? Least favorite? Tell me what happens after school/evenings/weekends. Have you and/or your family gone through any big changes? Who do you hang around with at school? What is the hardest thing about school? Is there anyone to help you at home? What year in school was your best/most difficult? (You may need to check Cum File, especially for younger students. Is there a language or other learning difficulty?)

Responses to these questions will identify what, if any, interventions may be helpful.

Level II

If indicated by the computer recommendation or information gathered in the interview, assign the student to a mentor, counselor, or peer assistant who can provide ongoing support and monitoring of the student's situation. If your school does not have a mentoring program in place, this may be done informally. The mentor needs to have regularly scheduled contact with the student and provide ''evidence'' that there is someone who cares. This might involve help with schoolwork or other problems, sending a birthday card and other little notes, and occasional activities together.

Schedule a parent conference. Explore the same topics you covered in the interview with the student. In addition, does parent appear to need help with parenting skills and/or training in how to help a child with schoolwork? You may be able to do this parent education during the conference. If more help is needed, refer the parent to school parenting and/or homework workshops, if available. Refer to outside programs if needed and available.

Provide academic assistance. Assign a tutor, if available, or guide student to outside tutoring programs. Arrange for or provide instruction in English as a Second Language, if needed.

Consider using a behavior modification program with the student, such as a daily contract for getting work done on time and correctly, with an appropriate system of positive responses.

Level III

Refer student to the student study team for evaluation and recommendations if there appear to be severe academic problems.

Refer student for counseling if the academic problems seem to be a function of personal problems. If the student is experiencing a life crisis, consider teaching skills for coping: recognizing feelings of anger, control issues, and depression; coming to terms with problems; and learning to hope. (Sample programs may include STAGES, small group counseling, and PAL.)

Question 11

The eleventh question is: Have you ever been suspended or expelled from school? If the student's response is 1, the following interventions may be recommended on your computer readout.

11. Have you ever been SUSPENDED or EXPELLED from school? (1) yes, (0) no

If student's response is (1), yes, the following interventions are recommended.

Level I

Interview the student for reasons, in order to select the appropriate intervention(s).

First, establish a caring and helpful environment/relationship with the student so that the student will trust you to give you information. You may share some information about yourself, that you care about students, that you work on special programs, that you experienced some challenging times growing up, etc. (whatever may be *appropriate*).

Topics for discussion may include: What do you think of/feel about school? What happened to cause you to be suspended? How are things at home? When did things get tough here at school? How are your relationships going (friends, family, etc.)? Anything you feel really angry about now? Have you or any family members been through any big changes in the last few years? This year? (Check Cum File.) How many times have you been suspended? What happens at home when this occurs?

The student's response will guide you in deciding which additional interventions, if any, are needed.

Level II

If indicated by the computer recommendation or information gathered in the interview, assign the student to a mentor or counselor who can provide ongoing support and monitoring of the student's situation. If your school does not have a mentoring program in place, this may be done informally. The mentor needs to have regularly scheduled contact with the student and provide "evidence" that there is someone who cares. This might involve help with schoolwork or other problems, sending a birthday card and other little notes, and occasional activities together.

Assign student to a peer advisor if your school offers such a program, particularly if the suspension may be partially a function of a poor choice of friends. (Sample programs may include peer assistance programs, PAL, etc.)

Have a parent conference. Explore the same topics you covered in the interview with the student. In addition, does parent appear to need help with parenting skills and/or training in how to help a child with behavior/anger management, etc.? You may be able to do this parent education during the conference. If more help is needed, refer the parent to school parenting and/or district/city/county workshops, etc. Refer to outside programs if needed and available.

Level III

If indicated, arrange for instruction in social skills if student's misbehavior reflects lack of knowledge in interpersonal communication and/or lack of social skills. Consider special instruction in these areas: understanding own personality style, making friends, being a friend, communicating needs, etc. (Sample programs may include STAR and PAL.)

Refer student to the student study team for evaluation and recommendations if there appear to be severe academic/behavior problems.

Refer student/family for individual or group counseling if the expulsions or suspensions seem to be a function of personal problems. If the student is experiencing a life crisis, consider teaching skills for coping: recognizing feelings of anger, control issues, and depression; coming to terms with problems; and learning to hope. (Sample programs may include STAGES, small group counseling, etc.)

Question 12

The twelfth question on the questionnaire is: Have you ever been disciplined for a behavior problem? If the student's response is 1, the following interventions may be recommended on your computer readout.

12. Have you ever been disciplined for a behavior problem? (1) yes, (0) no

If student's response is (1), yes, the following interventions are recommended.

Level I

Interview the student for reasons, in order to select the appropriate intervention(s).

First, establish a caring and helpful environment/relationship with the student so that the student will trust you to give you information. You may share some information about yourself, that you care about students, that you work on special programs, that you experienced some challenging times growing up, etc. (whatever may be *appropriate*).

Topics for discussion may include: What do you think of/feel about school? What happened when you were in trouble? How many times this year were you disciplined for behavior problems? Has this happened in other years at school? What was your best year in school? What was it you liked about that year? What was your worst year? Did anything happen that stands out in your mind? Have you or family members gone through any big changes? What do you do after school/evenings/weekends? How do people in your family usually handle anger? What happens? Usually students who are disciplined at school have a lot on their minds. What is happening in your life? Who do you hang around with at school/after school?

The response will guide your choice of interventions.

Level II

If indicated by the computer recommendation or information gathered in the interview, assign the student to a mentor or counselor who can provide ongoing support and monitoring of the student's situation. If your school does not have a mentoring program in place, this may be done informally. The mentor needs to have regularly scheduled contact with the student and provide "evidence" that there is someone who cares. This might involve help with schoolwork or other problems, sending a birthday card and other little notes, and occasional activities together.

Monitor frequency and severity of problems to see if problems persist. Consider referral to school counselor, if available. Consider a behavior modification program focused on reducing number of incidents of misbehavior and/or referrals, with appropriate rewards.

Hold a parent conference. Is behavior the same at home? If not, what does the parent think is wrong at school? If behavior is the same at home, offer help. If appropriate, discuss some of the options described below as possible steps the family might take. (Sample programs may include: STAGES for parents, Active Parenting, and district/city/county programs.)

If the behaviors seem to be a cry for attention, consider assigning a student "special friend" to give the student recognition and extra attention. (Sample programs may include PAL, peer assistance programs, etc.) Giving the student a special responsibility at school might also help.

Suggest new activities if the student needs alternative activities to replace the patterns that have gotten her/him into trouble. Provide opportunities for involvement in clubs, scouts, etc.

Level III

Arrange for instruction in social skills if student's misbehavior reflects lack of knowledge in interpersonal communication and/or lack of social skills. Consider special instruction in these areas: understanding own personality style, making friends, being a friend, communicating needs, etc. (Sample programs may include STAR, PAL, etc.)

Refer student to the student study team for evaluation and recommendations if there appear to be severe academic/behavior problems.

Refer student/family for individual or group counseling if the behaviors seem to be a function of personal problems. If the student is experiencing a life crisis, consider teaching skills for coping: recognizing feelings of anger, control issues, and depression; coming to terms with problems; and learning to hope. (Sample programs may include STAGES, small group counseling, etc.)

Question 13

The thirteenth question on the questionnaire is: How many times last semester were you absent? If the student's response is 2 or higher, the following interventions may be recommended on your computer readout.

13. How many times last semester were you absent? Responses will vary from 0 to 99.

If the student scored with a 20 or higher, the following interventions are recommended. *Note:* This number is designed for schools where a high absence rate is typical. The critical number may be less than 20 in some schools; consider the normal attendance profile for your school.

Level I

Interview the student for reasons, in order to select the appropriate intervention(s).

First, establish a caring and helpful environment/relationship with the student so that the student will trust you to give you information. You may share some information about yourself, that you care about students, that you work on special programs, that you experienced some challenging times growing up, etc. (whatever may be *appropriate*).

Topics for discussion may include: What kinds of things keep you at home? (Check Cum File or other records for a pattern of excessive absences.) What do you think of school this year? What do you like/dislike? Tell me about your friends. What do you think of your teacher this year? What does your teacher think about you? Have you or family members been through any big changes (new baby, financial, divorce, loss, moving, etc.)? What happens when you get sick? Who takes care of you? (Does the student have a neglected or undetected health problem? If indicated, consider additional interventions, working with your school nurse or community health programs.) How are things at home? (Check for any signs of abuse and make appropriate reports to your school team and Child Protective Services.)

Responses in this interview will direct you to other interventions, if any.

Level II

Monitor student absence. Consider a behavior modification program to improve attendance—some schools have special attendance clubs; individual teachers can also design a program of attendance incentives.

Assign student to an adult mentor to increase student's bonding to school—many students are convinced that, "Nobody cares whether I'm here or not. They probably don't even notice." If indicated by the computer recommendation or information gathered in the interview, assign the student to a mentor or counselor who can provide ongoing support and monitoring of the student's situation. If your school does not have a mentoring program in place, this may be done informally. The mentor needs to have regularly scheduled contact with the student and provide "evidence" that there is someone who cares. This might involve help with schoolwork or other problems, sending a birthday card and other little notes, and occasional activities together.

Refer student or family to school nurse or outside health provider if student has (or may have) unmet health needs.

If the behaviors seem to be a cry for attention, consider assigning a student "special friend" to give the student recognition and extra attention. (Sample programs may include PAL and peer assistance programs.)

If the student indicates that s/he was absent for reasons other than illness or for very minor complaints, the following interventions are recommended.

Level III

If student absence is due to parental neglect, babysitting, etc., hold a parent conference, with possible referral to district or site attendance personnel, and/or SARB, and, if necessary, report to Child Protective Services.

If absences seem related to emotional problems, consider referral for counseling. If student is experiencing a life crisis—serious illness or death in the family, divorce, birth of a sibling, etc.—consider teaching skills for coping. This includes learning to recognize feelings of anger, control issues, and depression; learning to come to terms with problems; and learning to hope. (Sample programs may include STAGES, STAR, and individual or small group counseling.)

Question 14

The fourteenth question is: How many times have you moved or changed schools in the previous year? If the student's response is 2 or higher, the following interventions may be recommended on your computer readout.

14. How many times have you moved or changed schools in the previous year? 1, 2, 3, 4, 5, 6

If the response is 2 or more, the following interventions are recommended.

Level I

Interview the student for reasons, in order to select the appropriate intervention(s).

First, establish a caring and helpful environment/relationship with the student so that the student will trust you to give you information. You may share some information about yourself, that you care about students, that you work on special programs, that you experienced some challenging times growing up, etc. (whatever may be *appropriate*).

Topics for discussion may include: Sometimes it's hard for people to move. What is moving like for you? Which move did you like? What was the hardest move? A lot of people have a hard time making new friends. How have you done with making friends? What do you like to do with your friends? What kind of things do friends like to do here at this school? How are things going at home? What do you think of school/your teacher? Have you or other family members been through other big changes in the last year? When there are lots of changes, it is sometimes hard on families. How are you doing? How is your workload here at school? How long do you spend on homework?

The student's responses will determine the interventions you select, if any.

Level II

If indicated by the computer recommendation or information gathered in the interview, assign the student to a mentor or counselor who can provide ongoing support and monitoring of the student's situation. If your school does not have a mentoring program in place, this may be done informally. The mentor needs to have regularly scheduled contact with the student and provide "evidence" that there is someone who cares. This might involve help with schoolwork or other problems, sending a birthday card and other little notes, and occasional activities together.

Level II interventions may also include informal discussion and brainstorming of alternative behaviors and teaching of social skills or self-esteem fundamentals. (Sample programs may include STAR, etc.)

If no mentors are available at your site, consider referral to an outside group that offers mentors. (Sample programs may include Big Sisters/Brothers, college or business mentoring programs, etc.)

It may also be helpful to assign a "Special Friend" to the student. Your school may have a mechanism for doing this: leadership team, peer assistance team, PAL, etc. If not, make use of your contact with and knowledge of the other students to find students who would enjoy doing this and who would also be in contact with you or other mentors, so that the peer does not feel responsible for the student's behavior.

Level III

If the student has been through family changes and is feeling sad, s/he may not understand this natural emotion. (Sample programs may include STAGES to help children manage reactions to changes.) The need may be in the area of social skills. (Sample programs may include STAR, HERE'S LOOKING AT YOU 2000, etc., that can help a student learn assertive social skills to reach out to peers.)

Individual or group counseling programs may help this student to talk with others who have been through changes and to learn coping skills.

If the student seems angry or depressed, referral of student to school/community counseling services may be necessary. Family referral to outside agencies may also be helpful. If the family has been through a major change, parenting resources through STAGES or other grief, adjustment, or district/city/community loss programs may be helpful.

Chapter 6

USING COMPUTER-ASSISTED INSTRUCTION FOR STUDENTS AT RISK OF SUBSTANCE ABUSE

Computer-assisted instruction (CAI) makes it easy for a teacher to create software that will help at-risk and other students who respond well to inter-action with a computer. We call the software *Creating CAI,* and any teacher can learn to fill in the screens by typing them on her/his word processor. Guidelines for using CAI are included, such as activities that offer extrinsic rewards to students at risk who may place limited value on education. The guidelines include strategies such as creation of an active and thoughtful learning setting, visible recognition of various types, creation of curricula that interest these students, setting clear goals, using positive reinforcement, cooperative learning, inducing a readiness to learn, encouraging student responses in class, teacher efficacy, self-concept development, tutorial ser-vices, flexible scheduling, and alternative schooling options.

CREATE AN ACTIVE LEARNING SETTING

Students at risk of substance abuse need to be challenged by active learning opportunities and many different instructional strategies. They are easily bored, which makes them difficult to teach. It is therefore worth extra effort on the part of the teacher to set up an active learning environment. Kierstead (1986) suggests teachers focus on sharing responsibility with students for creating an active learning setting.

While allowing students to operate independently through planning the use of their own time and by making decisions regarding pace, sequence, and content of the projects, the teacher never fully relinquishes control. Instead, the teacher establishes a set of rules, routines, and consequences which make it possible to monitor and guide what students are doing. For example, students are taught to follow a procedure which looks like the following:

1. Gather materials and equipment: They begin by gathering what they need to carry out their work. These resources are usually kept in a pre-established location, within easy reach of the students, so that they do not waste time searching for them or waiting for them to be handed out.

2. Carry out the task: Students know what is expected of them as they work:

They understand the rules for general behavior such as where they may sit, how much talking and walking about is acceptable, and whether they may work with other students;

Standards for the quality, quantity, and complexity of work have been established;

They know where and how to get help. Peer tutors or a student "buddy system" encourage them to share information and ideas with fellow students.

3. Have work checked and signed off: Students are responsible for asking the teacher to check and sign off on their work upon completion of all or a pre-determined portion of a project. At this point, they receive specific feedback and may be required to make a correction or expand the work and then return for another check before the teacher completely signs off on it.

4. Record that work is complete: Once the teacher has made the final check, the student indicates by a visual signal (usually by checking off on a class chart) that his or her task is complete. This allows the teacher to see, at a glance, how far each student has progressed during the project period.

5. Turn in completed work: Students usually place completed work in a central location so the teacher can look through it outside class time. This allows the teacher to assess student work and plan which students should receive special attention during the next project period.

6. Return materials and equipment: Students know how to care for and return materials and equipment to storage areas so that they remain in good condition.

7. Begin another activity: The student knows what to do once the first portion of a project is complete.

In addition to creation of an active learning environment, teachers should consider questioning strategies that encourage a "thoughtful classroom." This is especially important for students with poor self-images who have not been "quick" enough to play an active role in most classes in the past.

CHARACTERISTICS OF SCHOOLS THAT REDUCE POTENTIAL SUBSTANCE ABUSE THROUGH CURRICULUM STRATEGIES

- The teachers in each school emphasize communication between teacher and students and between students and other students.
- Classrooms are organized to use heterogenous groups rather than homogenous groups.
- Teachers use integrated curriculum where reading and science and social studies are blended together, as are art and mathematics.
- Instruction is given to small groups most often, and rarely to the whole class; heterogenous groups are constantly reformed into new ones.
- Teachers who work with at-risk students begin instruction by asking lower order questions such as, ''What color is this?'' and later move to higher order questions.
- Classes seem like families; teachers treat students like sons and daughters.
- Writing is going on constantly with prompts such as ''How do they feel?'' ''What do they think?''
- In the early grades, all writing is in Spanish in schools where many students do not speak English; in the third and fourth grades there is a transition to English.
- Teachers who are advocates for students and demanding of students.
- Teachers work autonomously and are clear about why they do everything; they argue strenuously with the principals to get to do what they want.
- Schools have a 90 + % parent involvement.
- Teachers refuse to refer students to remedial classes or special education; all problems are handled in class, often with the help of older students.

CREATING COMPUTER-ASSISTED INSTRUCTION USING PROBLEM-SOLVING APPROACHES

As schools throughout the country work to develop new means of instruction and assessment, computer-assisted instruction is a popular additional alternative. We have developed a simple means of programming so teachers can create their own CAI, with about an hour or less of time invested to learn the approach. Curriculum development can proceed most readily, we have found, if the team begins with mathematics, then moves to science, then to social studies, and finally to language arts. We work in this order in our project in Irvine Unified School District, Irvine, California, because mathematics is the easiest to measure in terms of identification of correct results.

Five aspects of instructional improvement that we use include

(*1*) Specification of the instructional approach

(*2*) Identification of critical teacher competencies needed

(*3*) Description of the context of instruction

(*4*) Selection of subject matter perceived as relevant by the learners

(*5*) Identification of required student background to proceed with the planned content.

When our curriculum development team works with teachers who are interested in learning to develop computer-assisted instruction, we use an approach that

- teaches how to convert course content into a problem-solving format
- utilizes state curriculum frameworks as a guide
- uses interdisciplinary teams; with cooperative learning encouraged
- utilizes computer-assisted instruction and the use of data bases
- designs curriculum for presentation at three levels: exploration, invention, and discovery
- provides the teacher many different models to use for different situations

Because	This staff development is designed to
• research indicates instruction is more powerful if it uses a problem-solving strategy	• help teachers evaluate the effectiveness of instruction with and without problem solving so they can know what works for them
• many school districts want teachers to increase the use of problem solving in their instruction	• make it easy for teachers to increase the use of problem solving by providing many different strategies that work in different situations

Because	This staff development is designed to
• teachers know from their own experience that students are more motivated if the instruction is oriented around problems that interest students	• provide teachers with materials on problem solving that will give them dozens of ideas to use when they get home
• student motivation is especially good if the problems are related to future occupational possibilities	• give teachers a list of types of problems and the occupations where these problems have to be solved
• teachers like to carry home something useful, they should bring copies of course content with them to the workshop to put in the problem-solving format	• provide each participant with the opportunity to create several new problem-solving approaches for the course content material they bring to the workshop

The following instructions guide teachers in using the Creating CAI software:

The [Creating CAI] program is a computer-aided teaching assistant (computer-managed instruction program) that allows an instructor to create her/his own managed instruction software for each course. It can also be called an authoring program and probably would be by people who are familiar with authoring programs. If you have ever tried to use one and found it was more trouble than it was worth, this program will please you. We have consciously kept it very simple. It uses just five symbols (commands in computer talk). These are *, #, +,], and -.

The text for the program is developed using a standard word processor, for example Word Perfect 5.1. The file must be saved as standard ASCII text (in WP51 it is called DOS text).

See Appendix B for the instructions that go with the software.

When teachers rely on questions with short, correct answers and call on students with their hands raised, they are encouraging recall in some students and ignoring others entirely. In contrast, teachers should do the following:

• Ask questions that have a range of appropriate responses, all of which require some explanation of the student's thinking.
• Wait five to ten seconds for all students to think.
• Call on students without anyone raising hands.

Math Drill and Practice.

By doing this, several important purposes are accomplished:

- All students know they are expected to think.
- They are given the time and silence to think.
- All students must be ready to communicate their thoughts (Report of Superintendent's Middle Grade Task Force, 1987).

VISIBLE RECOGNITION

The following activities offer extrinsic rewards to the potential dropout/abuser who may place little or no intrinsic value on education. These activities may have a positive effect by encouraging students to attend school:

(*1*) Award the most improved attenders a certificate of recognition.

(*2*) Provide special field trips for improved attenders.

(*3*) Reward improved attenders with paperback books.

(*4*) Hold a drawing for special prizes donated from local businesses which is open to students with the greatest improvement in attendance. Ask businesses to provide reduced price coupons for products and services that students like.

(*5*) Send letters of commendation home to parents of students with excellent improvement in attendance.

(*6*) Provide special lunchtime and end-of-school parties for students with improved attendance.

(*7*) Allow students with the greatest improvement in attendance to opt out of some examinations; base grades on classwork.

(*8*) Publicize attendance awards in your local newspaper; seek television coverage for attractive attendance-oriented events. Reward and publicize schools with the greatest improvement in attendance and related issues like reduction in tardiness.

(*9*) Schedule special assemblies and other attractive events on Mondays and Fridays when students are often absent.

Getting students to come to school and to stay in school are critical steps in improving attendance and instruction. Many schools are using computerized attendance programs that help administrators routinize parent contact by automating the personalized letters that are mailed to students' homes. Some programs offer period-by-period attendance record keeping as well. More expensive programs help administrators set up their attendance records so they link to the main student records, such as those discussed in Chapter 3, Development of a Student Information System. Making student records easy to access and use takes time and money, but improved attendance can easily pay for these efforts.

BUILDING AN INTERESTING CURRICULUM

Students are motivated in school when their studies relate to topics that have real interest to them.

(*1*) Use questionnaires to identify general and specific interests of students.

(*2*) Observe what students do in their free time to guide you to their real interests. Plan surprise activities and events. Use instructional games, especially those involving the computer.

(*3*) Consider how student interests can be integrated into the curriculum as starting points of lessons, examples of concepts, and applications of skills they have learned.

(*4*) Individualize by providing choices, so students have more opportunity to select assignments, activities, or projects that are interesting to them.

SET CLEAR GOALS

Students will move toward goals when they know what the goals are.

The goals need to be specific, challenging, and communicated as expectations for the results of learning.

(*1*) Involve students in some of the goal setting for the class and for themselves individually.

(*2*) State objectives in behavioral terms so you can measure students' progress and find out which of your approaches works best.

(*3*) Communicate your goals and objectives to students before each lesson, orally or in writing.

(*4*) Design new lessons that take advantage of your approaches that prove to be most effective.

USE POSITIVE REINFORCEMENT

Positive reinforcement can be used as a powerful extrinsic motivator. Effective employment of reinforcement strategies requires careful reading of the models, skill and understanding in establishing them, and patience and practice to finally refine them so they work for you.

(*1*) List the specific things students do that you want to reinforce so you can work consistently and systematically toward rewarding them for the appropriate behaviors.

(*2*) Use verbal and nonverbal reinforcers immediately after movement toward your target behaviors on the part of your students.

(*3*) Remind students of specific academic objectives or social behaviors that you will be looking for, and then acknowledge them and show your appreciation for the examples you see.

(*4*) Give specific praise for what you can find that is correct and successful in students' work.

COOPERATIVE LEARNING

Motivation can be enhanced by actively teaching students how to cooperate in achieving academic goals. Cooperation can build supportive relationships and group morale, as well as increase student motivation.

(*1*) Assign learning tasks to students in heterogeneous pairs, triads, or small groups. Group, as well as individual, grades and recognition may be given.

(2) Develop a "skill bank" of student experts where, to the extent possible, every student is expert at something and is asked to help other students.

(3) Teach small group skills directly. Let effective groups discuss how they work so they can serve as models to the other groups.

(4) Have students evaluate their own group processes and effectiveness; discuss these results in class when it is appropriate.

INDUCE READINESS TO LEARN

Effective teacher-motivators plan specific instructional activities that create interest in a topic about to be taught. Inducing readiness to learn requires planning and imagination. Try to build on the natural power of student anticipation.

(1) Ask thought-provoking questions that can only be answered in an activity that follows.

(2) Start with an event in school or community life and work back to the topic of the lesson.

(3) Use cartoons, pictures, newspaper headlines, taped excerpts from television programs, records, computer activities, and other strategies to liven up class and get students' attention.

(4) Design specific activities to introduce lessons, and then check to see if student progress is greater than it is for lessons where you have not done this.

ENCOURAGE STUDENT RESPONSES

Students need to be encouraged to respond to questions and to interact with each other during most lessons. At-risk students are often quiet, and special effort needs to made continuously to draw them out in class. If you, as a teacher, do not feel you are effective with these students, work with the administrators to put fewer of them in your classes until you have improved your skills (see Teacher Efficacy on the next page) in working with them.

(1) Ask students questions to find out what they know and do not know. Avoid questions that tend to trap, trick, or punish students. Allow students to demonstrate what they know, believe, and value.

(2) Give more "wait time" (time the teacher waits for slower students to react) to questions you ask. You may be pleased at the responses of students who never get recognized if you don't consciously wait for them.

(3) Ask questions that you do not know how to answer. About one in four at-risk students is gifted (and very bored), and this gives students an opportunity to explain things they know about to you and the class.

(4) Suspend judgment when students respond to queries. Instead of saying "right" or "not quite," move on and gather several responses before commenting.

These principles of motivation, when used by a competent teacher, can help turn routine instruction into exciting teaching. The thrill of catching the interest of a formerly apathetic student is a sweet memory for years to come.

TEACHER EFFICACY

As we mentioned in our Review of the Literature, Ashton and Webb (1986) have reported some research that can significantly help administrators who are working to assist students at risk. High-efficacy teachers create a more positive classroom climate than do low-efficacy teachers. They are less likely to punish students or scold them and, at the same time, more likely to accept their feelings and ideas than is true for low-efficacy peers. High-efficacy teachers also are more likely to include all students in their class in instruction and seatwork activities than is true for their counterparts (Ashton and Webb, 1986).

(1) Administrators might seek to schedule, to the extent possible, at-risk students into the classes of high-efficacy teachers.

(2) In order to be fair to the high-efficacy teachers who are receiving the difficult students to teach, the low-efficacy teachers could be asked to participate in training activities that help them improve classroom climate, strengthen human relations skills, increase their interest in motivating weak students, and strengthen their instructional skills through clinical supervision and similar strategies.

(3) Administrators could improve the organization of schools and teacher effectiveness by encouraging collaborative planning between teachers who instruct the same at-risk students, by involving

these teachers in key decisions that affect their problem students, and by seeking special funding that allows the teachers release time and needed resources to meet the special needs of students they have identified in their collaborative planning.

ALTERNATIVE INSTRUCTIONAL STRATEGIES

Some students are not successful in a regular classroom setting, but they can work effectively in less formal environments. They often need to be involved in transactional analysis or a similar program to improve their self-awareness and self-esteem in order to develop a positive attitude about pursuing their education. Emphasis may be given building a feeling of self-worth through the arts, for example, or wherever a sympathetic teacher is willing to give this effort their special attention.

(*1*) Tutorial strategies can use other students to help those likely to drop out/abuse.

(*2*) Similarly, peer-counseling efforts have been organized in scores of districts to help students learn how to work with substance-abusing students.

(*3*) Use of retired persons as volunteers in classrooms and as tutors has been a successful strategy in some districts.

(*4*) College students who are not as active socially as they would like to be make excellent candidates for crossage tutoring of secondary students. We operated an informal program of this type from the Admissions Office at Occidental College in Los Angeles some years ago.

(*5*) Retired teachers are another fine group to approach when a school is looking for tutors for students with special needs.

Harris has described the very successful tutoring program at Allendale School in Oakland, California.

Student tutors are recommended by their teachers on the basis of responsibility, conscientiousness, and reliability. During four training sessions, tutors learn their responsibilities, positive tutor behavior, and the content of their "skill-based" reading and math tutoring units. Tutors and tutees are matched on a one-to-one basis for the entire year. Tutoring sessions range from thirty minutes twice a week to thirty or forty minutes five times a week. Tutors meet once per month to share insights and problems. At least twice per month, the trainer meets individually with each tutor to discuss the progress of the tutee. A network of referrals among tutor, teacher, and trainer kept everyone working together. Thorough written evaluations take place at the end of the year. The program changes, grows, and improves each year. (Report of the Superintendent's Middle Grade Task Force, 1987)

Flexible scheduling may be a critical strategy for the administrator to consider as you consider the findings of Wehlage and Rutter cited in the Introduction. They call for students at risk to be divided into groups of 100−125, where they can have informal relations with their five or six teachers. In other situations, late afternoon and evening classes may prove to be the key to making it possible for some students to work earlier in the day and go to school later in the day.

PEDAGOGY OF POVERTY

Martin Haberman has written an article (1991) that argues that there is a "pedagogy of poverty" that is so powerful that an urban teacher who did not follow it would be regarded as a deviant. It is probably more true for high school than junior high teachers. The pedagogy consists of the following core functions of urban teaching:

- giving information
- asking questions
- giving directions
- making assignments
- monitoring seatwork
- reviewing assignments
- giving tests
- reviewing tests
- assigning homework
- reviewing homework
- settling disputes
- punishing noncompliance
- marking papers
- giving grades

The problem with this sensible-looking list of activities is that it does not lead to successful performance for most urban students. Teachers become enforcers of rules to minimally control student behavior, not successful educators. Research indicates that successful teachers have quite a different agenda, which is to

- involve students with issues they see as vital
- spend time discussing human differences
- teach major concepts and general principles
- involve students in planning what they will be doing
- apply ideals such as fairness, equity, and justice
- involve students in real-life experiences

Many of us would have no problem agreeing to this approach. The difficulty with implementing it is that students in urban schools have learned to control teachers by complying with the activities on the first list and by resisting the more complex activities that are used to implement the second list. If control is the name of the game, urban students have learned that, for them to succeed in controlling, the activities need to be simple. Haberman cites the example of the experienced teacher who has learned how to have a quiet, orderly classroom: "Take out your dictionaries and start to copy the words that begin with *h*."

We believe that urban teachers can begin to move in the direction of control of their classrooms by a political strategy that comes from the work of Gamson (1968). If students are divided into positives, neutrals, and negatives, teachers should give verbal praise and recognition to the positives; tangible rewards such as certificates of recognition, field trips, and paperback books to neutrals; and no recognition to the negatives.

Alternative schooling of many types appears attractive to students at risk. Some of the options include work experience, independent study of various designs, continuation schools, opportunity classes aimed at special interests, and a variety of nontraditional experiences that allow for teachers and students to operate in a casual environment. Teachers need to be interested in the personal lives of these students and their families and willing to work on the myriad personal problems that fill them in order to move toward success in their academic efforts.

POLICY RECOMMENDATION

Each district should consider developing activities that offer extrinsic rewards to students at risk who may place limited value on education. They include strategies such as creation of an active and thoughtful learning setting, visible recognition of various types, creation of curricula that interest these students, setting clear goals, using positive reinforcement, cooperative learning, inducing a readiness to learn, encouraging student responses in class, teacher efficacy, self-concept development, tutorial services, flexible scheduling, and alternative schooling options.

Chapter 7

USING WORK EXPERIENCE WITH STUDENTS AT RISK OF SUBSTANCE ABUSE

We believe that work experience and related occupational programs dramatically reduce dropout. Of the more than 400,000 students who enrolled in Regional Occupational Programs in California in the 1990−91 school year, 89% obtained employment or went on to advanced education. This is an 11% dropout rate compared to a state dropout rate of more than 20%.

Our data indicate that two-thirds of substance abusers drop out. Consequently, substance abuse prevention programs should focus upon careers and work experience.

Work-directed learning seeks to use the motivation of competence in one's chosen type of work to provide students purpose and drive as they prepare themselves for future accomplishment. Many students who are abusers or becoming abusers can be redirected by work-directed learning. It includes school-based and work-based learning and is, perhaps, the single greatest motivating force in United States society. Work-directed learning propositions are offered as part of a conceptual model that uses many paths to achieve its goal of preparing young people to obtain and advance in good jobs.

WORK-DIRECTED LEARNING

The programs in this model are called Work-Directed Learning (WDL). This phrase seems to capture the essence of what makes the programs succeed. In discussing the many definitions and models, we will indicate how each of them is work-directed learning, whether they are school-based or work-based programs. These include, to name a few, Experienced-Based Career Education programs (unpaid experience in naturally occurring jobs); Cooperative Education or co-op programs (school-supervised experience in paid jobs); Two + Two or tech-prep programs (last two years of high school and two years of community college organized around a career theme); and Career Academies (a school-within-a-school where a team of teachers offers a career-related academic curriculum to students in grades 10−12 or 9−12).

The purpose of work-directed learning is to use the desire for competence and income to motivate the learner. Program propositions include the following:

(1) If the learner sees a connection between what is to be learned and increased income, s/he will be motivated to complete the program.

(2) The learner is more likely to obtain a job and advance in his/her career if problem solving is integrated into the school-based and work-based aspects of the program.

(3) Both school- and work-based learning should include content knowledge, a variety of instructional approaches, planning strategies, problem-solving strategies, and learning strategies.

School-based propositions are as follows:

(1) School-based learning should include content that leads to a diploma or a certificate of competence.

(2) School-based learning should be built around existing career preparation courses and should be revised regularly. It should be designed so that an increasing proportion of student time is spent at the work site and based on a written agreement signed by the student and representatives from the school and work sites.

(3) School-based learning should begin as early as possible and not later than age sixteen. It should include life-coping and wellness skills and employability skills for getting and keeping a job, and each student should be guided by a teacher-adviser.

Work-based propositions include the following:

(1) Work-based learning should be integrated with school-based learning at the earliest opportunity in the school curriculum and no later than grade 11.

(2) Work-based learning should offer occupationally specific knowledge and skills, utilize sequenced learning, include a mentor from the job site, and result in a job placement.

Work-directed learning is a generic concept encompassing programs based both in schools and at work sites. It uses many paths to achieve its goal of preparing young people to obtain and advance in good jobs.

We move now to some specific suggestions for implementing work-directed learning. The method section (Taxonomy of Teaching Methods) was developed by Peterson (1992). We apply concepts to a present-day apprenticeship program later in the chapter so that the reader can see the types of changes that could be made as they seek to offer "employment bound training" (the curriculum) in a delivery system (instruction) that utilizes the new generic approach, focusing upon problem solving and critical thinking.

How Students Learn

There are four types of knowledge that students use in the learning environment. These include

(*1*) Content knowledge, such as conceptual and factual knowledge and procedures that relate to the field of interest, whether it be electronics, machine repair, accounting, or English

(*2*) Planning strategies, such as assessing needs, predicting future needs, and goal setting

(*3*) Problem-solving strategies that are based on successful experience, typically, and include problem identification, listing of alternative solutions, selection of a solution, implementation of the solution, and evaluation of effectiveness

(*4*) Learning strategies, which include learning to learn, identifying one's learning style, cooperative learning, listening skills, and adapting to new situations

Principles to Guide Instruction

(*1*) *Increasing complexity:* Tasks the students are asked to perform are increasingly complex as they move through the training experience.

(*2*) *Increasing diversity:* Tasks the students carry out are increasingly diverse and require more and varied skills.

(*3*) *Global before local skills:* Students should get a feel for the overall product or big picture prior to being asked to develop individual parts of the whole.

(*4*) *Context:* Work to carry out instruction in a context that facilitates what you are teaching. For example, teach writing where you have access to an electronic bulletin board where the students can write messages to each other.

(5) *Use of experts:* If you are teaching about using experts, go to a setting where the students can see an expert at work or show a videotape of an expert working.

(6) *Intrinsic motivation:* Intrinsic motivation comes from inside us and often follows extrinsic motivation such as pleasing someone. To help students understand this, invite someone to class, like an athlete who plays hard because it's fun.

(7) *Cooperative learning:* In this situation, students work together to solve problems and carry out tasks. It is easy to demonstrate this with two students at a computer. Typically, they will naturally cooperate to accomplish a task.

(8) *Competitive learning:* To make this constructive, the students should compete in using a sound process, rather than in terms of the product being produced. Realistically, the easiest thing for students to understand is a combination of competitive and cooperative learning as in teams working together to make a presentation and get a high grade.

The taxonomy in Table 7.1 can be especially useful for designing instruction for work-directed learning. Watching-doing methods at the bottom of the table are particularly relevant, especially the contract method, "hands-on" method, projects method, and simulation method (Peterson, 1992).

As we begin to think of the type of curriculum we need for work-directed learning and apprenticeship programs, in particular, it is appropriate to review our program requirements.

ACADEMIC CURRICULUM AND INSTRUCTION

The academic curriculum should consist of a program of study that meets state expectations, including proficiency in English, mathematics, history, science, and geography. There should also be modifications to the delivery of instruction to insure relevance to the workplace, especially in the areas of critical thinking and problem solving. Even if little change is made in curriculum, modifying one's instructional approaches to use problem solving and critical thinking is an important step, as we indicate in the apprenticeship model at the close of the chapter.

TABLE 7.1 *Taxonomy of common teaching methods.*

NATURE OF TRANSACTION	AMOUNT OF TEACHER DOMINANCE			USEFULNESS WITH GROUPS OF VARIOUS SIZES (NUMBERS OF STUDENTS)				
	HIGH	MEDIUM	LOW	1	5	10	15	30
Listening-speaking methods								
Lecture method	High					*	*	*
✓ Giving instructions	High			*		*	*	*
Recitation methods		Medium			*	*	*	*
✓ Drill method		Medium		*	*	*	*	*
Review method		Medium			*	*	*	*
✓ Questioning method		Medium		*	*	*	*	*
Oral exam method		Medium		*				
Discussion method		Medium			*	*	*	*
Film analysis method			Low			*	*	*
Debate method			Low				*	*
Oral report method			Low		*	*	*	*
Brainstorming method			Low		*	*	*	*

(continued)

TABLE 7.1 (continued).

NATURE OF TRANSACTION	AMOUNT OF TEACHER DOMINANCE			USEFULNESS WITH GROUPS OF VARIOUS SIZES (NUMBERS OF STUDENTS)				
	HIGH	MEDIUM	LOW	1	5	10	15	30
Reading-writing methods				*				
Textbook method	High				*	*	*	*
Workbook method	High			*	*	*	*	*
Chalkboard method	High				*	*	*	*
Bulletin board method	High							*
✓ Problem-solving method		Medium		*	*	*	*	*
Laboratory report method		Medium			*	*	*	*
✓ Team/cooperative learning method			Low		*	(Repeated w/entire class)		
Peer review method			Low	*		(Repeated w/entire class)		
✓ Peer tutoring method			Low	*		(Repeated w/entire class)		
Programmed instruction			Low	*	*	*	*	*
✓ Individualized instruction			Low	*		(Repeated w/entire class)		
Note-taking method			Low	*		*	*	*
Journal-keeping method			Low	*	*	*	*	*

TABLE 7.1 (continued).

NATURE OF TRANSACTION	AMOUNT OF TEACHER DOMINANCE			USEFULNESS WITH GROUPS OF VARIOUS SIZES (NUMBERS OF STUDENTS)				
	HIGH	MEDIUM	LOW	1	5	10	15	30
Watching-doing methods								
Demonstration method	High				*	*	*	*
Field trip method	High						*	*
✓ Contract method			Medium	*	(Repeated w/entire class)			
"Hands-on"/lab method		Medium		*	*	*	*	*
✓ Inquiry method		Medium		*	*	*	*	*
✓ Learning center method			Low	*		(Repeated w/entire class)		
Projects method			Low	*	*	*	*	*
Simulation method			Low			*	*	*
Games method			Low	*		*	*	*
✓ Exploration-discovery method			Low	*	*	*	*	*

Note: Checkmark (✓) indicates that the method is used in more than one kind of transaction: listening-speaking, reading-writing, and watching-doing.

Working on Study Skills.

Study Skills

There are other areas that also need to be included in the revised curriculum. These include basic skills such as the *hm* [sic] *Study Skills Program* for at-risk students, developed by the National Association of Secondary School Principals (NASSP) and mentioned in Chapter 8.

- learning to learn—skills for perceiving, organizing, making sense of, and using ideas and data
- learning style—gives insight into students' own style of learning and provides practice in their learning style strengths
- cooperative learning—many activities that support cooperative learning strategies
- listening skills—starts with these listening skills and uses them throughout each of the study skills programs
- creative problem-solving strategies for solving problems effectively and imaginatively
- adaptability—supports the development of adaptability by helping students to learn skills for managing and making sense of new conditions, ideas, and information

- personal management—teaches scheduling and goal-setting skills and offers instruction in studying and "testwiseness"

The NASSP Study Skills materials are being used in more than 7,000 classrooms nationally and are designed for at-risk students. Our suggestion would be to train the academic core teachers (English, mathematics, history, science, and geography) to use these strategies as they teach their regular content. This is the manner in which they are typically implemented in classrooms.

VOCATIONAL EDUCATION

Since most high schools have existing vocational education programs, it makes sense to build the internship/apprenticeship curriculum around the present vocational education courses if they are presently leading to jobs. If they are not, perhaps a supplementary structure such as the California Regional Occupational Programs needs to be put in place. Vocational education courses frequently include trade and industrial education, business education, agriculture, home economics, marketing education, and technical education. This will require some serious revision, however, since many existing vocational education courses do not reflect the new emphasis on problem solving and critical thinking that are critical in preparing students for the higher level cognitive requirements of the present and future job market.

At this point, the decision makers need to carefully consider whether the present teachers are willing and able to revise the existing courses to reflect higher order thinking skills. It may be that teachers whose present courses already reflect these strategies should play this role. You might think of a math teacher, for example, who has been teaching problem solving for years, as a consultant to the vocational education teachers for this task.

This is a serious issue, in that one of the main purposes of the Vocational and Applied Technology Education Act Amendments of 1990 was to introduce problem solving and critical thinking into the new vocational education curriculum. The old curriculum, "dumbed down" to the supposed level of the vocational education students, did not work. Only one-third of the students who completed the curriculum got jobs, in part because employers had learned that those students had a hard time learning to use new machines and technologies.

OCCUPATIONALLY SPECIFIC KNOWLEDGE

Work-based learning should consist of instruction in occupationally specific knowledge, skills, and abilities accepted by industry standards. It would also include a planned program of job training with specific identification of the tasks to be mastered. It would include the development of sound work habits and behaviors and training in the use of resources, working effectively with coworkers, and utilization of appropriate technologies.

Work-site learning and experience should take 20% − 50% of the students' time in the first year of the program and increase to 40% − 70% in the second year. This time should be used to help the student meet

- the academic requirements of the work place
- appropriate job training requirements
- other work place requirements as seen in the previous paragraph, such as the use of various technologies

The balance of student time would be used to meet the academic and other school diploma requirements. Disagreement over the allocation of time may lead to the development of a supplementary structure such as Regional Occupational Programs (ROPs), where 50% or more of student time is directed to the needs of the work site.

Written Agreement

Since there are many controversial features in a program oriented to the work site, a written agreement should be used to ensure completion of program requirements. The written agreement should include a commitment on the part of the student to achieve specific academic standards, to remain in school and attend regularly, to avoid alcohol and drug abuse, and to meet work-site requirements. In practice, the California ROPs have found little problem in students living up to these regulations, since all of the other people at the work site want to keep their jobs and tend not to violate them. Programs that are not employment oriented will have greater difficulties because students do not see the job and income payoffs for following the rules.

Parents should be asked to commit to support of students' school and work place requirements.

Employers are asked to help students acquire skills and knowledge in an orderly sequence, to provide them with a mentor at the work site, and to employ them after successful conclusion of the apprenticeship.

LIFE-COPING AND WELLNESS SKILLS

Life-coping skills are taught throughout the curriculum in the Irvine Unified School District, Irvine, California. The program has been carefully evaluated to be successful and is part of a K − 12 curriculum for drug prevention. Table 7.2 lists skills that are taught at grade 10.

CERTIFICATE OF COMPETENCY

The school should work to coordinate the successful operation of the program and to offer a high school diploma and a certificate of competency specifying the standards the student has met in the program. The agreement may include a second educational organization and postsecondary training. There should be provision for a wage scale, a schedule of hours of work expected in both the school and work-site portions of the program, and provision for termination of the agreement.

Materials for Career Awareness.

Table 7.2.

GRADE	LIFE SKILLS	WELLNESS SKILLS
10	COPING SKILLS FOR ANGER AND DEPRESSION (STAGES II) integrating six stages and reactions of change Applying knowledge of reactions to change Integrating knowledge of resources Integrating skills to cope with denial integrating the effects of anger Utilizing assertion skills to deal with anger Integrating the effects of bargaining Utilizing assertive refusal to cope with bargaining Integrating the understanding of depression Accepting and integrating reactions to STAGES Integrating skills to understand hope DEVELOPING EFFECTIVE PROBLEM-SOLVING SKILLS (PLUS) Developing effective problem-solving skills Understanding of difference between fact and beliefs Developing awareness of rational/irrational beliefs Differentiating between rational/irrational beliefs Developing the skill of problem-solving Developing understanding of self-talk Developing the skill of brainstorming Developing skills of alternative solution	USE AND MISUSE OF SUBSTANCES Recognizing alcohol dependency Recognizing effects of marijuana use Understanding alcohol and marijuana Physical and mental alcohol effects Learning about effect of other substances on self and others Differentiating between prescription and nonprescription drugs Learning about misconceptions and myths of alcohol and alcoholism Examining factors that influence decision not to use Analyzing the influence of advertising Developing resistance, peer, and media Benefits of giving up tobacco and other substances FAMILY HEALTH Recognizing family influences and differences Learning how the family meets basic needs Locating community resources and family assistance Developing awareness of individual rights and responsibilities in relationships Recognizing dysfunctions within families Identifying, preventing abuse Identifying proper steps in solving family problems

116

Table 7.2 (continued).

GRADE	LIFE SKILLS	WELLNESS SKILLS
10	COPING SKILLS FOR ANGER AND DEPRESSION (STAGES II) DEVELOPING EFFECTIVE PROBLEM-SOLVING SKILLS (continued) Understanding the consequences of brainstorming Recognizing skill of listing alternatives Recognizing consequences in problem solving Practicing implementing plan	USE AND MISUSE OF SUBSTANCES PERSONAL HEALTH Achieving and maintaining health Understanding how health choices affect quality of life Understanding when health changes require professional assistance

Advisement

The school should also be responsible for advising the student about occupational and career opportunities, work experience requirements, and possibilities for postsecondary education and career specialization. Advisement should also include information about how job-related competencies will be assessed and job descriptions of potential positions.

WORK-BASED LEARNING

A decade ago, one could make a case for teachers' concern that employers have too narrow a view of the skills students need and their desire to focus upon job-specific skills. Increasingly, employers recognize the need for broader skills, especially those that lead to improved problem solving. Consequently, it is easier now for high school teachers to link to local employers and feel good about the training students are receiving. This is a key factor leading to improved opportunities for apprenticeship development at the current time.

The big issue now becomes: ''What curriculum can we deliver that is sound academically, that is presented in an interesting manner, that is relevant to the work site, and that therefore meets student's needs?''

One example of a youth apprenticeship is the Astech/MCI approach seen below.

Apprenticeship Proposal between
Century High School and Astech/MCI
Written by Connie Mayhugh
Director, Career Development Laboratory
Santa Ana Unified School District
Santa Ana, California

Mr. George Weeks of Astech/MCI, a manufacturing firm, contacted Century High about the possibility of implementing an apprenticeship program between his corporation and the school. Mr. Weeks is a visionary for his company. He recognizes that, in the next five years, his employment force will undergo drastic changes as many reach retirement age, and the company will expand its customer base and application for its unique materials and processes. He is acutely aware that there is a lack of a skilled replacement employment force.

Century High School in the Santa Ana Unified School District has a relatively high dropout rate. This rate is attributed to both the community of learners and the programs being offered. In many incidents, the reason for students dropping out is due to family financial obligations. Putting food on the table often times takes precedence over achieving graduation from high school. The current programs offered may not provide the learner with the incentive to remain in school. The student needs to see that the programs offered are a viable means for him/her to become a productive member of society.

Mr. Week's proposal addresses both issues. He proposes a work experience training program between his corporation and Century students. The planning for this adventure is still in progress, but a basic outline for the program has been established.

To be in line with the work experience guidelines established by the state of California, students involved must be sixteen years of age. Students will be able to satisfy graduation units and obtain employable job skills while earning minimum wage. In an effort to illustrate to students the connection between good citizenship and employability, it is required by Astech/MCI that all participants must take a drug test. Once a drug test has been taken and passed and the requirements for work experience met, students will be enrolled in training courses at Astech/MCI. Mr. Weeks has arranged for his current employees to be a vital part of this training effort. Using the concept of mentorship in the program will allow the students to feel connected to an individual on staff, not just a teacher in a classroom.

Astech/MCI is a manufacturing firm whose product is aircraft engine exhaust systems. Their most renowned product has been the engine exhaust system for the United States' state-of-the-art F117 Stealth Fighter. The manufacturing process includes design engineering, manufacturing engineering, M & P Lab, purchasing, preparation of the metal prior to construction, construction through tooling and welding, and completion through heat treatment, quality control, and packaging. The knowledge of metallurgy, the use of machinery, and the understanding of technology are all integral in completion of the final product.

Training will consist of many areas. Introduction of the manufacturing process will begin with an understanding of the material used in the process, material handling, and product construction through the understanding of tooling and welding. It was agreed that, in the initial training phase, the emphasis would not be on product creation but on understanding the processes involved.

All training will be onsite at Astech/MCI, using materials provided by Astech/MCI and the expertise of the employees of Astech/MCI. Classroom instruction will lead to hands-on application of the knowledge learned. Assessment will be based on the students' understanding of information presented and the practical application of this knowledge. Upon completion of the course, students will be awarded certification in the processes from Astech/MCI and Century. The ultimate reward will be employment in a company that values and rewards its employees through continued opportunities for education and advancement.

This program is a benefit to all parties. Astech/MCI is building a workforce that is knowledgeable in the manufacturing processes and competitive in the field. The opportunity to allow students to complete their high school education, making available the aquisition of employable skills with a pay incentive may be the hook that the Santa Ana Unified District, or any district, may need to produce graduates who will be productive in society. Programs such as the one between Astech/MCI and Century High must be the trend of the future—society's future and education's future.

These youth apprenticeships will

(*1*) Integrate academic instruction and work-site learning and experience

(*2*) Provide a clear and appealing alternative to existing unpaid options

(*3*) Utilize national skill standards set by each participating industry and, if these are not available, work to create them

(4) Build on existing education and training programs such as the Regional Occupational Programs to serve eleventh and twelfth grade students

(5) Include postsecondary and community college candidates who seek opportunity to meet the skill standards in an industry of their choice

(6) Result in each candidate receiving Certificates of Competence (skill certification) or a Letter of Qualification (where skill standards are not yet established)

(7) Train high school, community college, and industry administrators to facilitate the development of skill standards and paid youth apprenticeships

Work-directed learning programs recognize the need to provide job-specific and job-related training for the 75% of students who do not go on to a four-year college. They require collaboration between business, labor, and education, something that has been more readily achieved in Germany and Japan than in the United States up to this time. California's Regional Occupational Programs, begun in 1967, are a notable exception. Perhaps the time has now come for their more complete development in this country; many of us will work to help this come true. Perhaps we have attempted to move too quickly to achieve the difficult new understandings and relationships between schools, unions and employers in the past. As the proverb says, it is ''hard by the yard but a cinch by the inch.''

We turn now to some guiding principles that can be helpful in developing work-directed learning programs.

WHAT IS AN APPRENTICESHIP PROGRAM?

One definition contained in proposed federal legislation speaks of a youth apprenticeship program, as one that

- integrates academic instruction and work-based learning (the community classroom concept)
- provides for work-site learning and paid work experience
- is offered to students beginning in the eleventh or twelfth grade
- results in receipt of a high school diploma or certificate of competency
- leads, as appropriate, to entry to a postsecondary program or permanent employment

The legislation indicates there should be a written agreement between the employer, the local education agency, the student, and the parent, which defines the roles and responsibilities in the program. Participating schools are asked to provide career exploration opportunities and academic programs that prepare students to participate in the apprenticeship. Employers are asked to assist schools in developing curricula that are relevant to the work place, to take primary responsibility for ensuring the success of the work-site learning and work experience (community classroom), and to provide the school with information about each student's performance. An advisory council should be established to review the various apprenticeship programs under its purview to ensure that they mesh with local labor demands and provide broad-based competencies and transferable skills that will allow the student to progress to more responsible positions in the appropriate trade or industry.

PROGRAM CHARACTERISTICS

Academic instruction should consist of a program of study that meets state expectations, including proficiency in English, mathematics, history, science, and geography. There should be modifications to curricula to insure relevance to the work place.

Work-based learning should consist of instruction in occupationally specific knowledge, skills, and abilities accepted by industry standards. It would also include a planned program of job training with specific identification of the tasks to be mastered. It would include the development of sound work habits and behaviors and training in the use of resources, working effectively with coworkers and utilization of appropriate technologies.

Work-site learning and experience should take at least $20-50\%$ of the student's time in the first year of the program and increase to $40-70\%$ in the second year. This time should be used to help the student meet 1) the academic requirements of the school and work place, 2) appropriate job training, and 3) other work place requirements such as the use of various technologies.

The written agreement should include a commitment on the part of the student to achieve specific academic standards, to remain in school and attend regularly, to avoid alcohol and drug abuse, and to meet work-site requirements.

Parents should be asked to commit to support of their students' school and work place requirements.

Employers are asked to help students acquire skills and knowledge in an orderly sequence, to provide them with a mentor at the work site, and to employ them after successful conclusion of the apprenticeship if that is feasible. Coastline Regional Occupational Program in Costa Mesa, California, has data indicating that, in 1991−92 74 of 141 (52%) employers hired participants. More than 90% of participants seeking employment were placed in jobs or further training, leading to a job; therefore, it seems wise to ask employers to carefully consider hiring trainees but not to make it a requirement. Often, another firm in the same industry is where the individual is finally placed for employment.

The school should work to coordinate the successful operation of the program and to offer a high school diploma and a certificate of competency specifying the standards the student has met in the program. The agreement may include a second educational organization and postsecondary training. There should be provision for a wage scale, a schedule of hours of work expected in both the school and work-site portions of the program, and provision for termination of the agreement.

The school should also be responsible for advising the student about occupational and career opportunities, work experience requirements, and possibilities for postsecondary education and career specialization. Advisement should also include information about how job-related competencies will be assessed and job descriptions of potential positions.

Many of the existing programs help educationally disadvantaged youth overcome the handicaps of low academic achievement and lack of skills. This is accomplished through a high school level curriculum related to work, especially computers and electronics. Emphasis is placed on English, mathematics, and science, as well as job experience with the promise of employment after the successful completion of the program.

Principles for Connecting School and Work

In order to understand how our education system needs to relate to business and industry, we need to first understand the changes that are taking place in the world of work. If there is little change in the technologies used in business and industry, as there has been historically, there is a gently moving timetable for education to adjust to the changes. *If, on the other hand, the pace of technological change accelerates as it*

Learning to Program.

has in the last several decades, education must speed up the pace of adaptation.

There is a second principle operating as well. The United States mass production system has historically utilized production workers with little training, thus minimizing the need for apprenticeship-type programs. Quality control has been accomplished through close supervision and careful management. Rapid technological change, shortened product life cycles, and increased foreign competition have led firms to change to a different approach requiring workers that are more highly trained and that uses fewer supervisors (Rosenbaum, 1992). These changes have led to the need for apprenticeships and related training approaches that require workers to use higher order cognitive skills and to engage in problem solving as they work.

As Rosenbaum indicates, jobs that require these higher skills have increased at two and one-half times the rate of lower skill jobs between 1975 and 1990. And this trend will continue into the coming decade.

What, specifically, are these higher order skills? Foundation skills include reading, writing, mathematics, listening, and speaking. Complex reasoning skills are needed for defining and solving problems, critical thinking, knowledge acquisition, and evaluating problem solutions (Stasz et al., 1990).

It seems clear that more highly trained employees will require a greater investment on the part of employers. This will, in time, lead them to make a greater commitment to keep their highly trained employees for a longer period of time. It will also lead to a greater business interest in and investment in training programs such as apprenticeships and related work-directed learning programs.

Who will train our 75% of students who will not graduate from a four-year college? Most likely, our present and future teachers. Some business leaders argue that many of our teachers don't care about these students and that we should introduce a voucher system to force them out of education by eliminating schools that are not chosen by parents and, presumably, the teachers in those schools.

HOW CAN WE BUILD APPRENTICESHIP PROGRAMS?

If we see an apprenticeship where most participants get a good job at the completion of the program as our goal, how can we move in that direction?

(1) Step One: Connect our program building efforts to existing programs that have built a foundation for a more potent connection to the business world.

(2) Step Two: Make sure the program offers the student sound foundations in core academic areas such as reading, writing, and computation and teaches students to solve problems, just as they will have to do on the job.

(3) Step Three: Look for employers that are hurting enough from their lack of employees that can solve problems to make a strong commitment to help train students and to provide adult mentors on the job. When the program meets employer needs, as the Regional Occupational Programs do (400,000 participants), employers become very positive and seek out the candidates.

(4) Step Four: Adopt an incremental change approach where you begin with the present situation and move toward stronger linkages as the school and employer learn to work together. Many of our present vocational education programs are good beginnings to work from.

Here are five principles to keep in mind for building school-to-work programs (Rosenbaum, 1992):

(*1*) Programs should use work-based learning methods that build on school learning and are connected to schools.

(*2*) School-based programs should build upon work experiences.

(*3*) Experience-based teaching in classrooms should develop cognitive, as well as practical, skills.

(*4*) School work linkages should reward school learning and effort with good jobs.

(*5*) Credentialing procedures should identify clear standards and certify attainment.

Powerful apprenticeships take a long time to build. The interim steps along the way will still provide our students with better access to good jobs than they may have at the present.

Chapter 8

SCHOOL POLICIES, LAWS, AND PROGRAMS THAT REDUCE ALCOHOL AND OTHER DRUG USE

In order to reduce substance abuse, school districts should develop policy statements that focus on school-based prevention and refer treatment to other agencies in the community. This chapter includes background about the field, software that contains information on drug prevention programs, curricular programs to reduce abuse within schools, a community involvement program, a law enforcement program, information on how to assess the extent of adolescent substance abuse, and strategies for parents to use at home.

BACKGROUND

Most states have developed guidelines to assist school districts in formulating substance abuse policies. The California guidelines include a philosophy of school-based prevention; a focus on dissemination of effective program descriptions; emphasis on affective, as well as cognitive, measures for prevention; stress on the importance of peer and family relationships; and strategies utilizing career and life planning. Suggestions for implementing a comprehensive school-based prevention program focus on curriculum design, in-service training, staffing, counseling, and parent and community involvement (Guidelines for School Based Alcohol and Drug Abuse Prevention Programs, 1982).

In the area of alcohol and other drug prevention, school policy and procedure is developed from state and federal guidelines, reaction toward substance use incidents in the school, and recommendations of community and administrative planning committees.

However the policies evolve, it is important to periodically review them at a school and district level. For example, some school policies

127

developed in the 1960s did not specify a clear ''no use'' message of alcohol and other drugs. This is important because history has taught us that we often get what we expect to get. Also, policies can best serve the students and the school system by clearly reflecting the goals and philosophy and by setting norms and standards for all staff and students to that end. With this framework, the policy should be proactive and specific within the limits of legal parameters (U.S. Department of Education, 1991).

A prevention policy that applies to students and staff sets the tone for a district to directly and humanely address alcohol and other drug (AOD) issues. A clear policy helps all understand the district's expectations and accept the position that the consequences are equitable. A clear policy can also provide motivation for staff and students to seek assistance for AOD problems.

A prevention policy is proactive when it

- enhances and supports student development
- encourages schools to link with community agencies for needed services not provided
- coordinates messages with other district policy and procedure for at-risk students
- assists self-referring students without punishment
- provides resource information to encourage school staff to seek treatment and requires AOD problem staff to participate in treatment
- addresses prevention policy needs in the areas of staff development, curriculum, student support services, parent education and involvement, community involvement, and evaluation.

A prevention policy must clearly address several issues with standards and procedure. For example, guidelines should specify how the policy and intervention program are to be implemented; procedures need to be developed that help the program function smoothly and that provide reinforcement to participating students.

The policy needs a strong legal foundation to insure that participating staff will be supported in their prevention efforts when they work within these legal parameters. The legal parameters include abiding by state and federal laws related to drug and alcohol use and should be reviewed by legal counsel. Steps to develop a school district prevention policy are

- education and awareness
- district philosophy

- formation of a working group
- development of a common language and common goals
- philosophy statement
- draft of the policy
- submission for board approval
- dissemination of the policy
- review, update, and re-dissemination of the policy annually

The policy regulations and procedures are developed either with the policy or shortly after so that the roles and responsibilities of school personnel implementing the prevention policy are clear. Disciplinary regulations and procedures that traditionally emphasize punishment, usually suspension, may be revised to include constructive alternatives, such as mandatory participation in workshops, support groups, assessment, or counseling.

The student support system developed is dependent upon the resources and administrative style of the school district. The roles and responsibilities of identification, preassessment, and referral of students may be shared between school staff, consultants, and community resources. Most programs have the following components:

- initial intervention strategies for classroom teachers who become concerned about a student
- a system of collecting information from several sources on students regarding AOD risk factors
- a system of reviewing and evaluating the referral information and determining the action needed
- strategies for involving and motivating parents, students, and school staff to support the intervention plan
- a system for monitoring the progress of students referred for intervention

CONFIDENTIALITY AND CONSENT IN STUDENT DRUG PREVENTION SERVICES

School-based alcohol and other drug prevention program personnel should have a thorough understanding of the legal parameters under which they operate. The reasons for this are well articulated by the Western Center for Drug Free Schools and Communities in their policy and procedure guide for school districts implementing alcohol and other drug or student assistance programs.

A complicated set of federal and state laws and regulations apply. Some laws apply to most student records regardless of the source of funds supporting the program, the educational subject, whether it is part of the core curriculum or an experimental program, or the purpose for which information is gathered and used. Other laws and regulations apply specifically to alcohol and other drug use programs and activities, or specifically to experimental programs, or only to federally funded activities.

Requirements regarding student records related to prevention and intervention programs include the following:

(*1*) Family Educational Rights and Privacy Act (FERPA) requires schools to release student record information to students over eighteen and to parents of students under eighteen. It also restricts release of this information to others, with certain exceptions.

(*2*) Student Rights in Research, Experimental Activities, and Testing (Hatch Amendment to the General Education Provisions Act) requires parent permission for students to participate in programs involving psychological treatment, or designed to reveal information pertaining to personal beliefs, behavior, or family relationships. It also gives parents the right to inspect instructional materials used in research or experimental projects. This amendment only applies to activities supported by funds from the U.S. Department of Education.

(*3*) Confidentiality of alcohol and drug abuse patient records regulations issued by the U.S. Department of Health and Human Services also applies to school-based programs supported by federal or state pass-through funds. These regulations prohibit information from being supplied to anyone about persons in an alcohol and drug-related program, with the following exceptions: student and parent consent; court order; disclosure to medical personnel in an emergency; or if the information is used for research, program evaluation, or audit purposes.

In general, these regulations mean school-based prevention programs need parent permission for student use surveys or program participation. However, some states, like California, grant minors acting alone the legal capacity to obtain treatment and give the required consent. Counseling services offered to schools by outside county and nonprofit agencies may not be aware of the legal complexity in this area, which can create liability for the school district and problems for the school administrator. Records for AOD student assistance programs should probably be kept separate from other student records to meet these different legal requirements. Information can, however, be released to school employees with a ''need to know,'' certain government officials carrying out their functions, and persons with a need to know for health and safety measures. Finally, any uncertainty regarding student participation in prevention programs or release of information is best referred for legal opinion.

SUBSTANCE ABUSE PREVENTION
CURRICULAR PROGRAMS

DIADS is computer software that helps school staff identify promising drug prevention programs. It includes a data base of over fifty prevention programs that have been reviewed by experts and found to be effective. These programs fall into the following categories: 1) comprehensive curriculum, 2) peer education/leadership/training, 3) student assistance, and 4) family/community education (Bosworth, n.d.).

Existing programs tend to be either content-oriented and cognitive or person-oriented and affective (Garfield, 1981). Content programs teach participants the facts so they can make wise decisions; person-oriented programs provide one with the means for acquiring the personal strength and values to resist involvement with harmful substances, according to the designers. Both approaches seem appropriate to many administrators, and, in fact, Schaps et al., in a review of primary prevention programs, found that a combination of cognitive and affective approaches seem to be most effective (Schaps, 1978).

Schulte, in a review of evaluation reports of fifteen widely used prevention curricula, found that the majority of the programs emphasized knowledge as their main objective (Schulte, 1985). Some of her curricular recommendations are as follows:

(*1*) HERE'S LOOKING AT YOU 2000, grades K−12, was the strongest program reviewed. It addresses knowledge and affective, behavioral, and skills objectives and the results are positive and statistically significant.[1]

(*2*) CASPAR (Cambridge and Somerville Program for Alcohol

---

[1]Contact: Comprehensive Health Education Foundation, 20832 Pacific Hwy. South, Seattle, WA 98188.

Rehabilitation), grades 3−12, showed significant gains in knowledge and attitudes.[2]

(*3*) School Health Curriculum Project (SHCP), grades K−12, showed significant gains in substance abuse knowledge.[3]

Another researcher, Boyd, surveyed sixty-eight school districts in southern California to identify substance abuse curricula in use, with the following results (Boyd, 1987):

Program Name	No. of Districts Using
HERE'S LOOKING AT YOU 2000	19
D.A.R.E.	14
QUEST	10
Project S.M.A.R.T.	8
District-developed curriculum	9
Starting Early	5
Project Self-Esteem	5
McGruff	4
STAR	2

Towers (1987) also suggests Project Charlie, The Alcohol/Other Drug Risk Reduction Project, Amazing Alternatives, and Refusal Skills.

COMMUNITY INVOLVEMENT

One of the most comprehensive programs we have encountered includes five parts, three within the schools and two that connect to the community. It is common for schools to link to the community for assistance in combatting substance abuse and Peer Assistance Leadership (PAL). Simpson (1987) provides a model for doing this.

PAL: Elementary School Level—Project Self-Esteem/Friendship Clubs

Teams of parent volunteers are trained to teach nine to twelve lessons

[2]Contact: CASPAR Alcohol Education Program, 226 Highland Avenue, Somerville, MA 02143.
[3]Contact: Center for Disease Control, Division of Health Education, School Health and Special Projects Office, 1600 Clifton Road, NE, Atlanta, GE 30333.

a year at grades 2 through 6. Selected fifth and sixth grade students are specially trained to be positive role models and provide friendship to new and troubled peers.

PAL: Intermediate School Level—STAR/Friendship Clubs

Seventh through ninth grade teachers provide up to fifty lessons a year on assertive communications skills, stress management, and drug use avoidance skills through the STAR program (IUSD, 1987). Selected students are trained to be members of a Friendship Club, providing help for new and troubled peers.

PAL: High School Level—Peer Facilitator Training/Service

Two faculty volunteers teach positive, caring, listening skills; an understanding of school and community referral resources; and procedures for helping a fellow student use these resources. Following the training, an outreach process is designed, which may include peer tutoring, socio dramas, student orientations, classroom presentations, rap centers, and other activities.

PAL: Community Level

PAL is part of a countywide substance abuse network that fosters coordination among youth-oriented agencies and concerned organizations. At monthly meetings, the members share resources and jointly plan activities.

PAL: Business Level

The corporate advisory board is the vehicle for recruiting business and industry assistance. The advisory board's function is to create a business awareness of problems related to substance abuse, to lend their organization's name in support of abuse prevention, and to assist in program planning and development.

PEER ASSISTANT SOFTWARE

This peer counseling discussion tool is designed to heighten participants' awareness of a possible likelihood for dropout or substance dependency. The program utilizes the same variables that Students-at-Risk, Inc. uses to predict dropout and substance abuse, as seen in Chapter 4. This program establishes a reference point at which peer counselors or school staff may open discussions with students who may be at risk. The intent of this program is not to predict dependency or label individuals. Properly used, it will assist peer counselors with the task of helping the program participants recognize their individual potential for dependency or dropout. This program is intended for use by peer counselors or school staff who have undergone a period of training designed to enable them to interpret the results. The program runs on Apple IIe, IIGS, Macintosh or IBM compatible hardware.

LAW ENFORCEMENT COLLABORATION

Substance abuse has reached epidemic proportions in many communities, and administrators will find police and other law enforcement agencies ready to collaborate in many ways to reduce abuse. One nationally known effort is Project DARE (Drug Abuse Resistance Education). This program was developed by the Los Angeles Police Department in collaboration with the Los Angeles Unified School District. It covers grades 5 – 12 and consists of seventeen lessons taught by district-trained police officers on full-time duty with the project.

The lessons include the following topics: practices for personal safety; drug use and misuse; consequences of using or choosing not to use drugs; resisting pressure to use drugs; resistance techniques: ways to say no; building self-esteem; assertiveness: how to exercise your rights without interfering with others' rights; managing stress without taking drugs; media influences on drug use; decision making and risk taking; alternatives to drug abuse; alternative activities; an officer-planned lesson for a particular class; role modeling: a visit by a high school student who is a positive role model; summarizing and assessing learning; composing essays or writing letters on how to respond to pressure to use drugs; and schoolwide assembly to award DARE students their certificates of achievement.

ASSESSING ADOLESCENT SUBSTANCE USE

One of the best known people in the field of substance abuse surveys is Professor Rodney Skager at UCLA. Here are some tips from his experience in carrying out surveys to find out if your situation is improving: 1) Identify who will use your survey information and the

These Seventh Graders Are Old Enough to Complete a Substance Abuse Survey.

minimum information they need; 2) secret-response items should be considered in a brief survey; 3) keep the survey as simple as possible; 4) report percentages, not complex statistics; 5) identify the proportion of at-risk respondents; 6) stay with your first instrument for year after year consistency; 7) compare your results with state and national figures; 8) never report results so comparisons between schools or districts can be made; and 9) provide confidential reports to principals and teachers (Skager, 1990).

DRUG, ALCOHOL, AND TOBACCO SURVEY

Figure 8.1 presents an instrument to assess tobacco use, as well as drugs and alcohol, which is called the Drug, Alcohol, and Tobacco Survey and is developed by the Orange County Department of Education, Costa Mesa, California.

We turn now to strategies for working with parents, who are so often the key to reducing abuse for young people.

PARENT STRATEGIES

Parents should take responsibility to identify agencies in the community than can help them if they suspect a child is a potential abuser.

1. What grade are you in now?
   a) 7th   b) 9th   c) 10th
2. What is your sex?
   a) Female   b) Male
3. Which one of the following would best describe you?
   a) White   c) Black   e) Other
   b) Hispanic   d) Asian
4. Most of the time with whom do you live?
   a) Two parents   d) One parent and one stepparent
   b) One parent   e) Other people
   c) Other members
      of the family
5. How much school do you miss?
   a) I never miss school   d) I miss some school every month
   b) I hardly ever miss school   e) I miss some school every week
   c) I miss 2 or 3 days a semester
6. How likely is it that you will graduate from a four-year college after high school?
   a) Definitely will not   c) Probably will
   b) Probably will not   d) Definitely will
7. How many extra school activities do you participate in regularly? (Fill in as many answers as apply.)
   a) None   d) Student Government
   b) Sports   e. Clubs
   c) Music
8. How many nonschool activities do you participate in regularly? (Fill in as many answers as apply.)
   a) None   d) Work
   b) Religious activities   e) Other
   c) PAL/coaching/4-H Club/youth activities

The following questions are about drugs and alcohol.

9. How old were you when you had your first full drink? (A drink is a can of beer, a full glass of wine, or a mixed drink)
   a) I have never had a drink   d) 13 or 14
   b) 10 or younger   e) 15 or older
   c) 11 or 12

Figure 8.1 The Drug, Alcohol, and Tobacco Survey.

10. If you drink, how much do you usually drink at one time?
   a) I don't drink
   b) Less than one can or glass of beer, wine, or mixed drinks
   c) One can or glass of beer, wine, or mixed drinks
   d) 2 – 4 cans or glasses of beer, wine, or mixed drinks
   e) 5 or more cans or glasses of beer, wine, or mixed drinks

11. Think back over the last month. How many times have you had five or more drinks in a row? (A drink is a glass of wine, a bottle of beer, a shot glass of liquor, or a mixed drink.)
   a) None
   b) Once
   c) Twice
   d) 3 – 5 times
   e) 6 or more times

12. Do you use drugs?
   a) Yes (Answer question 13)
   b) No (Go to question 14)

13. If yes, what kind? (Fill in as many answers as apply).
   a) Marijuana
   b) Cocaine
   c) Uppers
   d) Downers
   e) Others

14. Have you ever used drugs and alcohol together?
   a) I don't drink or use drugs
   b) No, never
   c) Once or twice
   d) Many times
   e) Usually

15. How do you usually get the alcoholic beverages you drink?
   a) I do not drink
   b) From home with parental knowledge
   c) From home without parental knowledge
   d) From friends
   e) I ask adults to purchase it, or I buy it myself

16. If you use drugs and/or drink and help was available, where would you feel most comfortable receiving it?
   a) I don't use drugs or drink
   b) At school
   c) Family/church or temple
   d) Doctor or counselor
   e) I don't need any help

17. Do you believe that using drugs will affect the health of the user's future children?
   a) Yes
   b) No
   c) Only the female user
   d) I don't know

Figure 8.1 (continued) The Drug, Alcohol, and Tobacco Survey.

How would your parents/guardian feel about your doing each of the following?

18. Smoking cigarettes or chewing tobacco?
    a) Approve
    b) Do not care
    c) Disapprove
    d) Greatly dsapprove

19. Smoking marijuana?
    a) Approve
    b) Do not care
    c) Disapprove
    d) Greatly disapprove

20. Drinking alcohol (such as beer, wine, wine coolers, hard liquor, champagne)?
    a) Approve
    b) Do not care
    c) Disapprove
    d) Greatly disapprove

21. Using drugs illegally?
    a) Approve
    b) Do not care
    c) Disapprove
    d) Greatly disapprove

22. Attending a party in a private home where alcoholic beverages were served?
    a) Approve
    b) Do not care
    c) Disapprove
    d) Greatly disapprove

The following questions are about tobacco.

23. Does anyone living with you smoke? (Fill in as many answers as apply.)
    a) No one smokes
    b) My father or stepfather smokes
    c) My mother or stepmother smokes
    d) My brother(s) or sister(s) smokes
    e) Other people living with me smoke

24. How many cigarettes have you smoked in the last week?
    a) None
    b) Part or all of one cigarette
    c) 2–4 cigarettes
    d) 2–20 cigarettes
    e) More than one pack

25. How many times have you chewed or dipped tobacco (snuff) in your whole life?
    a) Never
    b) Once
    c) 2–4 times
    d) 5–20 times
    e) Over 20 times

26. If you smoke, would you like to be helped to stop smoking?
    a) I don't smoke
    b) Yes
    c) No

Figure 8.1 (continued) The Drug, Alcohol, and Tobacco Survey.

27. Which one of the following is most likely to convince you not to smoke?
    a) Nothing would convince me
    b) Friends or family
    c) Doctor
    d) Someone famous or powerful
    e) Other

28. The best reason for me not to smoke is that (Select the one best answer.)
    a) I might become addicted
    b) I could get into trouble
    c) I might lose close friends who disapprove of smoking
    d) I would disappoint my parents or other adults who care
    e) It would be dangerous to my health

29. If I smoked cigarettes . . .
    a) most people would like and respect me a lot less
    b) some people wouldn't like it, but it wouldn't change the way they feel about me
    c) most people wouldn't mind at all
    d) people would think I was cool

What do you think?

30. At what grade level do you think drug, alcohol, and tobacco education should begin?
    a) 3rd or less
    b) 4th or 5th
    c) 6th, 7th, 8th
    d) 9th or 10th
    e) 11th or 12th

31. Do you think you know enough about the harmful effects of drugs, alcohol and tobacco on your health?
    a) I know nothing
    b) I know a little
    c) I know enough
    d) I would like to know more
    e) I know everything

32. Which of the following do you think is the most dangerous to a person's health?
    a) Using tobacco (smoking/chewing)
    b) Using illegal drugs
    c) Drinking alcohol
    d) Being overweight
    e) Other

33. Which of these health problems can be caused by smoking. (Fill in as many answers as apply.)
    a) Heart disease
    b) Cancer
    c) Lung disease
    d) High blood pressure
    e) Other

Figure 8.1 (continued) The Drug, Alcohol, and Tobacco Survey.

34. Do you think that the information gathered in this survey will help us control drug use in youth?
    a) Yes   b) No
35. Do you have any suggestions? If so, please write your response on the blank paper provided. Do not write your name on the paper.

Figure 8.1 (continued) *The Drug, Alcohol, and Tobacco Survey.*

In addition, they can become involved in the following ways (Young, 1987)

(*1*) Discuss issues with children early.

(*2*) Discuss issues with other parents.

(*3*) Know where children are when they are out of the home.

(*4*) Support children in developing friendships with other responsible adults.

(*5*) Practice social skills, such as those involved in clarifying communication, in the home.

(*6*) Take classes and be active in local substance abuse prevention groups.

(*7*) Know the early warning signs of substance abuse such as those listed in this chapter and in Chapter 4.

(*8*) Confront children in a caring and concerned fashion, as needed.

SCHOOL STRATEGIES

Ocean View School District in Huntington Beach, California, has a fine model for developing a district or school drug prevention program. Components of a successful program are to 1) be age appropriate; 2) reach across the K−12 curriculum; 3) focus on self-esteem enhancement; 4) teach decision-making skills; 5) provide opportunities for parent and youth involvement—put them to work; 6) have serious evaluation, both process and product; and 7) include school, religious, community, business, media, public and private agency, and police involvement. They have been recognized at the national level for their fine approach.

In summary, the role of the school is central in the battle to reduce substance abuse. It includes focus on curriculum design, in-service training, staffing, counseling, and parent and community involvement.

POLICY RECOMMENDATION

Each district should consider an effort to reduce risk factors and to increase protective factors in substance abuse reduction. In order to achieve this, the district should implement a comprehensive school-based program that focuses upon curriculum design, in-service training, staffing and counseling, in collaboration with parents, law enforcement agencies and community agencies.

Chapter 9

A DISTRICT PLAN FOR REDUCING ALCOHOL AND OTHER DRUG USE

The causes and the impacts of alcohol and drug abuse on individuals, families, schools, and communities are indeed far-reaching. Consequently, the prevention and intervention of abuse must also reach beyond the school district to consistently reinforce and support prevention and intervention. Often, the first step is to form an interdisciplinary school and community committee or task force to study the issues. A case study of the Strategies for Resiliency Project in the Irvine District illustrates the program components needed in a comprehensive plan.

PLANNING WITH THE COMMUNITY

The causes and the impacts of alcohol and drug abuse on individuals, families, schools, and communities are indeed far reaching. Consequently, the prevention and intervention of abuse must also reach beyond the school district to consistently reinforce and support prevention and intervention.

Communities and schools vary widely in their level of awareness of problems related to alcohol and other drug use; therefore, often, the first step is to form an interdisciplinary school and community committee or task force to study the issues. The care and support of a healthy community task force is assisted by being aware that

(1) Committee members often feel overwhelmed at first because they soon recognize that so much is needed in many different areas and levels, that there is little or no money, and that there is a great deal of denial by others.

(2) The primary reason why a school and community committee is

143

needed is due to the complexity of the problem. Progress can be slow; however, creative solutions and new resources often develop from the power of uniting agencies and interests.

(*3*) It is important to select committee members who feel a sense of long-term commitment to the project and who can view the problem from a broad perspective.

(*4*) It is important to educate members both formally and informally to develop a similar awareness level of the issues.

(*5*) It is important to have committee members who can impact and update their organizations regarding the committee's work or provide an open door for that impact by other committee members.

(*6*) Turf issues inevitably arise and must be resolved fairly over time to the satisfaction of group members.

(*7*) Group membership will change over time as interests and jobs change. It is important to maintain a functioning group that includes all segments of the community, e.g., parents, school representatives, city representatives, youth representatives, and treatment and nonprofit representatives.

(*8*) In larger communities, it may be preferable to develop several community groups to address the issues. Groups probably should have some similar members, update progress periodically between groups, agree upon a common general goal, and occasionally collaborate on activities of mutual interest.

This diversified strategy, in which a community-led group focuses on community issues, a parent-led group focuses on parent training, and a school-led group focuses on the school program, is the strategy that developed in Irvine over the years. The school district has a long-term commitment to and involvement in all three planning committees. A closer look at the school district's prevention and intervention strategy is described in detail.

DISTRICT PLAN OVERVIEW

Irvine Unified is a decentralized school district with 20,000 students in the Irvine community of 100,000 residents. The district plan for reducing alcohol and other drug use is centrally coordinated but is uniquely implemented at each site.

Districtwide strategies include

(*1*) A district prevention program advisory board representing staff, parents, community, and students to provide input for school-based services

(*2*) Collaboration with city staff and city council, as well as county staff, through a city task force to implement communitywide prevention, including limiting alcohol advertising and availability to youth, biannual use surveys of students and the community, and input from youth on needs and alternative activities

(*3*) Collaboration with Irvine Community Drug Prevention (a nonprofit parent/community group) to provide staff, parent, community, and youth trainings with conferences and other activities concerning drug abuse prevention curriculum, self-esteem, and strategies for at- risk students

(*4*) Board-approved district policy, procedure, and oversight of activities that support prevention, suppression, and intervention activities in the schools

(*5*) The development and implementation of a K − 12 curriculum matrix of alcohol and other drug prevention skills, including district-developed health and guidance materials (STAGES and STAR programs), enriched with the DARE program, through classroom presentations by police officers

(*6*) Systematic identification of at-risk students using computerized district-level, staff site-level, and student-level information

(*7*) Student support groups for at-risk K − 12 students facilitated by site support staff or guidance paraprofessionals (with district-level supervision and training)

(*8*) Ongoing grant writing, program development, research, and program evaluation to ensure the continuance of high-quality programs

Implementation at the site level varies according to developmental and other student population needs, as well as site-level planning styles. Areas of difference in programs include

(*1*) How prevention, identification, and intervention duties are distributed; definition and function of core team or resource staff

(*2*) Frequency of prevention assemblies and availability of alternative activities, such as peer leadership/assistance opportunities

(*3*) Frequency and characteristics of student support groups
(*4*) Location and extent of prevention curriculum infusion

INNOVATIVE MIDDLE SCHOOL STRATEGIES

A recent addition to the district plan is the Strategies for Resiliency Project. This project is in the third year of a five-year grant funded by the U.S. Office of Substance Abuse Prevention to develop a model demonstration for the prevention and early intervention of drug abuse among middle school youth. An abstract and program overview follow.

Abstract: Strategies for Resiliency Program

Purpose: To demonstrate the effectiveness of comprehensive holistic prevention and early intervention strategies to reduce risk for alcohol and other drug use and to increase resiliency in high-risk middle school youth.

Need: The use of alcohol and other drugs by children and youth is a serious national problem. Hundreds of thousands of children in this nation are endangering their lives and their futures. Crime, violence, and tragedy sear the lives of victims, families, and friends. The likelihood that a young person will use and abuse alcohol and other drugs appears to increase as the number of risk factors increase and the number of resiliency or protective factors decrease. There is a great need for prevention and intervention programs that focus on reducing the power of risk factors and that increase the potency of resiliency factors across several environmental levels.

Goals: 1) to decrease the incidence and prevalence of drug and alcohol use among high-risk youth; 2) to reduce risk factors for using alcohol and other drugs as they impact on individual high-risk youth and on the environments in which high-risk youth and their families function; 3) to increase resiliency and protective factors within high-risk youth and within their families and communities in order to reduce the likelihood that youths will use alcohol and other drugs.

Activities: 1) to develop a systematic, multidimensional identification of at-risk students; 2) to provide effective prevention and early intervention programs for middle school students; 3) to collaborate with the community to provide outreach services to families of high-risk students; 4) to provide training and educational resources for school staff; 5) to develop, evaluate, and disseminate effective strategies.

Evaluation: Product evaluation includes 1) assessment of student attitude and risk behaviors, including alcohol and other drug use, antisocial behaviors, personality factors, self-esteem, and resilient attitudes or behaviors as measured by parent, teacher, and student self-reports, the Risk Assessment Survey, the Family Apgar Scale, the Rosenberg Self-Esteem Scale, and various locally developed instruments; 2) assessment of basic skills improvement as measured by academic GPA and CTBS test scores; and 3) attendance as measured by district records. Process evaluation measures include the effectiveness of trainings, manuals, and curriculum in meeting project implementation goals.

Intervention Approach

The intervention objectives of the project are to decrease antisocial, aggressive behavior and to develop prosocial behaviors; to decrease the tendency to associate with drug-using peers due to passive behavior and lack of alternative activities; to improve parental drug-free information, attitudes, and skills related to family management, value systems, modeling, and communication of a no-use message; to increase student achievement and interest in school activities; to improve health and health attitudes; to increase awareness of personality needs and develop healthy alternatives and resources for high-risk students who may be sensation seekers, cognitively impulsive, isolated, and highly tolerant of deviance and/or who have low self-esteem.

A multilevel intervention system will provide prevention to all middle school youth and identify at-risk and high-risk students, facilitating their referral to school-based early intervention and community-based treatment programs.

The first level of intervention is the district's alcohol and drug abuse prevention program being provided to all middle school students through health class, teacher advisement, homeroom, elective classes, assemblies, small group counseling, and positive peer activities (such as the Conflict Resolution Program and Youth to Youth Conferences).

The second level of intervention provides identification and early intervention for students at risk for developing drug abuse problems by evaluating the students' risk levels and providing interventions to increase resiliency and prosocial development. Risk and resiliency levels are evaluated along the continuum of risk, thereby permitting a non-labeling proactive intervention program.

DEFINING RISK IN STUDENTS

Research has found that there are many paths to drug abuse (Oetting and Beauvais, 1987); therefore, interventions must also address many specific areas. A student's risk factors may be related to problems with school, family, peers, or personality and may be a combination of these areas. Students must also be identified by the degree of risk, since strategies that work with at-risk students may not work with high-risk students. A definition of these groups, as used in the project, follows:

- *At-risk youth* have a limited number of risk factors. They may be students with low self-esteem; passive or aggressive students, who are experiencing peer pressure problems; children who lack realistic information on destructive aspects of drugs; children experiencing failure in school; or students with behavioral or antisocial problems. They may be children of substance abusers and genetically at risk, representing the 25% of children affected by alcohol risk characteristics.
- *High-risk youth* experience multiple risk factors. These students have multiple problems with attendance, discipline, family, self-esteem, or academic matters and/or are observed, reported, and/or self-reported to have alcohol and other drug use problems at school or in the community.

High-risk students' school problems may be academic, behavioral, social, or personal. Family problems may be due to living in dysfunctional or abusive family environments such as homes where alcohol and/or drug abuse occurs or has occurred. Other indications of high risk are being a child of a substance abuser; being a victim of physical, sexual, or psychological abuse; dropping out of school; becoming pregnant; being economically disadvantaged; committing a violent or delinquent act; experiencing mental health problems; attempting suicide; experiencing long-term physical pain due to injury; or experiencing chronic failure in school.

PROCEDURE FOR IDENTIFYING AT-RISK
AND HIGH-RISK YOUTH

Students' risk and resilient characteristics are collected through a multidimensional data-gathering system, including information from school records; teacher, parent, or community referral; and student self-report, including

(*1*) A data base of all students in the district, identifying those most at risk based on district records of academics, low test scores, and at-risk behaviors. The data base combines some of the indicators for dropout and substance abuse and is designed to identify high-risk students in the areas of attendance, number of D's and F's, reading level, retention during school history, mobility from school/home, and adjustment factors that include substance abuse incidents, juvenile delinquency, citizenship, special education, and physical disabilities.

(*2*) Referral from teachers who have identified a problem with a student and a procedure for handling referrals and tracking disposition of each referral

(*3*) A Risk Assessment Survey, included in Chapter 3, administered with parent permission, to students identified in the screening process to define further the areas of risk and intervention needs of students

(*4*) A plan for tracking and evaluating student interventions and sharing information with participating student's parents and teachers

RISK ASSESSMENT SURVEY (RAS)

This self-report instrument (see Chapter 3), designed for grades 6–12, includes general demographic questions, including grade, age, gender, and parents' occupation. In addition, the survey includes questions designed to determine the number and level of inter-, intra-, and extra-personal risk factors related to drug use.

The need to develop the Risk Assessment Survey, as an assessment tool appropriate for the school setting and focused toward intervention, was based on the school's role to provide services for prevention and early intervention. Assessment instruments best suited to school address risk factors that precede drug abuse and are statistically related to them. Historically, educators have adopted clinical assessment scales and have often found them normed on adults and too heavily focused on psychopathology and drug history information. By using risk factor assessments, schools can view drug prevention from a "whole child" perspective and design prevention and intervention services to decrease specific risk factors related to drug abuse.

The Risk Assessment Survey was developed in three steps: 1) Specific items were selected from the most salient risk factors found in recent research literature; 2) a pilot study of the research items was conducted in the Pomona Unified School District, Pomona, California (Callison et al., 1990); and 3) the revised survey was cross-validated on Irvine students using district record data to validate the results of the self-report RAS survey (Richards-Colocino, 1991).

The results of the validation study in Irvine identified eleven significant risk factors through a discriminant function analysis that predicted alcohol and other drug use in middle and high school students. Specifically, this study validated the Risk Assessment Survey, found four significant variables in school record data, and defined three risk level groups that predict user status.

Validation Study Results

One major finding of the study was that the Risk Assessment Survey did significantly discriminate between nonusers (no use in one year) and users (weekly use of alcohol and/or marijuana or use of high-risk drug in the last year). In combination with the number of D's and F's from the school record and the student's grade level, the discriminate function analysis was able to *correctly classify 81.6%* of a random group of 341 students into user and nonuser categories. This finding allows schools to identify and intervene in a more specialized manner with students at greater levels of risk. Although it is important not to stigmatize identified students for needing drug abuse intervention, these high-risk students certainly need more intense and/or more numerous interventions than those with fewer risk factors.

Eleven risk variables were found to be the strongest predictors of drug use through the discriminant function analysis:

(*1*) Ever arrested

(*2*) Close adults with use problems

(3) Absent when not sick
(4) Use if a friend dared you
(5) Number of D's and F's
(6) Parents against using
(7) Parents know whereabouts
(8) How often angry
(9) Argue or fight with family
(10) Close friends who use
(11) Grade level

These most significant predictors of drug use explain 46% of the variance and represent risk factors influenced by personality, peer relations, and the environment. This finding supports the implementation of interventions that 1) specifically address the risks identified, 2) affect the influence systems that impact the student, and 3) start early in the development of risks that are associated with drug use.

The Risk Assessment Survey has adequate validity and internal consistency (.71 standardized item alpha) for use in school prevention programs. This finding and the brevity of the scale make it especially appealing in busy school settings.

The Risk Assessment Survey was made more useful to schools in identifying students through valid cut-off scores. The finding that the scale's scores significantly separated students into three user categories of nonuser, occasional user, and user is important. This finding means that students can be identified for prevention and intervention services by self-reporting on risk factors, without asking direct questions about a student's drug use or without waiting until drug use and/or abuse develops.

For those school administrators concerned about the validity of self-report data, further analysis was conducted on the 15.2% misidentified or high-risk nonusers. RAS (self-report) scores of low, medium, and high-risk nonusers were compared to their school record risk factor scores (derived from school record data). *The high-risk nonusers also had significantly higher school record risk scores*, indicating that these students are having more problems in school and implying three possibilities: the high-risk students 1) lied about being nonusers, 2) are at high risk to become users, or 3) are truly resilient. Therefore, when in doubt, school administrators can use school record data (grades, absences, and problem behaviors) as a check on the validity of survey findings. Caution in favor of prevention would indicate that high-risk students who also have risk indicators in their school records be included in prevention/intervention programs, even if they are not currently using alcohol and other drugs. This is especially true because comprehensive school-based programs address risk factors that can also lead to dropping out, delinquency, and personality disorders.

Four variables from school record data were also found to be significant predictors for drug abuse. These significant variables from school records – number of D's and F's, a weighted risk factor score, reading achievement, and language achievement – serve as a basis to intervene with students in a prevention or intervention program, even if individual data cannot be gathered. While the number of D's and F's was most highly

Substance Abuse Survey Items Can Be Administered as Part of Another Survey on Self-Esteem and Peer Relations.

correlated to drug use, this analysis also supports the validity of the weighted risk factor score and, to a lesser degree, reading and language achievement scores as associated with drug use. The use of school record data alone to identify students for intervention, though not as powerful, is often readily available and can function, along with teacher referral, to identify students for individual risk factor assessment.

Finally, several demographic variables in this study not found to be significantly related to drug use were gender, father's and mother's occupations, living situation, ethnic background, and special education placement. This result was also found in previous research (with a few exceptions), which supports the conclusion that these demographic variables are not related to drug use. This finding lends support to the universal nature of the problem of drug use.

Based on these research findings, the Risk Assessment Survey was revised into different formats for a variety of identification purposes. Specifically, four options for identification have been developed. Option 1 is a paper and pencil version of the survey with scoring procedures that are useful for identifying a small number of students quickly. Other identification options are: Option 2, computerized school record data; Option 3, Risk Assessment items plus assessment of peer relations, self-esteem, and drug access and perceptions, which is computer-scored; and Option 4, a computer-scored version of the Risk Assessment Survey, suitable for evaluating many students quickly. These assessment instruments are presented in Chapter 3.

Administration of Risk Assessment Survey

With parent permission, students in grades 6−12 are administered items in the written survey. An alternate and recommended administration technique is to ask the alcohol and other drug use items (#6, 8, 16, and 18) separately, on a survey that is specially coded to track decreases in use without identifying students. This procedure encourages honesty of answers over time and is viable now that the Risk Assessment Survey has been validated as an accurate predictor of use. In addition, students are assessed on attitudes towards drug use, self-esteem, and peer relations.

TRACKING STUDENT INTERVENTIONS

The Strategies for Resiliency Project being conducted in Irvine is an extension of the At-Risk Management Project. The aims of the At-Risk

Management Project were to develop a computer management system that 1) identified potential substance abusers and potential dropouts and analyze their risk levels and 2) use an expert system to connect identified students at risk with appropriate interventions that reduced student risk levels and records and tracked the interventions used. The At-Risk Management Project was part of a federal grant to Dr. William Callison at California State University at Fullerton and eleven participating school districts, including Irvine, that made up the Partnership Academy Committee. The project was funded over a two-year period to use new forms of technology in substance abuse prevention.

The At-Risk Management Project was designed to assist staff in the identification of students at risk for substance abuse and dropping out. Using the latest research on risk factors for both substance abusers and dropouts, software was developed for identification. An expert system (Comprehensive Risk Assessment) was used to connect the identification of at-risk students with one or more of the many interventions available in Irvine Unified School District (IUSD). The expert system can be used by teachers and other school personnel to identify early problem behaviors connected to potential for drug and alcohol use/abuse, to refer students for intervention, to process referrals, and to track the disposition of each referral.

IMPLEMENTING INTERVENTIONS TO DECREASE RISK FACTORS

Students vary in the degree and number of risk and resiliency characteristics they possess. Some student risk characteristics (such as having been arrested) and the resiliency factor of being from a small family cannot be altered. However, other risk and resiliency factors are open to intervention and are the central focus of the Strategies for Resiliency Project. A summary of the project's interventions by risk factor follows.

(1) *Antisocial, problem behaviors, and drug use risk factors:* A comprehensive classroom health curriculum is provided to all students, including drug and wellness education and social communication coping skills through the district's STAR and STAGES programs (Irvine Unified School District, 1987a, 1987b). These wellness skills are enhanced for at-risk students who get additional counseling, drug education, and practice in prosocial skills through small groups conducted by support specialists.

(2) *Peer risk factors:* The positive use of peer groups can be highly effective in promoting a drug-free, healthy lifestyle. The Strategies for Resiliency Project includes providing opportunities to participate in peer assistance and drug-free activities such as Youth to Youth Conferences. In addition, peer resistance skills are taught through the STAR program in health class, advisement, or small group.

(3) *Family risk factors:* To offset family-related risk factors, the Irvine District provides two parent programs: Active Parenting and Neighborhoods in Action. Active Parenting and Active Parenting of Teens (Popkin, 1983, 1990) is a six-session video-based program designed to improve communication and discipline skills of parents. Neighborhoods in Action (1990) is a three-hour video-based course that teaches parents effective drug prevention and intervention strategies and how to be better role models for their children. Parents of participating students are personally invited and encouraged to attend the trainings.

In addition, the families of participating students will be contacted regularly (through home visits, phone calls, and school interviews) for feedback, input, and data collection. Based on identified needs, school coordinators will refer families for needed services and follow up on the outcome of the referral.

(4) *School risk factors:* Student study teams and support staff screen and assist students who are academically weak or failing. Activities such as assigning a mentor, offering tutoring, and establishing a homework hotline may be implemented. The school team, made up of the school coordinator and a support specialist, monitor student progress and develop activities to increase students' interest and bonding to school through support groups and alternative activities.

(5) *Physical and emotional health risk factors:* Through health classes, students are taught the importance of physical and mental well-being. They are also taught the importance of wellness as a choice and ways to enhance their self-esteem. IUSD health curriculum, along with support group activities, emphasizes the importance of knowledge, decision making, nutrition, exercise, stress management, and a positive attitude in maintaining good health.

(6) *Personality risk factors:* One common personality characteristic found in at-risk students is chronic anger. Teaching students anger

control and coping skills for their emotions is an important part of the prevention process. Through the district's STAGES program, students are taught, both in the classroom and in small groups, a roadmap that guides them through major changes in their lives. In addition, individual counseling will be offered to address individual personality risk factors.

(7) *Environmental risk factors:* Environmental risk factors are addressed by school teams, the district advisory board, and the community task force on substance abuse. Periodic reviews of school and district policy, community availability of drugs, and student perceptions of use in the community are conducted to enhance the effectiveness of the program.

INTERVENTION SERVICES FOR HIGH-RISK YOUTH

Through the efforts of a site-level school coordinator, a paraprofessional support specialist, and other site staff, the following intervention services are offered to at-risk youth:

(1) Individual and group counseling directed toward improved coping and social skills, increased interest in and information about drug-free activities and group support of nonuse, and, when indicated, referral to community counseling services

(2) Family needs assessment, intervention, counseling, and referral, including parent education groups

(3) Development of activities to decrease risk and increase resiliency, such as tutoring, drug-free conferences, peer assistance, involvement in the community, and after-school programs

(4) Monitoring of student progress in interventions by a caring school team

(5) Participation in a comprehensive health education program that includes wellness and social and coping skills

STRATEGIES FOR RESILIENCY EVALUATION PLAN

The evaluation process started early in the life of the project and continues as an ongoing activity. Evaluative studies during the first year of the project provided identification data of high-risk students and

baseline data to assess students' antisocial behaviors, drug use, associations with drug users, behavior/emotional competencies, achievement, health knowledge and attitudes, attendance, self-esteem, and personality factors. The project assessed the progress of high-risk students in improving their areas of risk and increasing their resiliency to involvement in alcohol and other drug use, which is measured as follows:
A five-year follow-up procedure tracks participants as they progress

Dependent Variable	Instrument/Data Source
Antisocial behaviors	Risk Assessment Survey; school records
Drug use and association	California Substance Use Survey; Risk Assessment Survey
Parent practices	Family Apgar Scale
Behavioral/emotional	Friends Apgar Scale; Rosenberg Self-Esteem Scale
School achievement	Comprehensive test of basic skills; grades
Attendance	Attendance records
Personality factors	Risk Assessment Survey; Rosenberg Self-Esteem Scale

through middle and high school, providing important research information about the support needed for continued nonuse of drugs and alcohol.

EVALUATION FINDINGS OF STRATEGIES FOR RESILIENCY PROJECT (FEBRUARY 1990 – SEPTEMBER 1992)

The Strategies in Resiliency Project made substantial and measurable progress toward the achievement of its goals. Both formative and summative evaluation were conducted, and it was shown that the project had a significant impact on the reduction of risk factors and the enhancement of resiliency factors in the identified at-risk and high-risk youth.

• The results of the pre/postadministration of the Risk Assessment Survey indicate a substantial reduction of risk factors, as shown by a matched t test that measured a significant decrease between the pre- and post mean scores.

- An analysis of the frequency distribution of the risk assessment scale range was used to divide the group of identified students into three groups of low, medium, and high risk based on their pretest scores. These groupings were used to compare to other assessment data to assess differential growth dependent on the degree of initial risk level.
- An analysis of variance between risk levels and peer relations (as measured by the Friends Apgar) was performed. There was a significant difference between groups of low-, medium-, and high-risk students in the quality of their peer relations. The difference appeared between the low- and high-risk group and between the middle- and high-risk group. This indicates that low-risk students have better relations with peers in the areas of adaptation, growth, and affection than either the medium- or high-risk groups.
- There was a significant decrease in the use of beer, wine, or wine coolers, as shown by the results of a paired t test of the Alcohol and Other Drug Survey data.
- The results of a paired sample t test on the prepost data from the Rosenburg Self-Esteem Scale indicate no significantly higher scores in the areas of self-esteem. The length of time between pre- and postassessment, for the first cohort, was shorter than what would be considered optimal, thereby shortening the amount of time for the implementation of interventions. The project will greatly increase the time between pre- and postassessment during the following school year, thereby increasing the length of time that interventions are in place. It is believed that a change in self-esteem ratings will be demonstrated in later assessments.

Process evaluation indicates substantial progress in meeting objectives:

- School-based interventions have included screening and identification and interventions performed with all identified students; hiring and training of support staff to facilitate screening and interventions; providing individual and small group counseling; hiring and training school coordinators to act as liaisons between project staff, families, school, and community; and collecting extensive data.
- Family interventions have included parent education, increased

parent involvement in school activities, planning for a Parent Development Day, and the development and field test of a Parent Survey/Interview Form.

• Community-based interventions have included the establishment of the local advisory board; a multidisciplinary team approach with community organizations to provide alcohol and other drug education materials and information; and planning for linkages with community health services and coordinated services with the county, state, and other relevant agencies.

STRATEGIES FOR RESILIENCY AND THE AT-RISK MANAGEMENT SYSTEM

Irvine's Strategies for Resiliency Program presents an innovative design that establishes effective drug and alcohol abuse prevention and intervention. These strategies are included in the At-Risk Management System, which will also make a significant impact on reducing student drug use by creating a computerized delivery system for drug abuse prevention and intervention that utilizes the latest research to predict potential abusers and dropouts with an identification system that, in turn, links to some of the most effective interventions in the country.

It is apparent that a large number of school districts would be interested in a delivery system that addresses two of their most critical problems, students who use drugs and alcohol and students who are likely to drop out of school. Students At Risk (SAR) identification software will not only serve to predict potential abusers and dropouts; it can serve as a means for evaluation of the effectiveness of prevention programs. The software can also be used for individual and group evaluation or for district offices to evaluate the many interventions in a school system, through pre/post measures of assessment.

POLICY RECOMMENDATION

Each district should consider working to develop a comprehensive, holistic approach for the prevention and early intervention of alcohol and other drug use by high-risk youth. The program should seek to decrease the incidence and prevalence of drug and alcohol use among high-risk youth; 2) to reduce the risk factors for using alcohol and other drugs as they impact on individual high-risk youth and on the environments in which high-risk youths and their families function; and 3) to increase resiliency and protective factors within high-risk youth and their families and communities in order to reduce the likelihood that youths will use alcohol and other drugs.

Chapter 10

ALCOHOL AND OTHER DRUG PREVENTION PROGRAM COMPONENTS

The goal of district prevention and intervention services is to decrease risk factors that lead to drug use and abuse by students and to increase protective factors. Using well-established curricular-based prevention programs (STAR and STAGES), the program seeks to improve the district's resources to work with all aspects of dealing with at-risk youth.

GOALS AND OBJECTIVES OF DISTRICT PREVENTION AND INTERVENTION

The goal of district prevention and intervention services is to decrease risk factors and to increase protective factors. The achievement of this goal is based on the following objectives:

- to improve attitudes, skills, and use of resources to decrease risks and increase protective factors in individual students
- to increase student achievement and interest in school activities, i.e., to increase bonding to school
- to improve health and wellness attitudes by teaching developmentally appropriate health information, including information about alcohol and other drugs
- to increase awareness of personality needs and to develop healthy alternatives and resources for high-risk students who may be sensation seekers, cognitively impulsive, isolated, highly tolerant of deviance, and/or have low self-esteem
- to decrease the tendency to associate with drug-using peers due to passive behavior and lack of alternative activities

- to increase teachers' knowledge and skill in the delivery of effective drug abuse prevention and intervention strategies
- to improve parental drug-free information, attitudes, and skills related to family management, value systems, modeling, and communication of a no-use message, i.e., teach skills to increase bonding to family
- to collaborate with others to support a no-use message for students in the community by developing awareness of environmental pressures to use and by developing community resources to prevent or stop using, i.e., to increase bonding to the community

CURRICULAR ACTIVITIES TO ACHIEVE OBJECTIVES

The prevention program in Irvine begins with a strong core curriculum that has been developed over a number of years to meet many of the objectives stated above. The district's prevention programs are based on research that personal and social skills training, when combined with cognitive and behavioral coping strategies (problem solving and stress reduction), provides the most successful approach to prevention (Botvin, 1986). The latest research adds additional evidence that the skills taught in the Irvine's core curriculum are central to prevention. For example, two of the findings in a recent review of the components of 100 successful prevention programs (Dryfoos, 1990) were the use of personal social skills training to teach students coping mechanisms and the provision of early and continuous individualized attention.

All students in the district have opportunities throughout the grade levels in the classroom and in small groups to receive instruction on basic prevention and health-related skills. Instruction is based on a matrix of skills that are implemented in classrooms at grades K−6, in student advisement or health classes at grades 7 and 8, and in health class at grade 10.

Instruction in substance abuse prevention is implemented as a part of health instruction in the elementary and secondary grades. In addition, student advisement and life skills elective classes implement prevention curriculum at the secondary level.

Figure 10.1 is a detailed description of IUSD Alcohol and Other Drug Prevention Programs that are being institutionalized in grades K−12. Students are taught prevention skills and knowledge that are develop-

Grade	Life Skills	Wellness Skills
K	SELF-ESTEEM AND SCHOOL ADJUSTMENT THROUGH LITERATURE (STAGES) Developing "who I am" and positive self-esteem Identifying and understanding feelings Learning how people react to change Learning about different types of families Respecting self and others	POSITIVE LIVING SKILLS Learning how we feel DECISION FOR SAFE LIVING Exploring feelings in disasters Learning about safety and medicine
1	FEELINGS AND SOCIAL BEHAVIOR (STAR I) Developing the concept of "being myself" Reinforcing concept of "It's OK to be me" Introducing passive, agressive, assertive behaviors Introducing skill of making assertive "I" statements Using assertive requests Understanding effects of positive/negative communications Developing ability to give and receive compliments Developing ability to identify and express feelings Decision making based on feelings Integrating and reviewing lessons on feelings	HEALTHY HABITS Learning about physical growth and nutrition Learning how doctors promote health and well-being POSITIVE LIVING SKILLS Learning to recognize how we feel Learning how people differ Learning how families differ Learning how families grow and change Developing awareness of dangerous situations

Figure 10.1 Irvine K–12 Drug Prevention Curriculum.

163

Grade	Life Skills	Wellness Skills
2	INTRODUCTION TO THE REACTIONS TO CHANGE (STAGES) Learning how people and families differ Learning how changes produce stress Discovering the six stages of change Developing awareness of the stage of denial Developing awareness of the stage of anger Developing awareness of the stage of bargaining Developing awareness of the stage of depression Developing awareness of the stage of acceptance Developing awareness of the stage of hope Developing ability to identify the stages in review lesson	HEALTHY HABITS Developing awareness of healthy eating and nutrition Discovering how senses work POSITIVE LIVING SKILLS Recognizing family structures Reviewing types of families Learning about others' feelings Learning about positive and negative feelings
3	RESPONSIBILITY AND GOAL SETTING (STAR I) Establishing concept of agreements Establishing concept of consequences Using puppets to understand agreements Making agreements at home Relaxing through proper breathing Building awareness of positive and negative consequences Identifying habits and how they relate to agreements Identifying helpful habits Reviewing the accountability skills concepts	HEALTHY HABITS Learning about body structure and functions POSITIVE LIVING SKILLS Learning how emotions affect the body Learning about individual uniqueness Understanding ways to prevent accidents Discovering skills to make friends DECISION FOR SAFE LIVING Discovering safety procedures for emergencies and earthquake preparedness

Figure 10.1 (continued) Irvine K–12 Drug Prevention Curriculum.

Grade	Life Skills	Wellness Skills
4	MANAGING STRESSFUL CHANGES (STAGES) Introducing awareness of stressful changes Understanding the six stages of change Developing an understanding of denial Developing an understanding of anger Using art to handle stress Developing an understanding of bargaining Developing an understanding of depression Developing an understanding of acceptance Developing an understanding of hope Reviewing ways to identify and manage change	POSITIVE LIVING SKILLS Finding ways of reducing stress DECISION FOR SAFE LIVING Risk-taking: safe and dangerous risks Learning characteristics of substances Proper and improper use of drugs Discovering effects of tobacco and second smoke
5	PROBLEM SOLVING AND DECISION MAKING (STAR I) Recognizing a need for problem solving Introducing "think aloud," step 1 Introducing "think aloud," step 2 Introducing "think aloud," step 3 Introducing "think aloud," step 4 Remembering the "think aloud" technique Applying "think aloud" to academic problems Applying 4 steps to interpersonal problems Applying 4 steps to personal problems Applying "think aloud" to goal setting	POSITIVE LIVING SKILLS Understanding personality Learning abilities and differences DECISIONS FOR SAFE LIVING Learning why people take risks Discovering the risk that families take Seeing how we take risks with friends Making decisions involving risks Recognizing laws that affect decisions Discovering persuasion in advertising Building decision-making skills for times of disaster

Figure 10.1 (continued) Irvine K–12 Drug Prevention Curriculum.

165

Grade	Life Skills	Wellness Skills
6	INTERPERSONAL COMMUNICATION AND PEER PRESSURE (STAR II) Introducing concept of legal and personal rights Recognizing passive behavior Understanding consequences of passive behavior Recognizing aggressive behavior Understanding consequences of aggressive behavior Recognizing assertive behavior Introducing ways to manage stress Communicating assertively through "I" statements Communicating assertively through compliments Communicating assertively through requests Communicating assertively through assertive refusal	POSITIVE LIVING SKILLS Choosing healthy personal habits Understanding the concept of fitness Learning to live a safe drug-free life DECISIONS FOR SAFE LIVING Understanding the major influences in risk-taking Recognizing effects of smoking on the body and on others Learning how advertising influences Our decision to use or not use drugs Understanding the impact of alcohol on the body Deciding to not use alcohol Recognizing dangers of inhalants Identifying health effects of marijuana Learning stimulants' effect on the body Choosing ways to refuse substances Role-playing to resist using drugs Reviewing the major concerns of substance use and abuse

Figure 10.1 (continued) Irvine K–12 Drug Prevention Curriculum.

Grade	Life Skills	Wellness Skills
6	SAFETY, SELF-ESTEEM, AND DRUG PREVENTION (D.A.R.E.) Practice for personal safety Drug use and misuse Consequences Resistance techniques-ways to say "no" Building self-esteem Managing stress without taking drugs Media influences on drug use Decision making and risk-taking Form ing a support system (making friends) "DARE to be a STAR" culmination	

Figure 10.1 (continued) Irvine K – 12 Drug Prevention Curriculum.

167

Grade	Life Skills	Wellness Skills
7	PEER RESISTANCE SKILLS AND UNDERSTANDING OTHERS (STAR II)	FAMILY LIFE EDUCATION
	Reviewing passive, aggressive, assertive skill	Making choices that promote wellness
	Reviewing assertive refusal technique	Decision making and well-being
	Practicing skill of broken record	
	Managing stress using broken record technique	USE/MISUSE OF SUBSTANCES
	Practicing use of open-ended questions	Understanding legal and illegal drugs
	Developing awareness of criticism	Relating drug use and the spread of communicable disease
	Using negative assertion effectively	Differentiating kinds of dependencies
	Practicing the skill of fogging	Identifying effects of substances on body/mind
	Practicing the skill of negative inquiry	Discovering danger of smokeless tobacco
	Reviewing skills to handle criticism	Learning smoking reasons and ways to stop
	Practicing stress management skills	Discovering alternatives to drugs
	Introducing personality skills	Finding community resources for giving support and rehabilitating
	Recognizing extroversion/introversion traits	
	Recognizing sensing and intuitive personalities	
	Recognizing thinking and feeling personalities	
	Recognizing judging and perceiving traits	
	Recognizing the responsible personality	
	Recognizing the spontaneous personality	
	Understanding the feeling type personality	
	Understanding the thinking type personality	

Figure 10.1 (continued) Irvine K–12 Drug Prevention Curriculum.

Grade	Life Skills	Wellness Skills
8	MANAGING STRESSFUL CHANGES IN ADOLESCENCE (STAGES II)	
	Understanding stages of adolescent changes	
	Understanding stress in adolescence	
	Discovering resources available	
	Finding personal resources for stress	
	Coping with denial stage during adolescence	
	Dealing with denial through relaxation	
	Using assertiveness to deal with anger	
	Expressing anger in behavior	
	Coping with anger using relaxation	
	Using assertive refusal for bargaining	
	Managing bargaining stage with relaxation	
	Understanding adolescent depression	
	Managing depression stage	
	Using problem solving with acceptance	
	Managing acceptance stage in adolescence	
	Understanding stage of hope in adolescence	
	Setting goals, relaxing to manage hope	

Figure 10.1 (continued) Irvine K – 12 Drug Prevention Curriculum.

169

Grade	Life Skills	Wellness Skills
10	COPING SKILLS FOR ANGER AND DEPRESSION (STAGES II) Integrating six stages and reactions of change Applying knowledge of reactions to change Integrating knowledge of resources Integrating skills to cope with denial Integrating the effects of anger Utilizing assertion skills to deal with anger Integrating the effects of bargaining Accepting and integrating reactions to STAGES Integrating skills to understand hope	USE AND MISUSE OF SUBSTANCES Recognizing alcohol dependency Recognizing effects of marijuana use Understanding alcohol and marijuana Physical and mental alcohol effects Learning about effect of other substances on self and others Differentiating between prescription and nonprescription drugs Learning about misconceptions and myths of alcohol and alcoholism Examining factors that influence decision not to use Analyzing the influence of advertising Developing resistance, peer and media Benefits of giving up tobacco and other substances

Figure 10.1 (continued) Irvine K – 12 Drug Prevention Curriculum.

Grade	Life Skills	Wellness Skills
10	DEVELOPING EFFECTIVE PROBLEM-SOLVING SKILLS (STAR II) Developing effective problem-solving skills Understanding of difference between fact and belief Developing awareness of rational/irrational beliefs Differentiating between rational/irrational beliefs Developing the skill of problem solving Developing understanding of self-talk Developing the skill of brainstorming Developing skills of alternative solution Understanding the consequences of brainstorming Recognizing skill of listing alternatives Recognizing consequences in problem solving Practicing implementing plan	FAMILY HEALTH Recognizing family influences and differences Learning how the family meets basic needs Locating community resources and family assistance Developing awareness of individual rights and respon- sibilities in relationships Recognizing dysfunctions within families Identifying, preventing abuse Identifying proper steps in solving family problems PERSONAL HEALTH Achieving and maintaining health Understanding how health choices affect quality of life Understanding when health changes require professional assistance

Figure 10.1 (continued) Irvine K – 12 Drug Prevention Curriculum.

mentally appropriate and needed for social, emotional, and healthy life adjustment. The curriculum is primarily implemented by classroom teachers with assistance from D.A.R.E officers, nurses, counselors, paraprofessional support specialists, and outside speakers.

BACKGROUND AND DESCRIPTION OF CORE CURRICULUM

The development of the district's unique prevention curriculum started in 1979, when GOAL (Guidance Opportunities for Affective Learning) was developed as a Title IV-C project for grades K – 6. Project GOAL was originally designed to meet the need of teachers who felt unprepared to teach important social and emotional skills, especially to students in special education. Based on research and observation of students' needs for successful mainstreaming, GOAL lessons were developed in social skills, decision making, accountability, and stress management. GOAL was awarded exemplary dissemination status by the California State Department of Education for its strong evaluation demonstrating significant improvement in special education students' behavioral and academic growth.

Good programs stand the test of time and are enhanced by updating, as the prevention knowledge base increases. To this end, GOAL was revised in 1985 and used in school districts to help *all* students, including at-risk students not in special education. Even in 1992, GOAL was being revised and got a new name, STAR I: Social Thinking and Reasoning. This revision enhances this exemplary K – 6 curriculum with lessons for each grade level and integrates lessons with the latest research on effective strategies to decrease risk factors and increase protective factors in the areas of child abuse and children of alcoholics. The design of STAR I continues to teach important intra- and interpersonal skills, using activities and puppets. Students learn ways to communicate successfully, control impulsiveness and anxiety, and problem solve. They also learn how to enhance self-esteem, be responsible for their behavior, and cooperate with others.

STAR II: Social Thinking and Reasoning was developed in 1981 as an innovative Title IV-C project for at-risk middle school students. The STAR II Program is based on extensive research by Manuel J. Smith (1975, 1986) and others that assertion skills and understanding personality styles (Kiersey and Bates, 1978) can provide important coping skills for adults and children. STAR II has been evaluated, both as an innovative Title IV-C project and through a longitudinal evaluation for a total of six years of data. The longitudinal research demonstrated that students trained in STAR II had significantly higher grade point averages, attendance, assertive skills, and healthy attitudes, including less self-reported drug use, than untrained control group students (Richards and Smith, 1985).

STAR II meets the needs of middle school (grades 6−8) students through a skill-based curriculum that teaches social skills, personality styles, and stress management through the use of role-plays, stories, and discussion. Since the middle school student is especially vulnerable to peer pressures that lead to experimentation with substances, STAR II addresses these recognized student needs by teaching ways to overcome shyness, interact effectively with others, develop a positive identity and self-concept, and manage the stress associated with adolescence. STAR II also has student workbooks in Spanish.

In 1982, the PLUS (Promoting Learning and Understanding of Self) Program was developed for at-risk high school students as an extension of the successful STAR and GOAL programs. PLUS was designed to teach essential cognitive, interpersonal, and physiological self-control

Students Learning to Express Reaction to Changes in Their Lives.

skills, shown by research to prevent school failure. The Title IV-C evaluation of PLUS showed that these skills significantly incréased academic and behavioral skills of students in special education.

PLUS meets the needs of adolescents in grades 9–12 through the development of skills in communication, decision making, and stress management. These skills are vital to students who are at risk academically and at risk for substance abuse. Lessons (82) provide instruction in assertive social skills, problem solving, managing stress, increasing self-esteem, and responsible discipline techniques. Lessons may be taught in advisement, health, social studies, language arts, special education, etc.

In 1991 – 92, PLUS became STAR III: Social Thinking and Reasoning after a major revision that also integrated the latest research on effective strategies to decrease risk factors and increase protective factors, including special small group activities for at-risk students.

STAGES (Skills to Manage Stressful Changes) was also designed in 1982 for K – 6 students at risk due to a major change in their lives, such as divorce, death, or major moves. Staff observations of academic and behavioral problems by students experiencing a major change aligned with research findings (Gardner, 1970) to indicate the need to develop this innovative program for schools. The evaluation of STAGES, which was also a Title IV-C project, demonstrated significant student results in behavior and achievement.

STAGES includes K – 3 and 4 – 6 classroom lessons. Students learn a vocabulary of six reactions that may be experienced when faced with changes in friendships, changes in the family moving, loss of pet, and so forth. Group activities allow students to learn responsible ways to express reactions to change. Lessons may be implemented in health, social studies, English, and special education.

After a few years, STAGES was so successful and well implemented in many school districts throughout the country that a secondary level was created and named STAGES II for grades 7 – 12, teaching adolescents how to manage major changes in their lives with special emphasis on managing anger and depression.

Stages II is a skill-based curriculum that teaches adolescents in grades 7 – 12 to recognize strong reactions to minor and major changes in life. In addition, lessons are presented to teach skills and techniques that are proven effective to help manage reactions to changes in the family, graduating, relationships, moving, etc. Lessons may be taught in advisement, health, social studies and language arts.

After the equal success of STAGES II in helping older students cope, a STAGES II Independent Study Program was added for students in alternative programs who needed to learn the concepts individually. Through the STAGES II student workbook, students complete lessons to understand normal reactions to change and learn skills to manage strong reactions. Students may earn one to three credits to be applied to social science, health, language arts, or electives. The most recent addition is the STAGES II Spanish Version, in which the curriculum was translated into Spanish with special revisions by Spanish students to enhance its effectiveness with recent immigrants from many countries who are coping with the STAGES of acclimating to a new culture. The Spanish version of STAGES II has proven to have especially effective uses in the classroom and in peer- or counselor-led small groups.

In 1987, the Irvine District copyrighted these guidance resources materials upon the recommendation of the California State Department of Education, so that dissemination could continue after Title IV-C funding ended. Since that time, there has been continuing interest in the programs. Over the years, district staff have revised the curriculum materials to reflect current research and student needs.

Based on the positive results of the programs, the district health curriculum was revised to include these effective life skill programs (ten grade level lessons of STAGES and STAR), creating a comprehensive, skill-based wellness program. Lessons taught in this core prevention curriculum provide students with the following skills and knowledge: resistance skills, social skills, self-esteem, ways to handle criticism, decision making, differentiating between safe and unsafe drugs, understanding how the body responds to various substances, healthy living options over substance use, and learning how peer pressure and self-esteem affect our health decisions.

In 1988, the district core curriculum was enriched with the Drug Abuse Resistance Education (D.A.R.E) Program, in which police officers present lessons from D.A.R.E in sixth grade classes to complement teacher instruction in STAR II.

IDENTIFICATION STRATEGIES FOR AT-RISK STUDENTS

As described previously, a districtwide identification and intervention system involving students, parents, school personnel, and community resources has been developed. This process identifies potentially risk-involved or at-risk students. A computerized data base identifies students who fall in the lower quadrant in grade test scores and at-risk behaviors. This screening information is provided to a school study team, at-risk team, or core team at the school site, who also takes referrals on students from teachers and who implement an accountability and tracking system for identified students.

INTERVENTION AND COUNSELING SERVICES FOR AT-RISK STUDENTS

When students are identified as being at risk, the school study team reviews, plans, and evaluates intervention strategies appropriate for that student. One successful strategy used in many district schools is mentoring or assigning a staff person to become involved with each at-risk student and coordinate needed services. Referred students' parents are contacted, counseled, and referred to outside agencies, as needed, to meet students' needs.

Intervention strategies for at-risk students usually include formal or informal counseling. Counseling support services for at-risk and high-risk students are delivered individually and in small groups by school-based certificated support staff and paraprofessional support specialists. Small groups are created for all types of student concerns, from chemical dependency issues to personal issues. Support specialists are trained and supervised by guidance resources staff and also receive supervision from school support staff. Support specialists work part-time to enhance the school's intervention services. They are trained in implementing prevention curriculum and in guidance techniques.

SCHOOL-ORIENTED SERVICES

Ongoing in-service training designed to increase the understanding of the signs and symptoms of drugs, prevention curriculum, and strategies for at-risk students is presented to teachers, administrators, school counselors, and police officers through general awareness and specialized core team staff development activities.

Support specialists consult with teachers to implement prevention strategies in the classroom, as well as alternative drug-free activities, such as peer assistance, Youth to Youth Conferences, and Just Say No Clubs.

Research and evaluation are important aspects of district services to schools. Program components are constantly being reviewed, evaluated, and refined to continually validate strategies, add to the body of literature on prevention, and improve services and curriculum to better meet student needs.

COORDINATING COMMUNITY RESOURCES

The District Drug Prevention Advisory Board was formed by school, business, parent, student, and community representatives (city police and community service staff, county drug prevention agencies and nonprofit family counseling centers among others). The Drug Prevention Board meets monthly during the school year to complete the following activities:

- Planning, e.g., update board training on all aspects of drug prevention; conduct formal and informal needs assessments for prevention, suppression, and intervention needs; provide input on community and district prevention needs, board policy and procedure, and available resources; evaluate and refine existing services and curriculum; and support the development of funding strategies for program development and maintenance.
- Coordination of services, e.g., fostering interagency cooperation by coordinating community resources for referrals and speakers; developing awareness of interrelated issues such as gang and drug prevention; supporting the suppression role of the police; and identifying resources to meet identified needs.

COORDINATION WITH EXISTING
TREATMENT PROGRAMS

For students and families needing intervention beyond school-based prevention, early intervention, and aftercare services, trained school support staff contact parents and make referrals of students for intervention assessments from treatment agencies. With parent permission, school staff follow up on students referred to treatment programs and maintain contact with families in treatment to provide support and plan aftercare services. Cooperative working relationships with treatment agencies thereby ensure adequate communication and support of students in treatment and after. In addition, agencies such as the Orange County Drug Abuse Services conduct onsite support groups for students on drug issues. Alateen groups are also conducted on some campuses.

FAMILY-ORIENTED SERVICES

Parent contact is an ongoing activity of school-based support staff. Parents are encouraged to become involved to intervene in their student's at-risk behavior. Parents of at-risk students are also personally invited to participate in parent and community educational opportunities to enhance their skills and knowledge of prevention. Given the complex schedules of today's families, school staff are constantly seeking new ways to maintain contact, especially with parents of at-risk students. Parent education is a vital part of the district program.

A three-hour drug prevention program for parents, Neighborhoods in Action, which was developed by the Scott Newman Foundation, is offered by district schools to provide parent training on drug prevention and intervention. The program combines the resources of the school, the police department, and the treatment community to conduct the training. Through this video-based awareness training, parents learn signs and symptoms of drug use, characteristic effects of various substances, prevention techniques, and communication skills, as well as information on their community's drug-related statistics and resources for treatment, rehabilitation, and counseling.

The district has also had good success with parent training classes using Active Parenting, which is a six-week class based on Drieker's model for democratic parenting, rather than authoritarian or permissive parenting. The program teaches basic parent/child communication skills, ways to prevent drug abuse, including the setting of home rules; role modeling; alternative activities; and joint efforts with other parents and concerned adults.

SUMMARY OF PROGRAM COMPONENTS

(1) A K − 12 alcohol and drug use prevention program core prevention curriculum

(2) Ongoing staff development training in substance use prevention and curriculum implementation for all staff

(*3*) Identification, intervention, support, and referral for students at risk

(*4*) Parent involvement and education to support intervention needs of at-risk students

(*5*) Community cooperation to reinforce the drug-free message, provide treatment services, and plan joint prevention programs

PROGRAM DEVELOPMENT AND DISSEMINATION

Program development and dissemination is an important district activity. District staff have found that these activities help maintain a heightened awareness of current research and student needs beyond the local community. The dissemination of effective practices and project evaluation information is shared with other schools within and beyond the district. Visitation/demonstration visits for potential adopters/adapters are available, workshops are scheduled and implemented, and follow-up consultation is offered for adopters/adapters to assist replication of the model.[4]

POLICY RECOMMENDATION

Each district should consider developing an alcohol and other drug prevention program that seeks to:

• decrease antisocial, aggressive behavior and develop prosocial behaviors
• decrease the tendency to associate with drug-using peers due to passive behavior and lack of alternative activities
• improve parental drug-free information, attitudes, and skills related to family management, value systems, modeling, and communication of a no-use message
• increase student achievement and interest in school activities
• improve health and health attitudes
• increase awareness of personality needs and develop healthy alternatives and resources for high-risk students
• improve attitudes, skills, and use of resources to achieve individual goals

[4]For further information about any of the programs described, contact Irvine Unified School District, Guidance Resources Office, 5050 Barranca Parkway, Irvine, California 92714, (714) 552-4882.

ASSESSING PRESENT PROGRAMS FOR REDUCTION OF ABUSE

The following model is a series of steps that are recommended for school districts to utilize in assessing what programs they presently have operating that are used for assisting students at risk. It was implemented in Orange Unified School District, Orange, California. Most districts will want to identify those interventions that are now working for their students at risk prior to detailed planning so they can build on what is already working in some schools.

A MODEL FOR ASSISTING STUDENTS AT RISK

The model in this chapter is a series of steps for school districts to use in establishing a model for assisting students at risk.

- Adopt a schoolwide philosophy to promote a positive learning environment that ensures the success of every student.
- Assess needs by analyzing dropout and substance abuse statistics and by identifying major reasons why students drop out and abuse.
- Implement a preventive program that provides early identification of high-risk students.
- Train teachers and counselors in intervention strategies that are effective with high-risk students (see Chapter 5).
- Identify resources in the school and community that can be used to help students with special needs and problems.

Most districts will want to identify several interventions that are now working for their students at risk prior to detailed planning so they can build on what is already working in some schools. We have included the results of an At-Risk Program Survey, which was filled out by staff at each school to give the principal and district staff information about interventions that are now operating in each school. In the SAR model seen in Chapter 5, students would complete the Comprehensive Risk Assessment software self-report forms and be scheduled into appropriate interventions by the software.

The National Association of Secondary Schools and the National Association of Elementary Schools have recently published an important new resource titled the *hm Study Skills Program* (Burkle, 1986), which provides a rich array of interventions for students who have been identified at risk through our software or other means.

Most districts will want to combine efforts to work with both potential dropouts and substance abusers since two-thirds of students at high risk of abuse are also high risks for dropping out.

The following plan is offered as a means for initiating your effort to identify and work with potential dropouts and substance abusers:

(*1*) *Develop a districtwide plan:* Meet with key district and school site staff to begin the process of developing a districtwide plan for identification of students at risk (see Chapter 3). Focus upon the essential information needed for identification and placement into interventions.

(*2*) *Identify present means for identification:* Meet with key school site staff to identify present means for identification of potential dropouts, including informal remarks by classroom teachers. Look for forms and checklists already in use in your district. You may wish to use the Teacher At-Risk Referral Figure (11.1) to develop a list of students to fill out the Comprehensive Risk Assessment software.

(*3*) *Combined identification of abusers and dropouts:* Meet with staff who work with potential abusers, as well as those who work with likely dropouts. Discuss the possibility of both groups working together to use a combined set of predictor variables for identification of students at risk, as well as many of the same interventions.

(*4*) *Develop a list of interventions:* To begin the planning process, one can carry out a survey of principals and others who provide service to at-risk students to find out what programs they have operating to serve these students at present. To get an idea of what your results might look like, see the list developed in Orange Unified School

District, Orange, California, under section 3.0 of the Dropout Report to the Board of Education on the following pages. Students-at-Risk, Inc. has developed software to assist in this process which is titled Comprehensive Risk Assessment.

(5) *Develop a site utilization and intervention plan:* Meet with selected site-level pilot school staff from at least one elementary, one junior, and one senior high school to talk about utilization of district data on students at risk. Plan to link district data on student needs to appropriate interventions at various school sites. List present interventions that would not require new budgetary support.

(6) *Develop districtwide evaluation plan:* Meet with key cabinet member(s) to develop a districtwide plan for evaluation of services for students at risk. The Completion of Interventions Form seen in Chapter 5 can serve as a pre/postevaluation of the effectiveness of the software and related efforts. Using this data, which creates item by item analyses of student progress, decision makers are provided with information to use in judging the success of the various interventions. If the discrepancies are not reduced, the intervention needs serious revision. For example, if we compare the pre/post scores on an item such as anger control and find there is not a pre/post improvement, decision makers should consider changing the interventions used for teaching anger control.

The following planning outline is being used in the Orange Unified School District, Orange, California. It was written by Roger Duthoy, former Assistant Superintendent, Secondary Schools. It is focused upon dropout, which was perceived by many to be the key area of concern for at-risk students. There is good collaboration with substance abuse prevention, however, as the reader will note in the many substance abuse prevention programs that are used jointly with dropout prevention efforts.

DROPOUT REPORT TO THE BOARD
OF EDUCATION OUTLINE

1.0 HISTORICAL DATA

    1.1   Definition of a dropout: "A student in grades 10, 11, or 12 who stops attending school prior to graduation for 45 days or more, and has not requested that his/her transcript (academic record) be sent to another school or institution."

1.2 Three-year statistics

$$\text{Three-year dropout rate} = \frac{(D1 + D2 + D3) \times 100}{E1}$$

D1 = Tenth grade dropouts (Class of 1990)
D2 = Eleventh grade dropouts (same class)
D3 = Twelfth grade dropouts (same class)
E1 = Total tenth grade enrollment

1.3 For Orange Unified, the 1988 three-year dropout rate is 21.3%. (Statistics are generated by the CBEDS Report.)

$$\frac{(110 + 177 + 218) \times 100}{2370} = 21.3\%$$

1.4 One-year statistics (Class of 1989)

$$\text{One-year dropout rate} = \frac{(D1 + D2 + D3) \times 100}{E1 + E2 + E3}$$

D1 = Tenth grade dropouts (Class of 1991)
D2 = Eleventh grade dropouts (Class of 1990)
D3 = Twelfth grade dropouts (Class of 1989)
E1 = Total tenth grade enrollment
E2 = Total eleventh grade enrollment
E3 = Total twelfth grade enrollment

1.5 For Orange Unified, the 1989 one-year dropout rate is 8.7%. (Statistics are generated by the CBEDS Report.)

$$\frac{(105 + 197 + 218) \times 100)}{1892 + 2500 + 1612} = 8.7\%$$

2.0 CHARACTERISTICS OF A POTENTIAL DROPOUT

2.1 Frequently absent, truant from school
2.2 From low-income home (AFDC)
2.3 Transient family
2.4 Poor grades (retained or failed secondary courses)
2.5 Low basic skills ability (reading and mathematics)

2.6   Behind in credits earned
2.7   At-risk behaviors (poor citizenship, gangs, smoking, alcohol, drugs, sexually active, on probation, discipline problem at school, etc.)
2.8   Low self-esteem (dress, friends, goals, lack of participation in school activities, etc.)
2.9   Lack of attachment to school (no one at school knows them or, in their opinion, cares about them)
2.10 Nonsupportive family (lack of supervision, discipline, communication, models at home)

3.0 CURRENT INTERVENTION STRATEGIES IN ORANGE UNIFIED

Elementary Programs:
3.1   D.A.R.E (Drug Abuse Resistance Education)
3.2   Babes, Babes' Kids
3.3   Project Self-Esteem
3.4   Developmental kindergarten
3.5   Saturday school
K – 12 Programs:
3.6   CASA – Very active drug and alcohol effort by parents, students, and staff.
3.7   PRIDE – Parent to Parent Networking
3.8   Red Ribbon Week, Awareness Weeks
3.9   Categorical programs (Chapter I, GATE, ESL, etc.)
3.10 Summer school program
3.11 ''Successful Parents for Successful Kids'' Conference
3.12 Migrant education program
3.13 School study teams
3.14 Special education programs, I.E.P. teams
3.15 Gang information workshops
3.16 Good working relationship with the Orange Police Department
3.17 SARB (school attendance review board)
3.18 Quest International (Skills Programs)
3.19 Home and hospital
3.20 Independent study program
3.21 Co-curricular programs (clubs, student government, etc.)

Secondary Programs:
3.22 PAL (Peer Assistance Leadership)
3.23 Athletic programs
3.24 Choices program
3.25 Pregnant minor program
3.26 Child development program
3.27 Continuation high school program
3.28 Middle school philosophy (homeroom, interdisciplinary teams, child-centered, etc.)
3.29 Regional occupation program (ROP)
3.30 Opportunity class (grades 7−9)
3.31 Work experience programs
3.32 Decision-making skills class
3.33 Summer recreation program
3.34 Rancho Santiago evening programs
3.35 Hispanic youth, leadership conference
3.36 Career day, college and university nights
3.37 Academy program (El Modena High School)
3.38 Olivecrest program

COMMUNITY NETWORKING/OUTREACH

- Establish cooperative networks with schools, law enforcement agencies, and juvenile courts, as well as mental health, substance abuse, and other community agencies to provide effective referrals and services.
- Galvanize the support of community organizations, such as churches, businesses, and community members, in the war against alcohol/other drug abuse.
- Conduct vigorous outreach efforts through culturally appropriate media materials, statewide conferences, community presentations, rallies, and other visible events.
- Provide alcohol and other drug education to raise awareness and knowledge of youth, parents, teachers, other family members, and the community.
- Train teachers, healthcare professionals, community service agency counselors, day-care providers, and others on issues related to alcohol/other drug abuse and on how to identify and help young children of chemically dependent parents or adolescent gateway drug users.

ETHNIC/CULTURAL APPROACHES

- Recruit, train, and support the involvement of respected community members, such as businessmen and tribal elders, as positive adult role models for high-risk youth.
- Demonstrate staff sensitivity to the culture of the target population through recruitment of minority staff at all levels of prevention programs.
- Encourage cultural revitalization activities to eliminate cultural alienation among minorities, such as celebrating cultural festivals and teaching the traditional language, values, and rituals.

PARENTING HELP/SUPPORT

- Reach out actively to involve parents whose support is critical for improving the life chances of their children.
- Provide individual, group, and family therapy for youth and families.

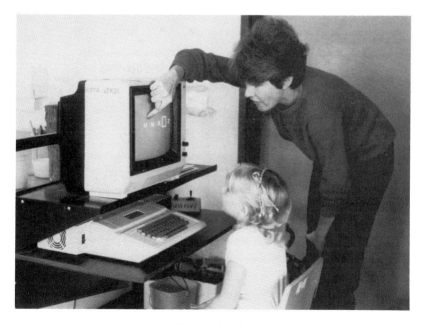

A Parent Tutoring.

- Offer parents help through parenting and other skill-building courses, support groups, and aid in accessing social services.
- Provide pregnant teenagers with prenatal and postnatal care, education about the effects of drugs on unborn babies, and treatment to help them stop their substance use.
- Offer day-care services for parents of preschool children.

YOUTH HELP/SUPPORT

- Provide life skills training (includes decision making, effective problem solving, coping with stressful situations, help in forming nurturing relationships and developing social skills, and refusal skills for resisting negative peer pressure) to build selfesteem and social competence in young people and enable them to make healthy life choices.
- Involve youth in community volunteer work or community development schemes, reintegrating them into their communities and reducing their social alienation.
- Organize drug-free activities, such as recreation and challenging wilderness trips that build self-confidence and teamwork among participants.
- Provide help with education, vocational counseling, job training, and job placement services.
- Provide health education, including courses on sexuality, birth control, and AIDS prevention

MENTORING AT-RISK YOUTH

One of the least expensive and most promising strategies for serving students at risk is the use of other students who have been trained as *mentors*. The Glasgow Intermediate School in Fairfax County, Virginia, has developed the following model (Aiello and Gatewood, 1989).

The Mentor Program has been in operation for four years. Designed to give personal support for at-risk students, each year, the school's guidance department first identifies and trains mentors, who are teachers and other staff members who volunteer to work closely and personally with one to three students. For instance, fifty-seven mentors volunteered for the program in the past school year. Together, the mentor and the student develop a warm, caring, and positive working relationship. The mentor also develops communications among parents, teachers, and counselors to provide support in both personal and academic growth. Improved academic performance, motivation, and self-esteem are primary goals of this interaction.

Each year, certain students are offered an opportunity to participate in the Mentor Program based upon teacher recommendations and/or low first quarter grades. Students (protégés) must then volunteer, and their parents must approve, their participation in the program. Out of a total school population of 850, eighty protégés participated in the 1987-88 program.

After an orientation meeting with protégés and their parents early in the school year, each protégé is matched with a mentor and placed in the mentor's homeroom. Aside from daily homeroom interactions, mentor and protégé meet together at least once a week after school for academic remediation and personal guidance. Monthly, group guidance sessions on study skills and self-concept are held. Once a month, all of the mentors and protégés have an after-school get-together for social activities such as games and informal discussions, as well as for assistance in homework and test preparation. The program concludes each year in June with a mentor-protégé softball game and awards ceremony.

Mentors receive four in-service training sessions a year on topics such as program goals and objectives, adolescent development, and research-based strategies to raise academic interest and achievement. In addition, monthly evening information and support sessions are held with parents.

The Glasgow guidance department is responsible for managing and assuring smooth operation of all aspects of the program. Counselors help prepare the *Mentor Program Guide* previously reviewed by a staff mentor committee, coordinate in-service and study skills planning, oversee data collection and dissemination, and provide overall support for both mentors and protégés.

SOME RESULTS

Formative and summative evaluation of the program is conducted each year with a variety of forms and assessment instruments. For example, teachers complete monthly logs, indicating the number of meetings they held with protégés. Students complete both a self-assessment survey on study skills and self-concept/motivation inventory. Teachers who have protégés in academic classes complete an assessment of their classroom performance.

In a recent academic year, the following major improvements of grades were reported: a 37% increase of grades of A, a 29% increase of grades of B+ through A, and a 7% increase of grades of C through A. Protégés decreased the number of D+ through F grades by 12%. In the three years of the program's existence for which there is data, the overall failure rate of program students has declined from 28% to 12%. In addition, the schoolwide failure rate has declined from 7.2% in 1984−85 to 5.8% in 1985−86, 5.0% in 1986−87, and 4.4% in 1987−88.

As you consider new strategies, you may find those developed by William Gray helpful (Gray, 1991).

ESSENTIAL COMPONENTS

Since 1978, researchers have identified certain generic components related to success. More than 800 researchers, practitioners, and writers have documented the importance of these components to varying degrees. These generic components must be carefully adapted to fit the contextual aspects of each situation, or success is not likely.

(1) Planned mentoring must be supported from the top, as well as at the grass roots, level so that voluntary participation occurs. Imposed programs seldom work as well as those in which people want to "buy in" as volunteers because they see the benefits for themselves and the organization, and because they can meet program expectations. To attract volunteers, the program's structure, organizational expectations, and anticipated benefits must be communicated to potential participants. Focus groups comprised of prospective participants and needed supporters provide useful input for improving the program's design. Having such input increases the support for the program.

(2) Each program should be designed around the specific goals (or intended outcomes/benefits) to be promoted. These goals relate to the need of participants, determining mentor and protégé selection and what type of training to provide.

(3) Begin small. Carefully plan a short (6−12-month) pilot program for a few participants (ten to forty) so that inevitable start-up bugs can be rectified. Employ a research and development approach to ensure that the pilot program is working as desired before expanding it to a larger audience.

(*4*) Prospective participants should receive an orientation to clearly outline items such as the organization's expectations related to intended goals, duration of mentoring, time requirements, etc. This orientation provides one means for enabling prospective participants to "buy in" and become committed volunteers.

(*5*) Carefully select mentors and protégés from amongst volunteers, and match them without forcing this. Match so that intended goals can be achieved. Some strategies for doing this include allowing protégés to nominate mentors and vice versa, with the nominated person being given right of refusal and letting the program coordinator suggest possible matches, with candidates being given the right to refuse, etc. Another useful strategy is to use a test instrument.

(*6*) Mounting research [e.g., PA Personnel Services (1986)] indicates that not training participants is the primary cause of unsuccessful mentoring in planned programs. Training must be provided for mentors and protégés so they know what is expected and how to fulfill those mentor-protégé roles and functions requisite to achieving intended goals. This can be done a number of ways. It is a mistake to assume that, just because mentors have greater experience and practical wisdom, they automatically know how to fulfill essential mentor roles.

(*7*) Primarily, mentoring is a close personal relationship and a process of working together to achieve agreed-upon goals. This relationship and process must be carefully monitored on a regular basis to resolve emerging conflicts and problems before a crisis develops. It is a mistake to assume that a training program, no matter how well-designed and -delivered, will automatically result in mentors and protégés correctly applying those skills taught in the training session. With this in mind, a key person within the organization is needed to provide ongoing monitoring and additional training when needed. This monitor is usually the program coordinator or a human resources development staff member.

(*8*) At some designated point in time, previously planned program goals should be formally evaluated to determine benefits for mentors, protégés, and the organization. Quantitative data from questionnaires can be collected as a means of measuring perceived group gains/benefits. Qualitative data from interviews is a means of obtaining in-depth information about worst and best case situations. Both types of data are then used to improve the pilot program until

This form is a communication aid designed to call attention to any student who may need help right away. It is sometimes difficult to separate "typical" adolescent behavior from what may be called "red flag" behavior, yet it is important not to ignore warning signs that may indicate that a student is experiencing special problems. When a student demonstrates several of the behaviors listed below, swift intervention may be the key.

After completion, please return this form to the school counselor.

Student _____ Date _____

Grade _____ Person Referring (name optional) _____

Look for unusual or sudden changes in the observable behaviors listed below. Please check appropriate boxes.

Grades and Attitude

Sudden drop in grades/achievement ☐

Decline in homework completion ☐

Citizen deterioration ☐

Other observed behavior (explain)

Attendance

Increase in absenteeism ☐

Tardiness ☐

Frequently needs to leave classroom ☐

Truancy

Other observed behavior (explain)

Extracurricular Activities

Loss of eligibility ☐

Sudden noninvolvement ☐

Dropping out ☐

Other observed behavior (explain)

Figure 11.1 Teacher at Risk Referral Form.

Physical Behavior

Smells of tobacco ☐

Smells of beer or stronger alcoholic beverages ☐

Glassy, bloodshot eyes ☐

Frequently wearing sunglasses ☐

Poor personal hygiene ☐

Neglecting physical appearance ☐

Sleeping in class ☐

Weight loss ☐

Weight gain ☐

Frequent physical injuries ☐

Other observed behavior (explain)

Disruptive Behavior

Sudden defiance of classroom rules ☐

Irresponsibility (blaming/denying) ☐

Fighting ☐

Cheating ☐

Obscene/abusive language ☐

Temper tantrums ☐

Hyperactivity/nervousness ☐

Dramatic attention getting ☐

Other observed behavior (explain)

Figure 11.1 (continued) *Teacher at Risk Referral Form.*

193

Social Behavior

Talks openly about drugs and alcohol ☐

Change of friends ☐

Depression ☐

Sudden mood swings ☐

Defensiveness ☐

Withdrawn ☐

Deceptiveness/deceitfulness ☐

Other observed behavior (explain)

Other Comments

Figure 11.1 (continued) *Teacher at Risk Referral Form.*

it is ready for expanded use with more mentors and protégés. It is important to note that since mentoring is such a personal experience and matching of mentors and protégés is so crucial to success, it does not make sense to randomly match mentors to protégés as required when using a rigorous control group research design. This means that relationships between program interventions (e.g., training, mentoring style, etc.) and other program outcomes must be determined in other, more appropriate ways.

POLICY RECOMMENDATION

Most districts will want to identify several interventions that are now working for their students at risk prior to detailed planning so they can build on what is already working in some schools. They can then include the results of an At-Risk Program Survey, which is filled out by staff at each school, in their planning document to give the principal and district staff information about successful interventions that are now operating in each school. Students could then be scheduled into them manually or by a software program.

Chapter 12

THE EFFECTIVE USE OF PARAPROFESSIONALS IN SCHOOL-BASED ALCOHOL AND OTHER DRUG PREVENTION PROGRAMS

A survey of school professionals and parents would undoubtedly confirm that only highly qualified staff should interact with students. The big problem is the cost in providing this service. Just as industry has looked for ways to cut costs and increase productivity, so schools have looked for creative ways to meet increasing student needs. An area of increasing need is to provide support for at-risk students, especially at the elementary level where credentialed counselors and social workers are rare. One way to meet student counseling needs is to refer students to local agencies or invite those agencies or professional volunteers to do counseling in the schools. These solutions may work well for a school if referrals are accepted and followed up on; counseling and financial resources are available to provide the services; and the considerable issues of programmatic supervision and liability have been resolved.

THE NEED FOR SUPPORT AND RELATED ASSISTANCE

Over a period of seven years, the Irvine School District has addressed the need for support and the related issues described above by developing and refining a district-run guidance assistant program. This district program supplements school psychologist or counseling services by providing small group, individual, and classroom instruction in coping and social skill development. Guidance assistants are college counseling interns or parent aides with natural counseling skills who receive extensive training and ongoing supervision to use district-developed curriculum materials with at-risk students.

The key to creating a successful cost-effective program is providing ongoing program support and continuity. This is important due to the nature of the noncredentialed staff employed in the program. Many are in school seeking training experiences required for their credentials, some are seeking hours for professional practice licenses, and others seek a meaningful part-time job that allows them to be available to their children and work within their community. Just as the personal needs of the staff change, so, too, does staffing, because of salary levels that are only slightly above that of instructional assistants. The guidance assistant program strives to match school and guidance assistant needs to create a workable service alternative. After seven years of program development, the program managers have turned art into science that can be shared with other districts and agencies seeking to serve at-risk students.

THE GUIDANCE ASSISTANT'S SURVIVAL TIPS

These suggestions have been prepared to provide guidance assistants with tips to which they may refer when beginning the process of working at elementary school sites in Irvine Unified School District, and they are compiled into a manual available from the Guidance Resources Office. Many of the same strategies are also effective at the secondary level, and a secondary level manual is also available. Persons interested in interviewing for positions as guidance assistants may also benefit from the "Survival Manual," as a guide to understanding the general duties of the guidance assistant position.

The information in the manual and presented here has been provided by present and former guidance assistants (GA's) who have contributed ideas from their first several months of experience. We hope these tips will assist new "GA's" to acclimate quickly and easily into the position of guidance assistant at their new school site.

Due to the fact that each school site has its own personality, the suggestions will, of necessity, be somewhat general. There are, however, certain situations that will be encountered at all sites. Rather than having new GA's reinvent the wheel, we hope to apprise them of methods that others have found useful in making the transition into a new school as easy as possible.

What Is a Guidance Assistant?

The guidance assistant in Irvine Unified School District is a part-time, classified employee who may work ten hours per week at one elementary school or up to 19.5 hours per week at two elementary schools. Guidance assistants who work at the secondary level may work up to fifteen hours at one school site. The GA positions are funded under various federal and state grants, which support substance abuse prevention, reduction in dropout rates, increased self-esteem, and improved social, emotional, and academic skills for students. These at-risk students need consistent, dependable adult models; therefore, the guidance assistant must be able to make a *full school year* commitment, usually from October through early June. The majority of time is spent in direct services to either small groups or individual students; therefore, the work hours will typically take place between 8:00 A.M. and 3:00 P.M.

In general, a guidance assistant is the link between the Guidance Resources Office and the individual school site. The GA will deliver direct counseling and educational services to students and keep Guidance Resources apprised of school site needs.

What Are the Duties of a Guidance Assistant?

GA's may have a variety of duties, including attending district training as a means of becoming familiar with Guidance Resource programs (STAR and STAGES). One may use these curricula in a small group setting or acquaint teachers with these programs for use in classroom presentations. Aside from district trainings, a guidance assistant will be expected to attend biweekly staff meetings for sharing information, further training, and supervision. At the school site, a GA will need to be a consultant to teachers regarding affective education lessons; a skilled communicator gathering referrals and background information on students, as well as working with staff in scheduling these referrals; a counselor conducting individual and small group sessions; and a Jack or Jill of all trades, possibly making home visits with families of at-risk students, referring students or families to community agencies, and participating in data collection for district research projects. Although not all GA's will need to perform all of these duties each week, the guidance assistant position is a challenging and exciting job requiring flexibility, adaptability, and social skills in addition to counseling skills.

The Interview Process

The first step in becoming a guidance assistant involves filing an application with the district personnel department. The position is a classified one, which requires that you fill out the Classified Employment Application, which has a general format. You should present not only an educational and employment history, but pertinent unpaid/volunteer experience that indicates your ability to work in the school situation for which you are applying.

The interview process usually consists of an initial interview with Guidance Resources staff to determine the applicant's experience, interest, and ability to undertake the role of guidance assistant (this interview is sometimes conducted by telephone). A second interview with principals, school psychologists, and/or other school contact persons will then be conducted to determine an appropriate placement at a particular school site. Although we know that interviewing can be very stressful, having experienced the process ourselves, we will make every effort to reduce the stress that seems to be a part of interviewing.

In assigning a guidance assistant to a particular school or schools, many factors are taken into consideration. It is of critical importance to the success of the guidance program that the guidance assistant and the supervising staff member are able to have a comfortable working relationship. Other factors that are taken into consideration are the assistant's personality and communication style and experience in working with children, as well as the goals of the school. Some schools are very familiar with the functions of a guidance assistant and have thoroughly integrated the programs into their system. Other schools may be in the early stages of fitting some or all of the available affective education resources into their already full schedules. These factors will obviously have an effect on GA assignments. In the former case, an important question might be: How well does this candidate fit into the existing scheme at the school site? In the latter case, the more pertinent question may be: Does this candidate seem confident enough to implement a new program in our school in a somewhat independent manner? In all cases, we understand the importance of placing people in situations where they are most likely to feel comfortable and successful, and a genuine effort will be made to accomplish that goal.

Training Opportunities

Among the many offerings available from the Guidance Resources staff, an opportunity for excellent training experiences is one of the most valuable. Our curriculum and training consultants travel the United States, delivering exciting and informative in-services to many school districts each year. New and potential guidance assistants in the district are offered free training in the rationale and implementation of several guidance programs that are specially designed for easy implementation by a variety of educational staff. STAGES is a program developed in Irvine Unified School District, which helps elementary school students (and teachers, parents, and others) to understand and accept their reactions to changes in their lives. STAR I (Social Thinking and Reasoning) is another Irvine program designed to assist elementary students in developing more successful social skills, critical thinking capabilities, and strategies for becoming accountable. Through the STAR II program, sixth through eighth grade students learn social thinking and reasoning skills appropriate to their age and activities, which is complemented by STAR III for high school. STAGES II allows middle and high school students to examine and begin to understand their reactions to change. Of course, the sooner one is trained to work with these curricula, the more ready one will be to begin working as a counselor.

In addition to the districtwide trainings directed at becoming comfortable with the guidance curricula, a great deal of training is conducted during biweekly mandatory staff meetings. Information and clinical issues addressed include recognizing and reporting child abuse, suicide prevention, and alcohol and drug abuse prevention, attention deficit, child development, play techniques, depression, family dynamics, and multicultural issues and case consultation. Other practical information about working at a school site, such as forming counseling groups, conducting groups, managing discipline, working as a team, and referrals and follow-up will also be shared on a regular basis.

Often, guidance assistants have areas of interest in which they possess a great deal of information and experience. In these cases, GA's are encouraged to share their expertise by conducting trainings for other staff members. Another way in which training may be achieved is through GA's attendance at seminars or workshops outside the district. Although our budget is limited for payment of fees for attendance at outside seminars, with approval, work time may be used to attend a pertinent training. Guidance assistants are encouraged to share pertinent information from trainings with the other GA's during a later staff meeting. Guidance assistants' input about areas of need for training will be essential to the staff providing training on the topics. As new and returning GA's become aware of their own training needs. There is a need to mention these to the coordinator who schedules ongoing trainings.

Working with the Guidance Resources Office

One role of the Guidance Resources Office is to provide support for guidance assistants. The office manager can be very helpful in getting materials such as curriculum binders, puppets, stress dots, and other products that will be helpful to you at your school site(s). The office manager is also the person who distributes and collects time cards (which are the means by which GA's keep a record of the hours they've worked) and delivers paychecks to all guidance staff. She knows the office inside and out and can be very helpful in answering almost all of your ''housekeeping'' types of questions, so make it a point to get to know her.

Other people to know are those listed as follows:

- The Guidance Resources program administrator manages the overall office, directing the day-to-day operation of the Guidance programs, managing budgets, personnel, and seeking ongoing support for the program through grant writing and public relations.
- The counseling coordinator serves as liaison between the Guidance Resources Office and the guidance assistants at each school site. Our coordinator was a GA for three years, so she knows the rough spots. If you have a question about your work, about how to approach a touchy situation with another staff member, or if you just want a sounding board for your ideas, or anything else, please call the coordinator.
- The evaluation psychologist does most of the research and data collection/analysis for evaluation of the Guidance programs. You may be asked to pre/post test your students and collect other important information for reports to funding agencies, depending on the requirements for funding the project or the district's own program evaluation needs.
- Guidance Resources trainers provide the curriculum training for guidance assistants and follow-up consultation and problem solving related to curriculum implementation. Our trainers are skilled presenters who travel the country training teachers, administrators, and counselors to implement the Guidance materials that GA's use in their counseling groups. In addition, they have written all of the curriculum materials used in the Guidance programs (with a little help from their friends).

There may be times when it will become necessary for the Guidance Resources Office to be able to contact you. The project is made up of very few full-time people and several (about twenty) part-time staff, all with varying schedules. By giving the coordinator your work schedule and work and home phone numbers, you'll enable her to reach you with schedule changes and updates and to return your phone calls. We will put together a list of guidance assistants' phone numbers and schedules so that GA's can contact each other, as well as the office for support and information. If your schedule should change over the course of the year, simply let the coordinator know your new hours.

Making Contacts at Your School Site

When beginning as a guidance assistant, it may begin to feel as though you're the only person at school who doesn't know everyone else and what all the rules are! In fact, it is this very feeling, experienced by virtually every guidance assistant we've talked to, that prompted the writing of the "Survival Manual."

Perhaps the most important thing to keep in mind is that becoming a guidance assistant is a *process*, and that all of your duties and skills will not need to be performed on your first day on the job. Former and current GA's have contributed their ideas to the manual in a sincere effort to make this process of "becoming" just a little smoother for you and future GA's. The following are, for the most part, suggestions rather than rules of conduct. If there is something that you really must do, we'll indicate that in the text.

Having gone through the two-interview process, new GA's will be called by the coordinator with an offer of the job and information about the school site assignment(s) that seems most appropriate.

Should you accept the offer and make the commitment, there will be a few simple administrative chores that you must attend to (being fingerprinted at the district office, having a physical exam, etc.). After that, you may want to call your new school to introduce yourself and set up an appointment to meet with your principal. If you've worked in a school system before, you know that the principal is the head administrator at your site. The principal may have a lot or a little direct involvement in the Guidance programs at your school; either way s/he is a very important person with whom to establish a working relationship.

Another VIP at your site will certainly be the school secretary. When you are in need of office supplies, use of copiers, or student information cards (these have parents' names, addresses, and home phone numbers) or when you have questions about how the school runs, the secretary will either know the answer or know where to find out. It's a good idea to introduce yourself or have yourself introduced to the secretary at the time you have your meeting with the principal. There may be some housekeeping issues concerning supplies or copying machine procedures that can be discussed at this early date, which will help everyone to avoid confusion later.

Presumably, you will have met your school psychologist or the contact person for the Guidance programs at your school during your second job interview. Shortly after accepting the position as guidance assistant, it will be important to set up another meeting with this contact person in order to get critical information about how the Guidance programs have been utilized at your site and the school's goals for the current year. Usually, some rapport will have been established with this person during the interview process, and this meeting will serve to further your working relationship. This may be a good time to ask questions about students with whom you will be working and teachers who have or have not referred students. You also may want to find out what the space considerations are at your school and in which nook, cranny, or classroom you will be conducting your group sessions.

Some school psychologists/contact persons will want to take you around and introduce you to teachers and students on your first day on campus. Others may wish to schedule a time during the school's staff meeting during which to introduce you to the staff en masse. Either of these methods are workable, but you may want to ask for some time at a staff meeting in the near future anyway, just to be sure that you develop a recognition factor among the teachers and other support staff. Another reason to be introduced at a staff meeting is that this is a perfect forum in which you can give the school staff information about the Guidance program and the service that you will be providing for their students. Many schools in the district have had guidance assistants for several years, and their staffs still value a brief "refresher" on what is available to their students; other schools have had less contact with the Guidance programs and will need you to clarify why you're there (refer to the section titled "What Is a Guidance Assistant?"). In addition, new staff are often unaware of the existence of our programs and will want to know about the curricula. You may even want to get started obtaining referrals of students from teachers that you talk to during this initial staff meeting or perhaps announce your intention to send referral requests in the near future.

During these first few days, it will be important for you to "become visible" at your school, i.e., spend time in the staff lounge during recesses and lunch time, getting to know the teachers and letting them know you; ask to observe in the classrooms or offer to make a classroom presentation about the Guidance programs or to present an actual lesson from one of the curricula; get information from teachers about what their concerns are with referred students. It's very helpful to let the teachers at your school know that you are there to provide them with a resource that, by helping their students feel better about themselves, may help them to achieve more in the classroom. A teacher's classroom is, to a certain extent, her/his domain, so it's wise to request observation time and offer support, rather than telling teachers what you are going to do.

Some Issues You May Encounter

Who's the Boss?

You may experience some confusion during the first days, wondering to whom you actually report. In all cases, the principal is the "Commander in Chief" of everyday school functions and administrative decisions. Your principal may want to be informed by you of all phases of your work, or s/he may prefer that you work with the school psychologist or another contact person and let that person keep her/him updated on your progress. Principals are particularly interested in giving their approval to correspondence going from any school staff member (including GA's) into the community. Thus, permission letters sent home to parents of students to be included in your groups must be approved by the principal or by the person delegated this authority by the principal. In any case, these are issues that can be resolved early by asking about them during those first meetings with your principal and school psychologist.

Supervision

Another issue that you may want to discuss early in your assignment is supervision. You'll need to know not only with whom you'll be working closely, but how often you'll meet. Some GA's have good results with a loosely structured format in which, when questions arise, the GA brings them to their contact person at the first convenient time. Others have found that, without regularly scheduled meeting times, they often go weeks without meeting to discuss questions and concerns about students, and important information is never shared. Because all school staff are very busy and time is in short supply, your contact person may not think to offer a regular meeting time for sharing concerns. If this type of support is helpful to you, you should take responsibility for requesting a regular meeting time. Most school psychologists will be willing to schedule this time with you if you clearly express a need for regular consultation.

Supplies

Art and games can be very important parts of group and individual counseling sessions. Obtaining paper, crayons, scissors, and other supplies may seem difficult unless you know who to ask. The place to start is probably with your school secretary. If the secretary is unable to help you, the principal and school psychologist will surely be of assistance. In this day of very tight budgets, your school may want you to have a small budget from which you can purchase supplies, or you may be given access to a general pool of resources at the school. You should not need to purchase necessary items out of your own pocket. However, if there is a particular game or other item that you have found useful in groups and that you would like to purchase and use with your groups at school, that is certainly permissible. Often, the school will have some games, puppets, toys, etc., that you may be able to use in your groups. Letting the staff know that you are interested in trying activities that they have found useful may serve to provide you with supplies and activities, as well as strengthen the bond between yourself and the school staff.

Office Machines

In most schools, you will find that there is one room that contains the office machines that the whole staff uses for preparing lessons. It's important to keep in mind that you will need to do some advance preparation of activities for your groups and classroom presentations and that it will be easier for you to accomplish this task if you can schedule prep time during off-peak hours during the day. Before and just after school and during lunch breaks and recess times are among the times of highest usage of copiers and other office machines by the teaching staff. If you can schedule yourself around those times, you're less likely to get "bumped" off of a machine. Also, keep in mind that you can spend prep time at the Professional Resource Center (PRC) in the district office and, when necessary, at the Guidance Resources Office as well.

Space Availability

Finding a space in which to conduct groups may be a challenge, since many schools are very full. Often it's possible to use the school psychologist's office on days when s/he is at another site. There may be other space that is going unused at your school as well. Talking to your principal and school custodian will help you to track down an appropriate spot to conduct groups.

Illness or Absence

It is very important to let both the school and the Guidance Resources staff know when you are ill or unable to work for any reason. Teachers and students need to be informed when groups will not be meeting at their regularly scheduled times. Confusion results from not informing the school and making certain that the people affected by your absence are told in advance, which can have a very negative effect on a GA's credibility at school, as well as on the GA's relationship with students in counseling groups. If absence is unavoidable, let the school secretary know and ask her to inform the people affected by your absence. Call the Guidance Resources Office as well, so they can help eliminate any confusion that might arise. Any absence should be written up afterward on a "Classified Absence Report" form, available from the Guidance Resources Office or at your school site(s).

Working with Groups

Why Work with Groups?

There are several reasons to do group work, such as 1) you will be able to serve more students, 2) students are used to groups in school, and 3) teaching some skills such as social skills are best practiced with others. The disadvantages of groups are also important to know that: 1) some students will not do well in groups, 2) some group members do not do well together, and 3) you will need a repertoire of behavior management techniques to be successful.

Getting Groups Started

It's possible that when you arrive at your school site, a list of students who have been referred for groups may already exist. You may then want simply to get information about these students and why staff feel they would be appropriate for group, send out parent permission letters, arrange a time schedule, and begin your groups. Somewhat more likely, however, is the scenario in which the school has been awaiting your arrival before beginning to consider who might be appropriate as group participants. In this case, you will probably find it necessary to request staff meeting time, which was mentioned earlier, as soon as possible.

Many GA's have found it very useful to develop a reusable referral letter, which may be sent to teachers, requesting that they recommend particular students who may benefit from group or individual counseling with you. This letter should give a thumbnail description of the content of the sessions, so that teachers will be reminded of which program might be most appropriate for which students. You can obtain valuable information by requesting that teachers write down their specific concerns about individual students on this referral form.

Often, teachers' comments and concerns can also be very helpful in deciding which students to include in particular groups. For instance, you may receive ten referrals from second and third grade teachers for students who would benefit from a STAR I group, in order to improve their social skills. If eight of these students are showing very aggressive behavior, however, you almost certainly will not want to include all of them in one small group! Or, if you did choose to have all these aggressive students in one group, you would (hopefully) have different expectations of how quickly you might progress with this type of group composition, as compared with a group of students with differing levels of social skills. In addition to requesting teachers' concerns about students, it's a good idea to ask for feedback on the students' strengths as well. Again, this information will be useful when deciding on group composition.

If you do not receive any response to your request for referrals from one or two teachers, don't be overly concerned. Some teachers are fortunate enough to feel that all of their students are doing fine and are not in need of extra affective education. Often, these teachers, after hearing positive comments from other teachers about the gains made by their students after participating in your groups, will notice certain of their own students who might benefit from group or individual counseling. It is quite likely that you will be able to fill ten hours at your school(s) working with students who are referred on the first letters you send to the teachers. If you have unfilled time, however, you may want to talk with those teachers who have not referred students. It is possible that they need personal contact with you before entrusting "their students" to your care.

As you receive referrals from teachers, you will have a decision to make regarding whether or not to conduct a pregroup interview with referred students. If you do conduct this interview, there are some advantages:

- You will give the student a chance to meet you and thereby reduce the anxiety level as group sessions begin.
- You will be able to "get a feel" for how each student feels about being referred for group or individual counseling.
- You will have an opportunity to compare your own experience with each student to the comments made by their teacher (or parent) when the student was referred and get an idea of whether the student has been appropriately referred.
- You can begin to get a sense of which students will be likely to work well together in group.
- You will get a sense, perhaps, of which students may benefit more from individual sessions than from group participation.

That's a lot to be gained, and the only thing that will be lost is time. Individual pregroup meetings, as beneficial as they are, do consume a lot of time, which may or may not be available to you. This will probably be a very good issue to talk over with your school psychology/contact person before deciding how to proceed.

As you receive referrals from teachers, you will need to begin the process of obtaining parental permission for students' involvement in the counseling opportunities at your school. Written parental permission *must* be obtained in order for a student to be included in group or individual sessions. Your principal will almost certainly want to review your permission letter before it is sent out. Do check on this. Your principal may also give her/his permission to include a student in counseling on a one-time-only basis before getting parental permission. Sometimes students are hesitant to even show a permission letter to their parents or are unwilling to have their parents sign until they have "checked out" what group or individual sessions are going to be like. If you can't seem to get that permission letter back signed, you may wish to call individual parents to get verbal permission. This will suffice temporarily, but you still have to get that parental permission *in writing* and keep it on file.

You may perceive that there will be some lag time between getting referrals and getting permission letters back from parents, so that you can start the actual process of counseling. This time can be used very effectively, so you need not feel as though time is being wasted in simply waiting. You may wish to use this time to work out a practical schedule of group meeting times, no small task when trying to take teachers' classroom schedules into consideration. *A few methods of schedule formulation* have been tried successfully:

(*1*) Put a sign-up sheet in the teachers' lounge, listing available days and blocks of time, and allow teachers to sign up for the time that's most convenient for them to have their students away from the classroom.

(*2*) Ask teachers to list as many convenient time blocks as they can on the referral sheet that you send out (ask for first, second and third preferences), and build your schedule around these times.

(*3*) Approach the teachers with two time slots available and have them select one. If neither is convenient, s/he will certainly let you know

Let Teachers Sign Up for Times When Students Can Be Away from Their Classrooms.

what they do need. This method is more direct and has proven to save days of scheduling nightmares!

You may develop your own method for scheduling, and if it works, we'd love to hear about it! It's very important to remember that you are at the school to provide a service to students, and if many students are not able to participate in group because of scheduling conflicts, then perhaps you need to rework the schedule. It can't be said too often that flexibility is a key part of your role at the school.

If a teacher seems hesitant to allow a needy student out of academic class time in order to participate in counseling, you may wish to inquire whether that student seems able to benefit maximally from her or his time in class or whether s/he might be better able to participate academically after receiving some counseling. Often, put in this light, teachers will consider making a change in their own schedules. If you find that, even with your best efforts, you're unable to fit a few students into your groups due to scheduling conflicts, remember that there will be future opportunities for these students to participate in group or individual sessions, and simply resolve to fit them into a group at the earliest possible time.

As you develop a schedule, you'll want to think about the number of meetings to schedule for your group and the number of individual sessions each week. Research conducted by the Guidance Resources Office recently found that the greatest change in students' self-esteem and behavior resulted from groups lasting approximately eight sessions. Please use this as a guideline for your groups and try to resist the temptation to work with the same at-risk students all year. The number of meetings per week, however, have varied from two sessions per week to once a week to once every other week. Deciding how often to meet with students will probably be a function of space availability, how many students you are working with, and your school psychologist's philosophy.

An important factor in group formulation is the number of students to include in a group. In general, it's probably safe to say that the younger the students, the smaller the group should be kept. While a group composed of seven or eight sixth graders may be manageable, that many kindergartners would probably turn your hair gray! With very young students, very small (two, three, or four students) groups meeting for relatively short periods of time (fifteen to twenty minutes may be as long as they can concentrate), using puppets, games, and limited amounts of very concrete verbal input may be a workable format. As the age of group members increases, so can the number of students in the group (within limits, of course), the time length for group sessions (up to about forty minutes maximum), and the amount of verbal "talk therapy" included in each session. Even older students enjoy puppets, games, and "fun" activities during group, and these can be a very productive source of learning about the different styles of interacting that are available to students.

As you think about the number of students to include in your groups, you'll also need to decide whether your groups are to be "open" or "closed." In other words, will you continue to accept students who are referred to group after the initial group is formed (open), or will you limit the group to only those students who were part of the group on the day it started (closed)? Different GA's feel differently about this issue. Open groups allow for needy students to be included in group as their need becomes apparent, rather than having to wait until the next series of groups begins. However, when a new member enters the group, time must be devoted to "catching them up" on group agreements, goals, and information that has already been covered by the rest of the group. This will certainly slow down the group process, and a ten-week group can become a twenty-week group all too easily! In a closed group, you may have to accept the fact that a student who has needs that might be met by the group is not able to join the group after the first session or two, that is, not until the next series of groups begins several weeks later. It is the dilemma of the good of the larger group being somewhat at odds with the good of the individual. And it's an issue to work out with the staff at your school, particularly your school psychologist/contact person.

In putting together groups, keeping a balance between different levels of social skills can be crucial to the group's success. One reason for this was alluded to earlier: a group composed solely of very aggressive children may be difficult to keep focused, while a group composed only of students who behave passively may prove overly compliant or may have difficulty in learning to express themselves assertively without some peer modeling of assertive behavior. It is sometimes helpful to include students with relatively high levels of skills in a group of passive and aggressive students. These more highly skilled students can serve as role models for the rest of the group members. When asking teachers for referrals, ask specifically about students with successful social skills who might benefit from group participation for some other reason. At any rate, when it's possible to balance a group with some students from each behavior type, you may find that it's worth the effort.

Other group composition issues to consider are the gender and age make-up of groups. First, gender: up to third and perhaps fourth grade, it's probably fine to have mixed gender groups. From fifth grade on (and perhaps with some fourth graders), issues around puberty and developing sexuality can impede the group's progress if boys and girls are included in the same group. Although this is not always true, enough students might be embarrassed to talk about particular aspects of their lives in front of the opposite sex so that, when possible, keeping groups segregated according to sex may be preferable. As students become older and more comfortable with their changing bodies this issue becomes less charged once again, and mixed gender groups can become very productive arenas for working on personal issues.

The issue of age composition of groups is similar: In general it's a good idea to limit the age differences within groups, simply because different aged students have different levels of verbal ability, physical attributes, and developmental skills. Some variability in age can be workable, however. For instance, a third grader can be included in a second grade group rather well, particularly if the third grader can become a sort of confederate of the guidance assistant. By acknowledging the age difference to the third grader (who will certainly notice it anyway) and inviting her/him to help the GA by modeling third grade behavior for the younger students, the third grader feels honored by being included in this group rather than being shamed at being "stuck" in a group of babies.

Another way to use your time while waiting to begin groups is to become more comfortable at your school site. Observing in classrooms, "hanging out" in the teachers' lounge in order to get to know and become known by the school staff, and making classroom presentations about the Guidance Resource programs can all be effective ways to become a part of your school. By announcing during your classroom presentations that you will be conducting small groups to help students learn more about themselves and how to deal with problems, make friends, and be more successful in school, you may find that some students will refer themselves once they know you're there for them. In general, an open referral process means that less stigma is attached to group participation, however, it may be necessary to prioritize needs.

Group Process

Once your groups are organized and scheduled and you have received parental permission for students to participate, it will be time to "begin." The types of groups that GA's conduct would come under the category of "educational," rather than therapeutic. Although much will happen during the sessions with the students, which will have therapeutic value for the children and their families, we do not "do therapy" in school. We educate students so they may understand themselves better, and, hopefully, they may have greater choices in their behavior. Rather than the three R's, we are teaching affective education—that is, education about how people feel in certain situations, react to change, deal with anger, get along with other people, and take care of themselves emotionally. We are trying to teach students more effective ways to interact with their environments by giving them information and opportunities to practice new behaviors. We help to strengthen our students' self-esteem by providing them a forum to successfully learn and exercise positive behavior patterns and self-understanding. As students' self-esteem grows, so, too, does their ability to say "no" to things and situations that may threaten their well-being, both now and in their future lives. This is no small thing to do!

As you meet with your groups for the first time, your students will naturally be curious about what it's all about. This first session is the best time to give an introduction of the curriculum, whether it's a short introduction to the STAGES material (coping with change) or STAR (social skills or problem solving) or whatever the group's main focus will be. A good way to get students involved in the process might be to ask them to state some goal related to the group's purpose that they would like to accomplish during the group's time together. This first session is also the time to go over the rules or agreements for acceptable group behavior. It's important to keep these agreements as simple and few as possible, while still ensuring that the group can accomplish its goals without disturbing the operation of the rest of the school. Some useful agreements might include

- I agree to keep my hands and feet to myself.
- I agree to take turns talking.
- I agree to get to group on time.
- I agree to participate in group.
- I agree to keep our group discussions confidential.

Students who are truly unable or unwilling to agree to this type of structure may be more appropriate for individual sessions or may simply not want to be in group at all. Other students may simply be displaying an aggressive behavior pattern by temporarily disregarding group agreements and will be able to learn better social skills via the group process. Talk to your school psychologist/contact person about what action to take in these cases.

Some GA's have found it useful to have some sort of reward system for students who keep the group's agreements. Candy, stickers, and trips have all been used to increase and reinforce students' positive behavior and participation during group.

Sometimes it appears that disruptive behavior on the part of one student may deprive the rest of the group of opportunities to accomplish anything positive in group. At these times, it may be best to have the student who is being disruptive remove him/herself from group by moving to another part of the room or even going back to class. This is certainly not an option to be used lightly or often, for the goal is to help these very students develop behaviors that will enable them to fit in with the group rather than be ostracized from it. However, since most students will not want to return to class and miss group time, sometimes the reminder that their behavior will affect their being included in activities of the group can effect a return to appropriate behavior.

It's important to keep in mind that, often, the student's negative behavior is being triggered by their reaction to some feeling(s) or some event, and bringing that into their awareness by asking what they think might be causing them to behave the way they are behaving can help them to understand their behavior better and help you to help them (rephrase) resolve whatever issue is going on with them. In other words, using student's behavior as grist for the group process can be therapeutic if done in a gentle, understanding, and nonblaming way.

If you find yourself having an angry reaction to a student's behavior, it's often very instructive to let them know, in an assertive way by modeling the ''I statement,'' how their behavior affects you. This can often help children understand the reactions that other adults have to their behaviors, also. One of the most useful concepts to remember about groups is that they are microcosms of the child's world. Anything that comes up in group can be used as a learning or therapeutic experience for its members, depending on how we, as guidance assistants, respond to the situation. If we yell, get angry, or withdraw from a student who is behaving inappropriately in group, we reinforce the idea that his/her behavior is bad and that it controls you and the group. This is a message that the student has probably already gotten, without positive results. If we, instead, ask the student how that type of behavior has helped or hurt her/him in the past and give assertive responses to the behavior itself, we give students an entirely different perspective about themselves.

Working with Individuals

Some students find it extremely difficult to function in a group setting and may benefit from seeing you individually. Most often, these are the very young students, kindergartners and first graders, who have not developed the social skills to interact successfully with their peers. If you have time in your schedule, it may be helpful to see these students one or, perhaps, two at a time, using a format that is less structured than that of the larger groups. Often, by being a "special friend" that the student can learn to trust through games, stories, and art experiences, you can help them, over a period of several weeks, to become more able to trust the group setting and be better able to develop healthy peer relationships.

Older students who appear unwilling to participate in group may be feeling stigmatized by their selection for "extra help"; they may also have issues that they are unwilling to share with schoolmates; or they may simply not feel in need of help. Usually, all of these reasons for not wanting to participate will be verbalized as being the last one: "I don't need (your) help." In general, it's unwise (not to mention impossible) to force a student to participate when they truly don't want to be in group. Often, offering them the option of attending for three or four sessions and then deciding whether they want to continue gives the uncertain student the "out" they are looking for. In most cases, the student will have acclimated to the group during those early sessions and will want to continue.

If a student is adamant about not participating in group, or continues to feel very uncomfortable after a few sessions, you may wish to give him/her the option of coming to see you on an individual basis for a period of time. Again, individual sessions may be difficult to offer to students because of time constraints, but, in certain cases, they may be the best direction to take. Your feelings about working with individuals, as well as your principal and contact person's ideas about how your time will best be spent, will help you decide whether to spend time in this way.

What types of activities to do in individual session will depend on what you feel comfortable with and what is going on with the particular student you're seeing. Games can provide a relaxed atmosphere in which to talk, and they approximate other social situations that the student may need to learn how to deal with appropriately. Art is very therapeutic and can provide you with a lot of information about what is going on with the student. Just your presence at the school, providing a place where the student can go and talk, can be very helpful in strengthening her/his self-esteem.

There will probably be times when you may be asked to intervene with individual students due to a situational need or crisis. As you become more accepted by the staff at your school, you will probably begin to be thought of as a resource in times of teacher stress. For instance, when there's a fight on campus, you may be asked to "deal with" one or more of the participants, especially if the principal and school psychologist are not readily available. This is an issue that you can resolve ahead of time by talking it over with those two people and deciding together how to respond to such "emergencies." If you feel comfortable in meeting with students in such a situation, and your staff contact people agree, that's fine, so long as it won't interfere with your normal schedule. Given that your purpose at the school is to help students learn social skills and how to deal with their feelings, you might suggest that the students involved in a situation that occurs become members in the type of group most appropriate to their current dilemma, as soon as your schedule allows.

Closure

All groups must eventually come to an end, even those open-ended, ongoing groups that some schools may prefer. Students come to depend on their group sessions and to look forward to the time they spend with you. To be told one day, "This is the last time we'll see each other for group," would be devastating for students, bringing up abandonment issues and undermining progress that had been made during group. Closure really should begin when the group begins, in that students can be informed at the beginning of your session just how many weeks you will be meeting. As group progresses, occasionally mentioning how many more times the group will be meeting will help to keep students aware of the passage of time and the approaching end of the group.

During the last few weeks of group, it will be important to address closure issues directly. You may wish to plan a special activity with each of your groups to acknowledge what each group member has accomplished towards achieving their own goals. This is the time to return to those goals the students stated at the beginning of group. Were those goals accomplished? Were other, unstated goals achieved? What was gained by the student through their participation in group? Some students may have difficulty in recognizing their own progress, and you can add to their sense of well-being by verbalizing the positive growth that you have observed in your students over time. You may have to look very closely and be generous, yet truthful, in this particular activity. Usually, the group can be very effective in giving itself evaluations. If group member David is having difficulty knowing whether he has made any progress toward his goal of being a friend, you might ask the group to provide examples of times when David listened to a friend, acted in a friendly way, offered to share, or talked about himself in an honest and serious way so his friends could know him better. When you ''front load'' the request for feedback by giving positive examples, you are most likely to receive positive responses. And if you get negative feedback, like ''Well, David was mean to me,'' you can gently remind other group members that, even though no one got perfect during group, now is the time to look for positive progress made during their sessions with you.

Starting New Groups

Once the earlier set of groups has terminated, the whole process begins again! You may have several students who were referred to you as you began the earlier groups. These students' needs will have priority now, since they have been waiting for a group placement. Sending out a new request for referrals about two weeks before the end of the earlier groups will probably garner enough referrals to begin again shortly after terminating those first groups. If you had students in those groups who continue to need to build more skills (which is more likely than not), you will want to decide whether to continue those students in the same type of group or in another type. Often, students who are needy in one area are also needy in several areas.

Working with Teachers in the Classroom

At the elementary level, *all* teachers have curriculum lessons available for teaching STAR and STAGES in the classroom. These consist of ten lessons at each grade level. First, third, and fifth grade teachers have ten

STAR I lessons, and kindergarten, second, and fourth grade teachers have STAGES lessons (for kindergarten, teachers have a comprehensive list of age appropriate books).

Some teachers are hesitant about beginning to implement guidance lessons. Guidance assistants can help to ensure that all of our students are receiving this initial amount of affective education by serving as consultants to the teachers in the classrooms. In this capacity, we can support teachers by demonstrating a lesson or two in their classroom; by acting as co-facilitators as they implement lessons; by offering informal in-service and consultation services; and, equally important, by providing communication between the teachers and the Guidance Resources Office.

It's important, when offering to provide assistance, to communicate to the teachers our *support* role in assisting them to work with materials that may be new to them. The teacher must retain her/his classroom responsibility and regard you as an assistant or guest speaker in the classroom. The first reason for our being so emphatic on this point is that, ultimately, the teacher will be teaching these lessons, and it would be unwise to become overly dependent on the GA to present them. In addition, most GA's are not credentialed teachers, and if a teacher leaves the classroom while the guidance assistant taught STAR I or STAGES, those students would not be properly supervised on campus. In most cases, as teachers observe you teaching these lessons or work with you to implement the first few lessons, their own comfort level with the lessons will increase, and the teachers with whom you work will quickly realize the ease with which they can teach the lessons themselves. In those few cases in which a teacher may want you to present all of the lessons, you may need to rely on your own assertive skills, setting limits on the number of lessons that you have time to assist with, and communicate that clearly to the teachers at your school.

Working with Parents

There will probably be times and situations in which it will seem a good idea to contact the parents of a student in your group(s). One of these might be the situation mentioned earlier, in which a student seems interested in participating in group, but a signed permission slip never finds its way back to you. In this case, call the parents/guardians and speak with them about the letter. Often, parents want a personal contact with you before they agree to their child's participation. Sometimes the permission letter has been misplaced because of the family's hectic lifestyle. This information may be helpful in working with the child, because a chaotic, super-busy home life often impacts the student's school performance.

Most parents are curious about what happens in group and are, perhaps, concerned about their child missing academic class time or anxious about other issues. By giving parents a brief description of group and reminding them of some of the teacher's concerns for their child, you may allay their concerns enough that they will give their permission for the child to attend group with you. The concern over missing academic time is appropriate, yet most students who need group are not able to perform as well as they might in class, due to the very difficulties that they would be working on in group. An understanding reminder of these factors will usually allow a parent to give their permission. However, if a parent is adamant about not allowing their student to participate in group, that is their prerogative. This should definitely be noted and mentioned to the school psychologist for follow-up.

If you detect a noticeable change in a group member's behavior or emotional state, it's a good idea to call the parent or guardian and inquire how things are going at home. This can be done in a nonthreatening way by informing the parent that you like to be in contact with parents on a somewhat regular basis, in order to know whether any of the skills that their child is working on in group are being noticed at home. Often, a child's acting-out behavior in group is directly tied to situations at home. By making the phone call, you may receive information that the child her/himself would not have perceived as having an impact on his/her behavior and feelings, but which you may then incorporate in some way into your group sessions. For example, if Mom tells you on the phone on Monday that Dad left home over the weekend, you can open up Tuesday's group by asking how folks might act/feel/think when someone important in their lives goes away. This will be helpful not only to that specific student, but to all group members who have experienced loss in the past.

Program Evaluation and Summary

Research studies on students' progress after participation in the district guidance groups have continually shown significant gains in behavior, self-esteem, and academic performance. Completed studies can be obtained for review from the Guidance Resources Office.

It has also become clear, for those interested in adopting a similar model, that the programmatic success depends on

- qualified supervisory staff dedicated to and experienced in service delivery
- continual efforts to maintain program funding and continuity over time
- school site cooperation and district-level support
- excellent and easy-to-use classroom and small group curriculum materials
- ongoing recruitment, training, and supervision of staff
- ongoing program evaluation and refinement

Chapter 13

A DRUG EDUCATION STAFF
DEVELOPMENT PROGRAM

The Pomona Unified School District (PUSD) has published a copyrighted drug education training manual for teachers titled *The Head of the Class*, which is a model that is being disseminated by the U.S. Department of Education-funded Substance Abuse Project at California State University at Fullerton, with Dr. William Callison as director. It is included in this chapter, and it is preceded by information about the district.[5] They are used as drug education staff development materials. In addition to this training effort, the district plans to identify potential substance abusers and potential dropouts and to place them in appropriate interventions, using Comprehensive Risk Assessment software.

AVAILABLE TRAINING

Staff of the Pomona Unified School District can provide training not only in the areas covered in this document, but, in addition, they can provide the following training:

- Drugs in the work place — A training for personnel with supervisory and management responsibilities regarding recognition of drug use and confrontation. This one-day workshop will fulfill the requirements required for agencies receiving federal funds.
- Parent education — A training for district personnel to implement a model parenting program. The model parenting program will allow the district and other interested agencies to deliver a parent

[5]Permission has been granted to Dr. William Callison from the Pomona Unified School District to use ''Understanding, Recognizing, and Confronting Drugs on Campus,'' which is copyrighted by the Pomona Unified School District.

221

education program that includes criteria for identification of at-risk youth, gang and drug awareness training, parenting the out-of-control adolescent, and training parent support groups.[6]

EXPERIENCE OF PUSD

Pomona Unified School District is a leader in substance abuse prevention education efforts. The district and the Pomona Police Department have collaborated on a drug prevention program called PRIDE (Pomona Resources In Drug Education). PRIDE includes the following: a twelve hour training for all district employees for understanding the dynamics and recognition of drug use and confrontation, implementation of the drug education curriculum, a parent intervention program for out-of-control adolescents, and referral to community agencies for drug-abusing youth.

The Pomona Unified School District conducted a student survey at the fourth, sixth, eighth, and tenth grade levels regarding drug use during the 1988−89 school year. Some 65% of the eighth graders have used alcohol more than once. Over 21% of the eighth graders reported using marijuana more than once. When asked if they had drunk alcohol within the last four weeks, 35% of the eighth graders responded yes. When asked if they had used marijuana within the last four weeks, 8% of the eighth graders responded yes. Comparing the 6th graders, some 48% of the sixth graders reported using alcohol at least once, and 6% reported using marijuana. When asked if they had drunk alcohol or used marijuana within the last four weeks, 16% of the sixth graders had used alcohol, and 2% had used marijuana. The general trend is increased use of drugs as the students get older; therefore, it is critical to have a variety of strategies for intervention.

DESCRIPTION OF THE STUDENT POPULATION IN PUSD

The target population served by Pomona Resources In Drug Education is 95% minorities in makeup, about 60% of whom are Hispanic.

[6]If you are interested in training staff in "Understanding, Recognizing, and Confronting Drugs on Campus" or the other programs listed, you may write or call Frank Garcia, Program Supervisor−Alcohol, Drug, and Tobacco Education, Pomona Unified School District, 800 South Garey Avenue, Pomona, CA, 91766, (714) 397-4854.

The 1989 – 90 California Assessment Program (CAP) data indicates that the district socioeconomic index is below Los Angeles County and state averages. This information is underscored by the fact that 36% of district students are eligible for Aid to Families with Dependent Children (AFDC). The 1990 R-30 Language Census Report shows that 36% of students have other than English language ability. The 1989 – 90 CAP data indicates a growing population of limited English proficient, exceeding county and state averages. This data indicates a significant number of students and families at risk.

Understanding, Recognizing, and Confronting Drugs On Campus

Introduction

There certainly is no easy solution to the problems caused by drug and alcohol use in our schools today. However, most experts agree that if we are to successfully cope with this epidemic, the following steps must be taken:

1. Establish a comprehensive K – 12 drug education program in all schools.
2. Train educators to better detect and cope with student drug use.
3. Provide adequate rehabilitation and counseling programs for students.
4. Insure that parents know how to recognize and intervene in adolescent drug use.

Although each of these steps is essential to the success of any program, it is the nature of drug abuse that makes training in early detection critical. This booklet has been specifically designed to help educators better understand, recognize, and confront substance abuse. We hope you will find the information useful.[7]

Cocaine, marijuana and heroin affect neurotransmitters and neurohormones that are crucial to pain relief, stress reduction, mental stability, time control, and motivation.

Continued drug use can result in permanent damage to receptor sites, neurohormones, and neurotransmitter activity.

Depleted reservoirs or a damaged neuro-system can cause a craving or physical need for the drug (biologic addiction). This process may also cause behavioral changes that can help us to identify drug use.

[7]Special acknowledgement and thanks are given to Dr. Forest Tennant for his work in the field of chemical dependency and assistance with this manual.

Negative Feedback of Some Drugs of Abuse

Drug	Neurotransmitter/Neurohormones Affected
Amphetamines	Dopamine Possibly Norepinephrine
Heroin	Endorphin Adrenocorticotropin Hormone (ACTH) Follicle Stimulating Hormone (FSH)
Cocaine	Norepinephrine Dopamine Serotonin
Marijuana	Norepinephrine Endorphin Follicle Stimulating Hormone (FSH) Luteinizing
Phencyclidine (PCP)	Possibly Serotonin Possibly Endorphin Possibly Dopamine
Nicotine	Possibly Acetylcholine

The Dynamics of Chemical Addiction

Neurochemistry and Addiction

For years, chemical dependency has been referred to by the experts as either being "physical" or "psychological" in nature.

It is now clear that both physical and psychological factors exist in every person who uses drugs compulsively. The term "biologic dependency" is becoming increasingly popular when referring to drug addiction.

Recent advances in neurochemistry have also given us a greater understanding of the addiction process, as well as the genetic factors that can lead to addiction during very early stages of use.

A basic understanding of neurochemistry will help us to better understand and recognize drug use, dependency, and the behavioral change exhibited by the abuser.

Neurotransmitters and Neurohormones

Simply put, *Neurotransmitters* are chemicals in the brain that carry electrical impulses (messages) between brain cells. They are also referred to as brain stimulators.

Neurohormones are chemicals made in a gland that act on nerve tissue to maintain equilibrium in the body. The pituitary gland (located at the base of the brain) produces neurohormones that are responsible for pain relief, stress relief, and mental stability.

Some of the more important neurohormones and neurotransmitters are listed below. Those greatly affected by drug use are *italicized*.

Neurotransmitters	Neurohormones
Norepinephrine	*Endorphin*
Serotonin	Cortisone Releasing Factor (CRF)
Acetylcholine	Thyrotropin Releasing Factor (TRF)
Dopamine	*Follicle Stimulating Hormone (FSH)*
Histamine	*Luteinizing Hormone (LH)*
Somatostatin	*Prolactin*
Neurotensin	*Adrenocorticotropin Hormone (ACTH)*
Substance P	*Vasopressin*
Gastrin	Oxytocin
Cholecystokinin	Enkephalin

Behavioral Change

As teachers, you will be more likely to observe behavioral changes in your students than objectives symptoms of use in the classroom.

One or two behavioral changes may be no more than normal adolescent growth. They may also be indicators of more serious problems, like drug abuse.

When any of the following problem behaviors are observed, a loving confrontation and good listening skills will be invaluable in heading off more serious problems. When three or more of these behaviors are observed, drug use should be suspected.

Look For:

1. Time distortion
   a. Sleeping in late
   b. Difficulty in waking up
   c. Late for appointments
2. Changes in personal hygiene
   a. Dirty clothes
   b. Dirt under fingernails
   c. No make-up
   d. Less attention to appearance

3. Lack of motivation
4. Good to poor work habits
5. Sudden depression or happiness
6. Sudden quiet or withdrawal
7. Less interaction with family/home activities
8. Sudden outburst of anger
9. Constant depression
10. Anxiety
11. Inability to concentrate
12. Increased moodiness
13. Change of friends
14. Frequent mistakes or sloppy work
15. Increased accidents
16. Clothing glorifying drinking or drugs
17. Drop in grades
18. Possession of suspicious substances (unknown powders, pills, leafy substances, small crystalline-like rocks, etc.)
19. Circles under eyes
20. Acne
21. Isolation
22. Abnormally pale complexion
23. Sudden appetite, especially for sweets
24. Imprecise eye movements

Teachers should also be aware of students with large amounts of cash and students with pagers.

The Examination Process

When trying to determine whether or not a child is under the influence of a drug, just ask yourself the following questions:

1. Does he/she seem unusually hyper or lethargic?
2. Are his/her eyes bloodshot or watery?
3. Does he/she seem to be uncoordinated?
4. Are his/her reactions slow?
5. Is his/her speech too fast or slurred?
6. Is his/her mouth dry?
7. Is he/she confused?
8. Does he/she have a blank expression?
9. Is he/she giggling or crying?
10. Is there a smell of alcohol or marijuana about his/her breath or person?

There are also several tests that are designed to determine sobriety. Some can be given to an entire class at once as part of a game like "Simon Says."

1. "Standing with your feet together and hands at your side, look up and close your eyes for ten to fifteen seconds."
   Is excessive weaving noticed or does the child have to open his/her eyes in order to maintain balance?

2. "Standing with your eyes closed, arms extended out in front, and index fingers touching, move your arms back until they are straight out from your shoulders. Now keeping your eyes closed, bring your arms back to the same position and touch the tips of your index fingers together."
   Can he/she bring fingers together or are fingers two or more inches apart?

3. "Stand on one leg, close your eyes and count to ten."
   Can he/she maintain balance? Do eyes open or does the leg come down?

4. Have the child step up onto a curb.
   Does he/she over or under step the rise?

If the answer is yes to three or more of the questions asked, or if the child fails two or more of the tests given, the probability of drug use is very high, and confrontation is warranted.

The Confrontation Process

"Confronting Problematic Behavior"

One of the most difficult tasks of a teacher is that of confronting problematic behavior. In fact, confronting our students can be so difficult at times that we are often tempted to ignore the problem, hoping it will go away. Unfortunately, the opposite is true. Especially if the problem we ignore is that of substance abuse.

Teachers who fail to confront their students can logically expect one or more of the following to occur:

1. The problem will become worse.
2. There will be a drop in class morale.
3. The student will lose respect for the teacher.
4. The class will probably develop an informal leader.
5. There will be a drop in overall class performance.
6. The teacher's job will become more difficult.

Inappropriately addressing behaviors can have a negative impact on both the student and class in general.

The following guidelines should be met to help insure a successful exchange:

1. Meet with the student as soon as possible after the incident or behavior has been observed. However, never confront a student while still angry (timing).
2. Develop a plan or outline to insure that you cover everything you want to discuss.
3. Choose a private, neutral location for your talk.
4. Hold all calls. Keep interruptions to a minimum.
5. Prepare yourself for the worst.
6. Explain the reason for your meeting (be tactful, but direct).
7. Demonstrate your concern for both the student and his/her behavior.

What to Expect

1. Anger
2. Denial
3. Defensive attitude
4. Personal problems

How to React

1. Actively listen to your student.
2. Remain calm.
3. Return to the reason for the confrontation (behavior or incident).
4. Reiterate your concerns.
5. Offer your or other assistance if appropriate.
6. Make your expectations of the student's future behavior clear.
7. End the meeting on a positive note. ''I have faith in you, I know you can do this,'' etc.
8. Follow through!

Remember that the three most important traits or qualities a teacher can possess when dealing with problem behavior are:

1. Concern
2. Consistency
3. Follow through

Confrontational Advice

Reason vs. Demand

Children are forever asking why? It seems fair for concerned teachers to explain the ''whys'' to students once, or even twice. However, as teachers, we would do well to remember that reason is an ineffective tool in dealing with emotionally generated behavior.

So what does that mean? Generally speaking, kids are driven by emotion. "I want, I need, I have to . . ."

Example:

Picture yourself relaxing with the evening paper when your 16 year old daughter floats into the room and announces that she is "in love." Struggling to cover up the fact that you have just torn the newspaper in half, and hoping your voice has returned to something resembling normal, you ask, "Oh? and who is the lucky boy?"

"Charlie", she sings.

"Charlie who?" you ask.

"Charlie Manson," she replies, as though they were the two most beautiful words in the English language.

"Who?!", you repeat, not trusting your own ears.

"Charlie Manson," she answers.

Glancing nervously at the tattered paper you are still clutching, you discover that the parole board, in its infinite wisdom, has indeed released the mass murderer, Charles Manson, and that he now resides in your city.

Unable to control the panic any longer, you say, "I forbid you to see this man!" "But WHY?", she pleads.

With great confidence in the power of reason, you tell her that her precious Charlie is a mass murderer, an ex-con, and mentally deranged! Appealing to her own sense of reason, you explain that he has no job (and never will), that he will abuse and brainwash her, that he will keep her from her family, and that he may just kill her. "Mass murderers are very unpredictable, dear."

For three days your daughter's sister, brother, close friends, and relatives bombard her with every reason they can think of to convince her not to marry this man. Her only response: "But I love him!" Why? . . . because reason is an ineffective tool in dealing with emotionally generated behavior.

So explain to your children once, maybe even twice, the reasons why. Then focus on the rule or demand. The handy words, *nevertheless* or *regardless* can be a teacher's friend.

Communication

There have been entire books written on the art of effective communication. While we're not going to write another, there are a few points we would like to make about conversing with your students.

1. Children who are *listened to* will be more likely *to listen* when we have something important to say.

2. Never condemn the child, just the behavior.

Bad	*Better*
You're so stupid!	That wasn't thought out very well.

3. The questions we sometimes pose, also condemn or degrade our students.

   Why don't you *ever* . . . ?

   How come you *never* . . . ?

   Surely you realize . . . ?

   How many times do I have to tell you . . . ?

   Better

   What was your understanding of our conversation regarding . . . ?

   Did you stop and consider . . . before . . . ?

4. When listening to your students, stop what you're doing and look at them (active listening). Remember, you can communicate a lot through body language.

5. Converse in terms of feelings, not intellect. Everyone experiences the same feelings, but not everyone possesses the same intellect.

   Example:

   Let me tell you how that makes me feel. . . .

6. Avoid arguing with your students. Arguments have their own energy and before we realize it, they have turned into screaming matches. Accept your student's feedback or reasonable questions, but do not argue.

   Words like nevertheless, regardless, or "uh-huh, is there anything else," are very effective in ending the discussion and, as stated earlier, can be a teacher's best friend.

Remove "You" and "I"

Running late one night, a husband burst into the house and, as he ran upstairs, said to his wife, "Honey, I'm late. I want you to have dinner ready by the time I come down."

Now based upon the manner in which he directed his wife, what do you think her response was?

You guessed it. "Go to Burger King! They may do it your way."

We often make the mistake of focusing on what we want, instead of on the task at hand. We also have a tendency to direct our students in the same, or in a worse fashion.

If we can learn to remove you and I from the directions we give, it will allow others to focus on the task at hand, and not on the fact that we want it done.

Example:

"Honey, I'm late. Let's have dinner as soon as possible."

Example:
"Jeff, I want you to do your homework."

Better
"Jeff, do your homework."

It will take some practice, but directions without the you or I will result in much less grumbling. After a while, the child will think of it as his task and not as one directed by you.

Poor communication skills result in poor class control and in negative student reactions. For example:

Action	Reaction
Blaming/accusing, name calling, threats	Defensiveness, guilt, lies Rage, self-fulfilling prophesy challenged and defiance or fear and reclusiveness
Commands	Anger, defiance, resistance
Sarcasm	Embarrassment, humiliation
Hitting	Anger, revenge, poor model
Lecturing and moralizing	Bored, irritation
Warnings	Fear, discounts the action, challenged to test the limits
Prophesy	Sense of doom, defeat
Comparison	Irritated, anger at person compared to
Bribes	Youth holds out for bargains
Long explanations	Irritation, tunes out adult

Some of the substitutes for inappropriate actions seem obvious and yet, regular review and reemphasis can make a difference in the daily operation of a school.

Instead of threats	Try persuasion, pointing out positive aspects of desired behavior
Instead of interrogating	Try resolving disagreements with both parties explaining their needs and views
Instead of preaching	Try modeling, setting an example
Instead of bossing	Try challenging, appealing to the students' competitive desire to do well
Instead of shrieking, yelling, shouting	Try distancing; be aware of when you are out of control, even leaving the scene if someone else is there to supervise the class

Action	Reaction
Instead of prolonged silence	Try ignoring undesirable behavior
Instead of public criticism	Try talking with the youth in private
Instead of harping	Try not holding a grudge; don't keep reminding the child of the mistake
Instead of begging or pleading	Try contracting, spelling out the specific behavior and specific reward or punishment
Instead of bribery	Try rewarding
Instead of just letting things go	Try establishing routines/expectations
Instead of over-reacting	Try being under control of your emotions while disciplining

General Behavioral Guidelines for Staff

Do

1. Do maintain full supervision over every student in your charge at all times.
2. Do make your presence known by your interested alertness and initiative and by taking action when needed.
3. Do remain objective, fair, and consistent in dealing with your students.
4. Do call for help or ask instructions for handling an explosive situation before it gets out of control.
5. Do watch your language, dress, and deportment. The students are watching and modeling after you.
6. Do assume your share of responsibility for the behavior of the entire school population.

Do Not

1. Do not leave any student or group of students unsupervised at any time, anywhere.
2. Do not forget that slackening supervision means surrendering control.
3. Do not attempt to handle alone any emergency which is beyond your resources.
4. Do not be a poor model for students by your dress, language, or behavior.
5. Do not limit your supervision to those in your immediate care. You are a staff member representing the entire school.

POLICY RECOMMENDATION

Each district should consider establishing a comprehensive K–12 drug education program in all schools. The program should train educators to better detect and cope with student drug use, provide adequate rehabilitation and counseling programs for students and insure that parents know how to recognize and intervene in adolescent drug use.

Chapter 14

DEVELOPMENT OF A CULTURALLY COMPETENT PREVENTION AND INTERVENTION PROGRAM

As prevention and intervention programs have grown, researchers have been concerned about the high number of students from minority backgrounds who are at risk for school failure, dropping out, substance abuse, delinquency, and teen pregnancy. Most ethnic populations (except Native Americans) have lower use rates of alcohol and other drugs (AOD) than whites. As ethnic groups become acculturated to America, their use increases. Although most ethnic populations have lower AOD use rates than whites, they suffer more behavioral and health problems associated with use. Researchers believe this is true because of the accumulation of other associated risk factors, i.e., poverty, unemployment, discrimination, lack of access to health care, and despair.

RESEARCH FINDINGS

The research findings on substance abuse and ethnicity as described by Bonnie Bernard (1991) in *Moving Toward a "Just and Vital Culture": Multiculturalism in Our Schools* have many implications, including those listed above.

(*1*) Most ethnic populations (except Native Americans) have lower use rates of alcohol and other drugs (AOD) than Whites. As ethnic groups become acculturated to America, their use increases. Researchers indicate the still lower use rates of ethnic minorities are perhaps due to their cultural values of cooperation, interdependence, and social responsibility, which serve as protective factors. This is in contrast to some American culture values of individualism, independence, and competition, which can be risk factors that lead first to alienation of vulnerable youth and later to AOD problems.

235

(2) Although most ethnic populations have lower AOD use rates than Whites, they suffer more behavioral and health problems associated with use. Researchers believe this is true because of the accumulation of other associated risk factors, i.e., poverty, unemployment, discrimination, lack of access to health care, and despair.

The following are highlights of key findings regarding specific ethnic minorities from Prevention Research Updates Number 2-5, reported in Bernard's (1991) work.

Native American Youth

- Native American youth have the highest use rates for almost all drugs.
- The rate of alcoholism is two to three times the national average.
- Heavy drinking has been found to be the main reason that Indian students don't finish high school.
- Native American adolescents are profoundly alienated and depressed and experience high rates of delinquency, learning and behavior problems, and suicide. This situation is a result of persistent and deep sociocultural and economic exploitation, which has made them the most severely disadvantaged population in the United States.
- The main risk factors for Native American adolescent drug abuse are 1) a sense of cultural dislocation and lack of integration into either traditional Indian or modern American life, 2) community norms supporting use, 3) peer group support for use, and 4) lack of hope for a bright future.
- Prevention efforts must focus on 1) community involvement in community development with youth playing a major role and 2) educational interventions that allow Native American youths to develop bicultural competence, i.e., to develop skills necessary to be successful in the dominant culture while retaining their identification with and respect for traditional Native American values.

Black Youth

- Substance use is lower among black adolescents than among whites or any other group except Asian-Americans.

- While blacks are more likely to be abstainers or have lower use rates, they experience more drinking-related problems, especially binge drinking, health problems, symptoms of physical dependence, and symptoms of loss of control.
- Compared to whites, adult blacks are more likely to be victims of alcohol-related homicide, to be arrested for drunkenness, and to be sent to prison rather than to treatment for alcohol-related crimes.
- At even moderate levels of use, the adverse consequences of substance abuse are exacerbated by the conditions of poverty, unemployment, discrimination, poor health, and despair that many black youth face.
- Drug trafficking adversely affects the ability of the entire black community to function and deal with its problems.
- Black communities are particularly exploited by the alcohol industry through excessive advertising and number of sales outlets in these neighborhoods.
- Prevention efforts must 1) involve the community in community development efforts that include an active role for youth; 2) facilitate the development of racial consciousness and pride; 3) include public awareness campaigns that counter the alcohol/tobacco industry's advertising; 4) be broad-based, i.e., providing access to a range of social economic services and opportunities; and 5) restructure schools to provide opportunities for academic success.

Latino Youth

- Hispanics are one of the largest, youngest, and fastest growing of the nation's subgroups (half of the Hispanic population is under the age of eighteen).
- While Hispanics, in general, have no higher levels of use prevalence than whites or other ethnic groups, some research has found that Hispanics have more drug-related problems and that drug abuse is a serious, chronic, and multigenerational problem in many Hispanic families and communities.
- Hispanic youth who do drink consume heavier quantities and experience more drinking problems than do other adolescents. Heavier use patterns beginning in late adolescence appear to result from a blending of the drinking patterns of the donor cultures with those common among American youth and reflect the value that the right to drink is a rite of passage.

- Differential acculturation can produce stress in family relationships and behavior problems in immigrant children who may acculturate to the American culture at a faster rate than their parents.
- Prevention efforts must 1) encourage biculturalism and bilingualism, building on cultural strengths and pride while facilitating the development of skills necessary to succeed in United States society; 2) involve the community in community development efforts, especially the development of cultural arts centers; and 4) involve the community in public awareness campaigns to counter the efforts of the alcohol and tobacco industry in Hispanic communities.

Asian-American Youth

- Other than Native Hawaiians, whose drug and alcohol use is more similar to whites, Asian-Americans have the lowest levels of use compared with other ethnic groups.
- Consistent with their low levels of use, Asian-Americans suffer less from substance-related problems than do other ethnic groups, and most of these problems are male owned.
- Drinking in Asian society is governed by social norms that condemn excessive use and encourage moderation.
- A concern among some researchers and practitioners is that Asian-American substance use problems are underreported because of their ''model minority'' stereotype status and because they do not want to bring shame on their families.
- Prevention efforts should focus on 1) encouraging biculturalism, 2) involving youth in community prevention, and 3) providing indigenously owned family counseling and support services.

THE IMPACT OF POVERTY

Reeves (1988) found that poverty is the most predictive risk factor for school failure and dropping. Since significantly more ethnic minority children live in poverty (38.7% of Hispanics and 46.2% of blacks) than white children (16.1%), it follows they would be more at risk for dropping out. When ethnic minority groups continue to experience a lack of opportunities afforded others in America, they often feel and act hopeless. Feelings of alienation often follow, which puts large numbers of youth at risk for problems of substance abuse, dropping out, delinquency, and teen pregnancy (Nobles, 1984).

RACISM VERSUS MULTICULTURALISM IN THE SCHOOLS

Few educators want to believe that they are supporting racism as they battle to educate students. Yet schools are a key institution in society, controlling access to the skills and knowledge to be successful, and large numbers of at-risk youth are not benefiting from the present distribution of those resources. In other words, schools have an opportunity to give minority students a chance in society or maintain the status quo. Substance abuse prevention focusing on risk factors offers a fresh opportunity to address these issues. The following keys to change through prevention are summarized from Bernard (1991):

- active involvement of a multicultural task force involved in program planning
- school prevention policies that include an appreciation of diverse cultural needs and assets

Multiculturalism Can Work.

- restructuring of classrooms and schools so that 1) all students are given opportunities to work together, make decisions, and be responsible and to be resources to each other and 2) minority students are formally instructed in specific ways to achieve power in the dominant culture
- providing a rich curriculum for at-risk students and high teacher expectations that includes cooperative learning study of cultures, support for the value of speaking different languages, use of a variety of teaching styles, and personnel who match the student's ethnicity or have received extensive training to teach and encourage development of minority children

CULTURAL COMPETENCE IN COMMUNITY PREVENTION

As described in *The Future by Design* (OSAP, 1991), when values of the dominant society and values of many ethnic communities differ, as they do in America, it is the dominant society values that are applied to all, with others' differences seen as inferior traits or habits.

To have cultural competence in conducting community prevention, one must first understand the community values and, second, act in accordance with those values. That means sensitivity toward the people processes needed for effective community prevention and willingness and encouragement to ensure that community participants shape the outcome of the prevention initiative.

It is important to recognize both the hierarchical and gender differences in different ethnic groups, as well as the diversity that dwells within groups of the same ethnic origins, such as Asians. All people come from ancient civilizations with unique contributions to the world and also with unique world views. Another common mistake is to assume that different generations of immigrants hold the same world view. As assimilation affects the generations, differences occur. Language and symbols and why individuals immigrated to this country are all important elements of effective work with ethnic communities.

Developing trust between community members can take a long time. Trust, however, is a prerequisite to really dealing with important issues and making progress.

Focusing on a community's strengths and competencies is a very effective strategy. Since many ethnic communities have so many risk factors, a focus on resiliency, good health, and prevention can help transform problems into opportunities for growth and well-being.

Finally, cultural competence is not a knowledge base to be learned but the acquired ability to identify and use the community's knowledge to shape prevention to serve its citizens well.

CULTURAL COMPETENCE IN PROGRAM EVALUATION

Developing a culturally competent prevention and intervention program is an important goal for preventionists. Being culturally competent means using academic and interpersonal skills that allow individuals to increase their understanding and appreciation of cultural differences and similarities within, among, and between groups. This requires a willingness and ability to draw on community-based values, traditions, and customs and to work with knowledgeable persons of and from the community in developing focused interventions, communications, and other supports (Orlandi et al., 1992).

To attain a high level of cultural competence in program implementation and evaluation, OSAP recommends attention to ten basic principles:

(*1*) Demystify program evaluation by collaborating with stakeholders to problem solve and strategically plan the implementation and evaluation design.

(*2*) Reach consensus on the definition of important terminology in reference to ethnic grouping, for example.

(*3*) Share information openly to increase knowledge and look for common ground where views differ to impact attitudes.

(*4*) Remain creative and open to seeking areas of agreement with those who do not value or support the evaluation methodology.

(*5*) Be aware of the funding agency's role to influence evaluation methodology and how that affects issues of community ownership and shared decision making at the project and community level.

(*6*) Include and train as many racial and ethnic representatives as possible to enhance the implementation and evaluation.

(*7*) Do not confuse the culture of poverty with racial or ethnic identification. Design and report project findings so that others don't have similar confusion.

(*8*) Do not underestimate the importance of within culture subgroups in designing projects and in analyzing data.

(*9*) Develop internal program and community skills in the area of evaluation, both to increase skills in understanding evaluation results generally and to provide program support for future evaluation tasks.

(*10*) Consider that more complex community and program settings require more complex evaluation skills, especially those with cross-cultural evasion needs.

In summary, training is needed for evaluators and program and community stakeholders with a goal to create culturally competent individuals who are knowledgeable, committed to change, highly skilled, and constructive.

Chapter 15

EVALUATION OF SYSTEM EFFECTIVENESS

A model for evaluation of a program for students at risk of substance abuse is presented, which utilizes the intervention placement pre/post data gathered with the student self-report forms. Staff who have been involved in delivering interventions fill out the Intervention Completion Form at the end of the year, and a report is prepared using the Intervention Completion Software, which indicates the extent of completion, together with the student's substance abuse prediction score. Hopefully, if many of the interventions are completed, the prediction score will go down, indicating success. If the score does not go down, specific recommendations are made about which interventions were 1) not completed and/or 2) not well designed.

SYSTEMIC EVALUATION

The evaluation of effectiveness of a prevention/early intervention program can take many forms. The first question many ask is, "Why evaluate?" Indeed, evaluation takes time, many data collectors do not prefer the task, and "garbage in, garbage out" also applies to evaluation. The answer to the question, "Why evaluate?" is that, without evaluation, we would not know what works or why. Sometimes even after evaluation analysis, we do not know, because of the complexity of the program, the effect of interventing variables, or poor evaluation design strategies. However, the probability is that we will know more than if we didn't do an evaluation. The goal of evaluation is to bring the information about many varied activities together in a form so that they can be assessed or compared.

243

In designing an evaluation of a program, the first question to ask is about the purpose of the evaluation. Some purposes include

- Were the objectives and activities completed?
- Is the program effective (summative evaluation)?
- How did the program achieve its effectiveness, or lack thereof (process)?
- How cost-effective are the program services?
- Was any change due to the program?
- Would the program be effective with other groups?

STUDENT EVALUATION

The students at risk comprehensive model for program evaluation is adapted from the conceptual work on dropout prevention conducted by Novak and Dougherty (1980). Categories include Centers on the Student, Serves All Students, Offers a Comprehensive Scope of Services, Coordinates Resources and Personnel, and Incorporates Feedback and Evaluation into the System.

One way to use this evaluation model is to give each item two ratings on a 1 (low) to 10 (high) basis. The first rating is the extent to which the intervention is now being implemented; the second is the extent the rater believes it ought to be implemented. This then provides the administrator in charge with a sense of needed changes to improve the program with those items with the highest discrepancy receiving priority in the future.

Centers on the Student

The broad goal of any prevention or intervention effort is to help students by decreasing risk factors and increasing protective factors. An effective evaluation could focus on formal assessment of the student utilizing grades, test data, and staff entries in the student's permanent record. Informal assessment might be developed from observation of student behavior, school record analysis, and teacher interviews.

Grades

Grades provide a convenient way to quickly identify students who are in academic difficulty. Grades also allow us a convenient way to measure student improvement, individually and for the program as a whole.

Scoring: Rating for "is now being implemented" as described previously _____; rating for "ought to be implemented" as described _____.

Test Scores

Test scores serve the same function as grades, in that we can readily see which students are in difficulty (using district proficiency scores) and, at the same time, record scores pre and post to find out if they are improving. These data can then be used to analyze individual students and the program as a whole. See Appendix D for help in learning to use statistics in program evaluation with the EasyStat Software.

In Appendix D you will find the Documentation for using EasyStat. You can see at once how uncomplicated it is to use the standard statistics used in many studies in education and the social sciences. Following the EasyStat Documentation we have included the Introduction to the Teaching Assistant: Statistics Manual to give you an idea of its level of difficulty and our notion of how it can be used.

Prices

EasyStat Software and Documentation	$25.00
Teaching Assistant: Statistics Software and Documentation	25.00
Teaching Assistant: Statistics Manual	10.00

Order from Students-at-Risk, Inc., 1260 Brangwyn Way, Laguna Beach, CA 92651.

Scoring: Rating for "is now being implemented" _____; rating for "ought to be implemented" _____.

Staff Entries in Permanent Record

The written notes that teachers and other staff make in the student's cumulative record are a fine indicator of student progress and, especially, difficulties. The prevention staff member can then begin to build a student case history from information in the cumulative folder.

Scoring: Rating for "is now being implemented" _____; rating for "ought to be implemented" _____.

Student Behavior

Student behaviors of discipline incidents, truancy, etc., are helpful in assessing progress of interventions.

Scoring: Rating for "is now being implemented" _____; rating for "ought to be implemented" _____.

School Record Analysis

The records we consider are the cumulative folder and the case history folder. The emphasis here is on analysis. After a careful reading of both folders, the staff member attempts to see patterns and look for changes due to recent interventions.

Scoring: Rating for "is now being implemented" _____; rating for "ought to be implemented" _____.

Teacher Interviews

The teacher interview schedule should give us specific information that we cannot get any other way. For instance, is the student now

- reporting for special help as assigned
- using care in doing homework and getting it in on time
- completing make-up work on time
- bringing required materials to class
- taking accurate and useful notes
- using class time well
- taking an active and positive role in class discussions
- learning to work independently
- respecting the rights of others

Scoring: Rating for "is now being implemented" _____; rating for "ought to be implemented" _____.

Serves All Students

Identification of each student's needs is the key concept, and, to the extent possible, programs are inclusive. At the same time, some groups of students may need additional attention to bring them to a satisfactory level of performance and behavior, in reading or social skills, for example. We can typically build more support from teachers and parents for programs that serve all students, such as proficiency testing and analysis, than we can for services designed for a narrow group, such as predicted dropouts or substance abusers. The key is then to set minimal performance and behavior standards, such as the 40th percentile in reading, and to work to bring every student up to that level. Many of the difficulties faced by potential dropouts and substance abusers are problems to a lesser degree for other students. We then build in assistance for students as needed. Following are some examples and techniques that may help.

Hyperactivity

The student is unable to sit still in class and pay attention. Give the student medication as prescribed, extra gym time, extra shop time, and permission to leave class and go to study hall/gym/shop when class is too "talky."

Disorganized Behavior

There is a tendency to move from one activity to another without purpose or thought. Try to focus on topics of special interest to the student such as photography or automobiles. See if the student can finish one activity if it is made very brief. Construct activities in a step-by-step fashion so one can start in the middle after a break.

Poor Written Expression

The student hates to write reports, letters, or anything that will show him/her to be "stupid." See if you can teach the student to write by "writing down her/his own words" from tape-recorded answers s/he makes to questions s/he doesn't mind answering about a friend or a hobby.
Scoring: Rating for "is now being implemented" _____; rating for "ought to be implemented" _____.

Offers a Comprehensive Scope of Services

The range of services must be as broad as the varied problems students have, some of which are mentioned previously. These services might include instruction in basic and social skills, tutoring in areas of individual need, counseling to help work on personal problems, testing to identify areas of competence and interest, and developing a supportive learning environment. Following are several examples for each category of service.

Instruction in Basic and Social Skills

- special offerings of basic/social skills in summer school
- flexible curriculum with basic/social skills offering
- individualized courses with basic skills options
- resource teachers who offer basic/social skills

Scoring: Rating for "is now being implemented" _____; rating for "ought to be implemented" _____.

Tutoring in Areas of Individual Need

Peers can be utilized to

- listen to the student read
- provide individualized content help
- play instructional games
- work through programmed materials
- drill on a specific academic skill
- assist with development of a motor skill

Scoring: Rating for "is now being implemented" _____; rating for "ought to be implemented" _____.

Counseling on Personal Problems

Counseling is very important, especially when giving special attention to

- involving the student's parents
- providing a relaxed atmosphere
- being a responsive listener
- discussing strengths as well as weaknesses
- starting and ending conferences with a positive comment

Scoring: Rating for "is now being implemented" _____; rating for "ought to be implemented" _____.

Testing to Identify Areas of Competence and Interest

- achievement tests – norm-referenced, where the student's score can be compared with a national mean score, and criterion-

Tutoring in Language Arts.

referenced, where the student's score can be looked at with reference to a specific instructional objective
- questionnaires – used to measure attitudes, opinion, or judgments
- observation instruments – used to measure involvement or process behaviors
- logs, records, and checklists – used to record informal, but key, information

Scoring: Rating for "is now being implemented" _____; rating for "ought to be implemented" _____.

Supportive Learning Environment

A supportive learning environment offers

- academic tutoring by referral
- flexible placement in regular school, school within a school, or some other appropriate setting
- variable time/day scheduling
- opportunity classes that move at a slower pace
- fifth year of a four-year high school option
- pregnant teenager and child care option

- small group instruction option
- big brother/sister connection

Scoring: Rating for "is now being implemented" _____; rating for "ought to be implemented" _____.

Coordinates Resources and Personnel

The comprehensive services suggested in the previous section may all be available through a school district, but a potential dropout often would not know about them or how to get them. Hence, there is need for a staff member to coordinate the efforts of teachers, librarians, counselors, health staff, and contact persons in business who can provide training and employment opportunities.

The following areas of coordination between the dropout program and school staff presently exist.

Administrator

- supports and participates in in-service efforts pertaining to the dropouts and substance abuse program
- visits program activities frequently
- allows programs staff access in a timely manner

Scoring: Rating for "is now being implemented" _____; rating for "ought to be implemented" _____.

Special Education Coordinator

- discusses students of mutual interest on a regular basis
- develops educational plans for students of mutual interest
- develops in-service on special education topics for project staff
- shares administrative and instructional materials of interest
- exchanges information about students of mutual interest on a timely basis
- jointly selects materials that would be of use to both programs

Scoring: Rating for "is now being implemented" _____; rating for "ought to be implemented" _____.

Resource Staff

The resource staff includes a reading specialist, speech therapist, social worker, language/math specialist; bilingual specialist, job placement coordinator, work experience coordinator, and vocational education coordinator. The staff

- discusses students of mutual interest on a regular basis
- develops educational plans for students of mutual interest
- develops in-service on relevant topics for project staff
- shares administrative and instructional materials of interest
- exchanges information about students of mutual interest on a timely basis
- jointly selects materials that would be of use to both programs

Scoring: Rating for "is now being implemented" _____; rating for "ought to be implemented" _____.

Out of School Resources

Parents, advisory committees, citizens, organizations, business-industry-labor, social agencies, and other education providers can offer the following types of help:

- improving the school's public image
- providing services to help meet the needs of at-risk students
- providing feedback to increase the quality of the program

Scoring: Rating for "is now being implemented" _____; rating for "ought to be implemented" _____.

Incorporates Feedback and Evaluation into the System

The evaluation aspect of the evaluation plan is critical in that so much of the effort is one-on-one by its nature. It is very difficult to keep staff informed about what is working and what isn't unless a strong effort to evaluate is implemented. A case system is one way to organize the effort, where each student with special needs is dealt with by a team of professionals who diagnose needs and suggest treatment and/or remediation as appropriate. All of these efforts are recorded in a permanent folder or computer record.

The following materials can be taken from the student's permanent record or gathered separately if needed:

- basic personal data
- home background
- school background and progress
- attendance record
- entrance and withdrawal information
- health and physical development reports
- academic record
- test results
- data explaining the differences between test results and classroom achievement
- social and personality characteristics
- interests and activities (in-school and out-of-school)
- vocational interests and plans
- educational interests and plans
- work experiences
- comments, observations, and summarizations
- guidance notes
- follow-up data (Novak and Hammerstrom, 1976)

Scoring: Rating for "is now being implemented" _____; rating for "ought to be implemented" _____ .

POLICY RECOMMENDATION

Each district should consider providing a substance abuse program evaluation. The Centers on the Student category should include formal assessment of the student, utilizing grades, test data, and staff entries on the student's permanent record. Also included could be informal assessments based on observation of student behavior, school record analysis and teacher interviews.

Chapter 16

ESTABLISHING AND IMPROVING A PEER ASSISTANCE PROGRAM

In this chapter these are suggestions for key elements to consider in starting a new peer assistance/counseling program or enhancing the one you have. They include peer assistance software, a list of relevant materials for schools, using risk factors and recommended interventions, a model sponsoring agency for a county or city, peer assistance program, a sample parent letter and return form, a peer assistant report form, a Risk Assessment Survey: Paper and Pencil Short Form, a teacher referral form, and a curriculum guide.

INTRODUCTION

One of the critical resources for schools seeking to reduce dropout rates is your own students. Most school staff are familiar with the use of students as peer tutors, especially the use of older students to help younger students. This model suggests the use of same age students with their peers to help them become aware of the great risks they run by exhibiting behaviors that lead to dropout, such as the use of alcohol and drugs. Two-thirds of substance abusers drop out of school.

PEER ASSISTANCE SOFTWARE

The purpose of the peer assistance software, produced by Students-at-Risk, Inc., is to provide a student who has been trained to use the software a tool for carrying on a somewhat intimate conversation with another student who has been referred by a classroom teacher as a potential student at risk. Two-thirds of substance abusers eventually drop out of school, so this software, which is directed toward substance abuse, is also relevant for dropout prevention.

Figures 16.1 – 16.17 show the screens of the software.

Before the two students have been placed in front of an Apple II series, Macintosh, or IBM compatible computer to see the software, the school, staff member in charge should do the following:

(*1*) If your school has an operating peer assistance program or the equivalent, go to step 2 below. If you do not, you should see that a letter is sent home to the parent/guardian of the student who has been referred by a teacher as one who may be at risk of dropping out or becoming a substance abuser. See Figures 16.18 and 16.19 for samples of a parent permission letter and return form. Figure 16.20 presents a peer assistant report form.

(*2*) Peer assistance leaders should be identified and trained to use this software. At the minimum, this should include having the student sit and view the program on the computer you are using with the teacher or counselor in charge. There should be role-playing of possible difficult or confusing responses that at risk students might make.

(*3*) If your school does not have a peer assistance program or the equivalent, and you would like to develop one, you can purchase a training manual by Dr. Barbara Varenhorst titled *Curriculum Guide for Student Peer Assistance Training*. You can purchase this book and the other items mentioned in this chapter from Guidance Resources, Irvine Unified School District, 5050 Barranca, Irvine, CA 92714.

This program is designed as a peer counseling instrument to be used in programs which have a focus on factors of teenage substance abuse. This program is not intended to predict substance dependency in an individual. Rather, it is intended to be used as a part of a larger substance abuse program by trained peer counselors under adult supervision.

Press < return > to continue

Figure 16.1 Screen One.

Interview questions' instructions:

Respond to the following multiple choice questions by entering the number of the answer which best describes how you view yourself.

Press <return> to continue

Figure 16.2 Screen Two.

I view myself as

1. A nonuser of drugs or alcohol
2. An occasional user (that is, you have used drugs or alcohol within the last year, but not on an average of once a week)
3. A frequent user of drugs and alcohol (that is you have used marijuana or illegal drugs, prescription drugs or alcohol an average of one or more times a week during the past year)

Please Enter a number

Figure 16.3 Screen Three.

How important is it to you to get good grades in school?

1. Very important
2. Quite important
3. A little important
4. Not important

Please Enter a number

Figure 16.4 Screen Four.

Do you learn anything from drug prevention activities at school?

1. Very frequently

2. Frequently

3. Sometimes

4. Not at all

Please Enter a number

Figure 16.5 Screen Five.

How many of your closest friends use alcohol or other drugs?

1. None

2. One or two

3. Three or four

4. Five or more

Please Enter a number

Figure 16.6 Screen Six.

How much do some other members of your family drink or use drugs?

1. Not at all

2. Sometimes

3. Frequently

4. Very frequently

Please Enter a number

Figure 16.7 Screen Seven.

How much do you think your family is against drug and alcohol use?

1. Very much against

2. Quite a bit against

3. A little bit against

Please Enter a number

Figure 16.8 Screen Eight.

How many days have you been absent from school in the past year?

1. Zero to five times

2. Six to ten times

3. Eleven to fifteen times

4. Sixteen or more times

Please Enter a number

Figure 16.9 Screen Nine.

How many D's or F's did you receive in the last marking period?

1. None

2. One or two

3. Three or four

4. Five or more

Please Enter a number

Figure 16.10 Screen Ten.

How many times have you moved to a new residence (home) in the past year?

1. None

2. One or two times

3. Three or four times

4. Five or more times

Please Enter a number

Figure 16.11 Screen Eleven.

Based upon the responses which have been entered into the computer during the interview section of this program, the score total is _____.

This compares with scores on the following chart:

 9 to 16 Low potential

17 to 25 Medium potential

26 to 35 High potential

Please <return> to continue

Figure 16.12 Screen Twelve.

Instructions: the following questions are designed to be the starting point for peer discussions.

Recently, a midwestern state surveyed 7,000 employers to find out what their number one concern was when hiring new employees. The overwhelming majority put substance abuse in first place.

Please <return> to continue

Figure 16.13 Screen Thirteen.

There is a growing trend nationwide by employers to require drug testing as a condition of employment. These tests routinely look at both illegal and prescription drug levels, as well as alcohol levels in the human body. Recognizing that the effects of substance abuse stay with the body for long periods of time:

1. What kind of employment do you hope to have as an adult?
2. How will you react to employment opportunities that require you to submit a urine, blood or hair sample for drug analysis? What are some of the alternatives in this situation?
3. What are five advantages of working with other employees who are abuse free?
4. List five ways that activities you participate in outside of your job affect the company and its employees while you are on the job.

Please <return> to continue

Figure 16.14 Screen Fourteen.

259

By the year 2000, employment opportunities for high school dropouts will be severely restricted. Traditional areas of employment for dropouts and undereducated persons are being increasingly automated, or those activities are being filled by higher qualified persons as the trend toward underemployment continues. Suppose, for the purpose of these questions, that you have chosen to drop out of high school.

As a dropout:

1. Describe the type of life that you would like to live as an adult.
2. Describe a picture of what you consider to be an ideal family life.
3. List five kinds of long-term or steady employment opportunities that would be available to you.
4. Give three examples of ways that you might be able to improve your future while working full time.

Please <return> to continue

Figure 16.15 Screen Fifteen.

Ancient saying states that:

People can be measured by the friends that they associate with.

1. What percentage of your friends (those people that you frequently associate with) do not use or experiment with drugs?
2. What changes would you have to make in your life to establish firm friendships with five more persons who are not substance abusers?
3. What value do you see in high school graduation based on your observations of the lives of others who have graduated? Why?
4. What changes would you have to make in your life to establish firm friendships with five or more persons whom you feel will graduate from high school?
5. What percentage of your friends do you think will graduate from high school.
6. What actions would you have to take to set an example with your friends, family and relatives, as a person who will become a successful, dependency-free adult? Are you willing to try? Why?

Please < return > to continue

Figure 16.16 Screen Sixteen.

This concludes the discussion program.

This starts you on the pathway to success.

PLEASE REMOVE THIS DISK FROM THE COMPUTER DISK

DRIVE NOW AND TURN OFF THE COMPUTER.

Figure 16.17 Screen Seventeen.

Dear Parents:

As you are aware, drug abuse has become a serious problem across our nation. Research shows that many users begin using drugs as early as elementary school. Schools and parents need to unite to prevent the continual spread of drug abuse, so that students are given the opportunity to reach their learning potential.

We know you share our interest in eliminating drug abuse in our community. Therefore we are asking you to give permission for your child to participate in this project. Thank you for your cooperation and support in this matter.

Sincerely,

Assistant Superintendent

Figure 16.18 Sample Parent Letter.

Dear Administrator:

I have read the above letter and I give my permission for my son/daughter

_____ to participate in the Peer Assistance program. I understand my child will participate in a computerized survey with another student to learn about the risk involved in drug use. It is my further understanding that:

- The student peer assistants are trained to keep information confidential and to respect student participants' privacy.
- Interview data will be thrown away.
- Students will be identified only by number.
- Students will not be labeled.
- Student participation will not affect school performance.

Parent Signature _____

Date _____

Figure 16.19 Sample Return Form.

```
┌─────────────────────────────────────────────────────────┐
│                         Report                            │
│                                                           │
│   Name of Peer Adviser _____   │
│                                                           │
│                                                           │
│   Name of Peer Assistant _____  │
│                                                           │
│                                                           │
│   Name of Student Participant _____  │
│                                                           │
│                                                           │
│   What were the key problem areas discussed?              │
│                                                           │
│                                                           │
│                                                           │
│   What suggestions were discussed?                        │
│                                                           │
│                                                           │
│                                                           │
│   Signatures                                              │
│                                                           │
│                                                           │
│   Peer Adviser _____  │
│                                                           │
│                                                           │
│   Peer Assistant _____  │
│                                                           │
│                                                           │
│   Student Participant _____  │
│                                                           │
│                                                           │
│   Date of Report _____  │
└─────────────────────────────────────────────────────────┘
```

Figure 16.20 *Sample Peer Assistant Report Form.*

263

(4) Select your at-risk students for participation in the use of the peer assistance software. If your school already has a means for identifying at-risk students, you should use it, or you can use the results of the comprehensive risk assessment software. This software is designed to identify students who are potential substance abusers and potential dropouts. This is critical, but districts find they also need to set up effective interventions in order to assist students at risk. Irvine Unified School District has developed many such interventions, which have been carefully evaluated and found to be effective. These are now for sale. Your district, no doubt, has a number of interventions that are also effective. Finally, districts need a quick and reliable way to place students who have been identified into these interventions. We can now do this with the comprehensive risk assessment software. Lists of students for placement into interventions are printed out, and these are sent to student study teams or the equivalent for final decision about placement. This saves precious teacher time. The study team then needs to initiate a tracking and follow-up system to make sure that the students actually attend the interventions and that they are improving. This is judged by entering new data about their performance each semester and printing out their new, and hopefully improved, risk scores. At the end of the year, you can have your staff complete the completion of interventions form as part of your program evaluation.

(5) The staff member in charge then arranges for pairs of students to meet and view the peer assistance software, with the peer assistance leader playing the role of host.

(6) If the at-risk student scores as a moderate- or high-risk individual when his/her score is reported in the software program, the peer assistance leader should indicate this to the staff member in charge. Many schools like to use an informal, verbal report in this situation in order to keep the process low-key and nonthreatening. The peer assistance software is designed so that it does not save student responses, nor does it print them out. We feel this also reduces the likelihood of the process being perceived as threatening by the student at risk.

(7) Once the moderate- and high-risk students have been referred to the staff member in charge, s/he refers them to the principal or his/her designee for appropriate assistance. Chapter 5 of this book is helpful in guiding teachers to effective interventions.

(*8*) If you decide to establish a peer assistance program, one or two of your teachers will need to be trained to be trainers of the student peer assistance leaders. The training focuses upon the following areas:
- communications
- listening
- decision making
- problem solving
- understanding teenage issues
- referral system policies and procedures
- the role of the peer assistant

LIST OF RELEVANT MATERIALS FOR SCHOOLS

Middle and High School Materials

(*1*) *Real Friends;* a book young people can read and use for self- and peer facilitation. Written by Dr. Barbara Varenhorst, formerly from Palo Alto Unified School District; order from Harper and Rowe Publishers, Keystone Industrial Park, Scranton, PA 18512.

(*2*) *Caring and Sharing: Becoming a Peer Facilitator;* a student handbook for learning helping skills. Written by Robert D. Myrick and Tom Erney; order from Educational Media Corporation, P.O. Box 21211, Minneapolis, MN 55421.

(*3*) *Telesis;* Telesis Peer Counseling and Training Curriculum with workbooks in English, Spanish, Laotian, Cambodian, and Vietnamese. The curriculum addresses self-awareness, group dynamics, decision making, pharmacology, communication, counseling, and peer leadership. Order from Telesis Corporation, 3180 University Avenue, Suite 640, San Diego, CA 92104.

Additional Junior High and Middle School Materials

(*1*) *Starting Conflict Manager Programs;* tells how to set up a school program to reduce conflict. *Training Middle School Conflict Managers;* tells how to train middle school students to help other students reduce conflict. Order from Community Boards Center for Policy and Training, 148 Ninth Street, San Francisco, CA 94103.

(*2*) *"Just Say 'NO' " Guide*; for adult leaders of ''Just Say NO Clubs.'' Order from ''Just Say NO'' Foundation, 1777 N. California Blvd. # 200, Walnut Creek, CA 94596.

Elementary School Materials

(1) Project Self Esteem; a personal/social skills curriculum for second through sixth grade students, taught by teams of parent volunteers or teachers. Written by Sandy McDaniel and Peggy Bielen; order from Enhancing Education, P.O. Box 16001, Newport Beach, CA 92656.

(2) Training Elementary School Conflict Managers; tells how to train elementary school students to help other students reduce conflict. Order from Community Boards Center for Policy and Training, 148 Ninth Street, San Francisco, CA 94103.

(3) "Just Say 'No' " Guide; for adult leaders of ''Just Say NO Clubs.'' Order from ''Just Say NO'' Foundation, 1777 N. California Blvd. # 200, Walnut Creek, CA 94596.

High School Material

(1) Choices: A Teen Woman's Journal for Self Awareness and Personal Planning and *Challenges: A Young Man's Journal for Self Awareness and Personal Planning;* designed to assist young women and men to develop skills in the areas of goal setting and decision making. Appropriate for youth and as a training guide for adults; written by

Training Conflict Managers for Grade 4.

Bingham, Edmandson and Stryker. Order from Mission Publications, P.O. Box 25, El Toro, CA 92630.

Middle and Elementary School Materials

(*1*) *STAR Curriculum;* a social skills curriculum of fifty lessons for sixth through eighth grade students. Written by Guidance Resources staff, Irvine, USD. Order from Guidance Resources, Irvine Unified School District, 5050 Barranca Parkway, Irvine, CA 92714.

(*2*) *STAR Kit;* one curriculum, fifteen student workbooks, one set of task cards, audiotapes, workbook, activity cards, and one student and one parent handbook. Written by Guidance Resources staff, Irvine USD. Order from Guidance Resources, Irvine Unified School District, 5050 Barranca Parkway, Irvine, CA 92714.

(*3*) *Friends Can Be Good Medicine;* K – 12 curriculum about relationships and well-being. Written by staff at the California Department of Mental Health. Order from California Department of Mental Health, Publications Unit, 1600 9th Street, Sacramento, CA 95814.

(*4*) *More Teachable Moments;* K – 12 curriculum that helps develop expert listening skills using student and teacher awareness of the ways we sometimes do not listen. Written by Cliff Durfee; order from Live, Love and Laugh, P.O. Box 9432, San Diego, CA 92109.

Grades 3, 5, and 7 Materials

(*1*) *Y.E.S. Curriculum;* Unique model prevention curriculum designed to help infuse current anti-drug/gang messages into subject area curricula. Order from Orange County Department of Education, Media Services Unit, P.O. Box 9050, Costa Mesa, CA 92628.

RISK FACTORS AND RECOMMENDED INTERVENTIONS

This is a more complete list of risk factors than are used in the comprehensive risk assessment system; those used in that system are marked with an asterisk (*).
Response selected is in parentheses.

(*1*) With whom do you live? (any other answer than two parents)
• Interview student to determine any associated problems.

- If indicated, teach coping skills for major change, i.e.,
  STAGES (Irvine Unified School District, 1987a) lessons.
- If indicated, provide parent support group or refer for
  counseling.

*(2) How important is it to you to get good grades in school? (not
important)
- Interview student to determine reason.
- Check school records for grades and achievement.
- If indicated, refer for special education screening.
- If indicated, teach study skills.
- If indicated, conduct activities to increase student's bonding
  to school, i.e., opportunities for recognition.

(3) Do you ever argue with teachers? (often or very often)
- Interview to determine reason.
- If indicated, train in (STAR) assertive communication,
  (GOAL) accountability, or (PLUS) problem-solving skills.
- Train teacher(s) in cooperative discipline.

*(4) Are you absent from school when you are not sick? (4−7 days)
- Interview to determine reason.
- If indicated, implement school bonding activities, i.e.,
  assign to a staff mentor.
- Monitor and/or contract for school attendance.

*(5) Have you ever been suspended or expelled from school? (yes)
- Interview for dates and specifics.
- If indicated, monitor student behavior and/or increase school
  bonding.

(6) What do you learn from school prevention activities . . . ? (nothing or a little)
- Interview for reason.
- If student is high risk (has several risk factors), provide
  secondary drug prevention activities, i.e., more intense drug
  education/counseling in small group.

(7) How many times have you used a prescription drug without a
doctor? (2−6 or more times)
- Provide specialized drug education/counseling in small
  group.

(8) Where did you learn most of what you know about drugs? (other
than school or parents)
- If indicated, provide correct drug education information.
- Train parents how to talk to youth about drugs.

(9) How many of your close friends use alcohol or drugs? (3 − 5 or more)
- Compare to student's own level of use.
- If indicated, teach (STAR) peer refusal skills.
- Provide opportunities for interaction with nonusing peers.

(*10*) How many times have you used marijuana? (6 or once a week for past 3 mo.)
- Provide specialized drug education/counseling in small group.

(*11*) What would you do if a friend asked you to use marijuana? (I'm not sure or I would try it)
- Interview for reason.
- If indicated, teach (STAR) refusal skills.

(*12*) How often do you feel angry? (often or very often)
- Interview for reason.
- Provide opportunity for counseling.
- If indicated, teach (STAGES) coping and anger management skills.
- If indicated, teach (STAR or PLUS) relaxation skills.

(*13*) How often do you argue with your family? (often or very often)
- Interview for reason.
- If indicated, refer for family counseling.
- If indicated, refer parents for education on family communication.

(14) How much are your parents against your use of drugs? (not at all or mildly)
- Interview for reason.
- If indicated, refer parents for education on clarifying/communicating values.
- If indicated, counsel student on being responsible for self.

(15) How much do adults you are close to use drugs? (often or very often)
- Interview to determine relationship (parents, sibs, or other) and impact.
- If indicated, provide student counseling support for family member's use.
- If indicated, counsel student on being responsible for self.

(*16*) How often do you smoke cigarettes? (1 − 2 or more a day)
- Educate about risk factors for drug abuse.

*(*17*) Have you ever been arrested? (yes)

(*18*) How old were you the first time you were arrested? (any answer)
  - Interview for reason and date.
  - If indicated, monitor for antisocial tendencies.
  - Create opportunities for prosocial behavior.
  - If indicated, teach (GOAL or PLUS) self-control skills.

(*19*) How old were you when you had your first alcoholic drink (more than a sip)? (under 15 years)
  - Educate about risk factors for drug abuse.

(*20*) How often did you drink last year? (once a week or every day)
  - Educate about risk factors for drug abuse.

(*21*) How many times have you been drunk or high? (3−6 or more times)
  - Provide drug education and counseling.
  - If indicated, provide opportunities for alternative high experiences.

*(*22*) When you are away from home, after school and evenings, how often do your parents know where you are? (seldom or never)
  - Interview for specifics.
  - If indicated, refer parents for education on limit setting.

(*23*) If you had a personal problem, with whom would you talk? (not mother or father)
  - Interview for extent and balance in student's support system.
  - If indicated, refer parents and youth to improve communication skills.

(*24*) Does your family have rules and are they enforced? (none or a few)
  - Interview for outcomes of rule enforcement.
  - If indicated, refer parents for education on limit setting.
  - If indicated, counsel student on self discipline skills.

(*25*) How many times have you tried illegal drugs? (3−6 or more times)
  - Educate on risk factors for drug abuse.

A MODEL SPONSORING AGENCY FOR A COUNTY- OR CITYWIDE PEER ASSISTANCE PROGRAM

The Orange County Substance Abuse Prevention Network

A major issue facing society is the extent and depth of substance use and abuse among our youth. Concerned adults commonly ask questions such as

- How can we keep children from experimenting with drugs in today's chemically oriented society?
- What can we do if a child is experimenting with drugs?
- Where can we go for help?

The Orange County Substance Abuse Prevention Network is a coalition of public/private agencies and organizations providing substance abuse prevention and treatment services in Orange County. Participants include parents, educators, treatment providers, law enforcement officers, and social service representatives.

Objectives

- coordinate countywide prevention efforts
- participate in the planning and funding of drug abuse prevention projects for Orange County
- provide training and technical assistance
- seek legislative support and funding for prevention projects
- participate in regional, state, and national prevention planning efforts

Agencies

- Agape Counseling and Therapy Services
- Breakaway Health Corp.
- Care Action
- Center for Creative Alternatives
- Center for Family Counseling
- National Council on Alcoholism
- Neidhardt, Ryan & Waln Counseling Assoc.
- Orange County Alcohol Program
- Orange County Drug Abuse Services
- Orange County "Just Say NO" Clubs
- Orange County Trauma Society
- PAL Program
- Phoenix House
- Charter Hospital Long Beach
- CompCare – Care Units
- Cypress Police Dept.
- Junior League of Orange County

- KIDS of Southern California
- Project NODS
- Project Self-Esteem
- Psycho Neurological Institute
- Second Chance Adolescent Program
- Straight Talk Clinic, Inc.
- Western Center for Drug-Free Schools
- Youth and Family Recovery Center

Parent Groups

- C.A.S.A., North Orange County
- CASA, Orange Unified School District
- Irvine Chemical People
- Parents Who Care—Newport Beach
- Parents Who Care—Tustin
- PRIDE—Newport Mesa

Chapter 17

FUNDING PREVENTION AND EARLY INTERVENTION PROGRAMS

Having needs for service can be very frustrating when there is no money to meet those needs. Working in a high-need situation over time can lead to staff burnout, because good ideas stop and energy is used, instead, to distance and protect the self from feeling overwhelmed by the needs we do not have the resources to meet.

Unfortunately, there are no automatic answers to funding programs and maintaining good morale in school-based prevention workers. However, there is often a high correlation between well-funded and implemented programs and a high sense of efficacy among staff and program participants.

INTRODUCTION

There are several successful techniques that have been used to achieve stable or increased funding, and it all goes back to caring, energetic staff with good ideas. A plan to stabilize funding over time should include a number of strategies. It's a lot like the mutual fund concept in that you don't want to be overly dependent on any one income source. In addition to writing proposals for increased funding, which we will describe in detail, program planners may want to try other strategies as well, including the following:

(*1*) Review who benefits from your service, either directly or indirectly. Have you asked them to contribute in some way? Contribution could be through matching funds, in-kind services, or as volunteers, perhaps. If you can't find *some* support at this level, perhaps your service is not valued as it exists and needs to be restructured or your service population may need education regarding the benefits of the service.

(2) As a work group, develop or review your mission statement, purpose, or goal statement. Are your program activities related to it? Time management is easier and programs are better implemented and funded when you focus time on tasks relating to the mission. A mission helps you see the big picture, as well as the current needs you are striving to meet.

(3) Think creatively about how you do what you do. This is often done best in a brainstorming group session. Is there another way? What resources, human, technical, or communicationally based do you think would make it work better? How do you know it works? Can you find out?

(4) Maintain an attitude that experimentation (willingness to change) is positive, and look for new things to try, while keeping what works and discarding or revising what doesn't work (even if it was *your* idea). The habit of focusing on positive outcomes, with the belief that good ideas will appear, goes a long way toward maintaining good morale.

(5) Can you expand your vision in a way that is complementary to the mission and brings in resources, such as training or providing materials to others? Related to this is the need to let others know about what works in your program. Sharing information through newspaper articles, publications, presentations, and networking can start new income sources you hadn't even thought about.

(6) Focus some energy on getting resources to try out your ideas. You can often do this quickly on a small scale or pilot by convincing key supporters how it will benefit them or something they care about. Persuading key supporters to operate differently or to contribute manpower or financial support usually involves writing a case statement, which details why an institution merits support, with considerable documentation of its services, resources, needs, and potential for greater services and future plans. A case statement should focus on a positive outcome (i.e., helping youth become productive citizens, not stopping delinquency), as well as address the information needs of the target audience, not internal reviewers (Kappel, 1993).

(7) Identify funding resources that are interested in funding your ideas and write proposals to them. Since many innovations get started

through governmental or private competitive funding of proposals, this is described in greater detail.

WRITING PROPOSALS FOR OUTSIDE FUNDING

Certainly, one of the more enjoyable ways to develop identification and intervention services for at-risk students is to apply for and receive additional funds from government or private sources. Although grant writing is labor-intensive and not guaranteed, receiving a grant, like childbirth, makes up for a lot of pain. The key to successful grant writing is, first, to clearly think though your idea, get excited about it, and then describe it clearly in writing.

The second important key to grant writing is to carefully follow the directions given by the funding agency, e.g., clearly respond to each grant section. Typical grant headings include an assessment of need and identification of the target group, identification of project aims, background and significance of the new effort, description of objectives and activities for the project, project design and methods, formative and summative evaluation, plan of operation, budget and cost-effectiveness, and commitment and capacity.

Here, we have included brief "starter" sentences from proposals to illustrate the various sections. These sections would typically be reordered and renamed to fit the suggestions of the Request for Proposal from the funding agency. Chapter 9 provides the type of detail seen in a typical proposal.

Need/Target Population

A winning proposal typically includes a strong presentation of need for the activities that are listed in the proposed project. Take time to gather information from staff and other research sources about the special need for your new effort. This is often a good section to define the target population with lots of descriptive words and numbers to present the need. Try to show how some promising things have been accomplished, but that more resources will really make all the difference in building the new approach. Example:

The magnitude of alcohol and other drug abuse problems has caused increasing nationwide concern among educators, policymakers, and the community at large. Although the rates of drug use have declined

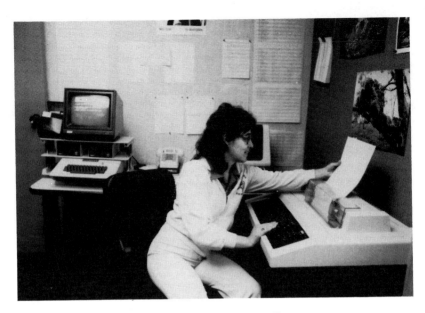

Identifying Potential Substance Abusers.

recently (NIDA, 1988), smoking and drinking are still very prevalent teenage activities. In fact, high school students in the U.S. are more involved with illicit drugs than youth in any other industrialized nation (Johnson et al., 1989). A recent survey of drug use and dropouts in California and Irvine found . . .

Project Aims

Present the purpose of the project clearly, demonstrating an understanding of what research indicates is effective. Example:
The aims of the District At-Risk Management Project are to develop a computer management system that will a) identify potential substance abusers and potential dropouts and b) use an expert system to connect identified students at risk with appropriate interventions that will reduce student risk levels.

Background and Significance

Describe background steps logically, leading to the current proposal. Example:

Project activities were developed during the past eight years from needs assessments with staff and students and a review of the current literature on high-risk and substance-abusing students. Components respond to the research findings, particularly the research on high-risk factors for adolescents.

Objectives and Activities of the Project

Present a plan for accomplishing the aim of the project, describing the objectives to be accomplished and the activities that will lead to the completion of these objectives. Example:

The proposed program offers a comprehensive holistic approach for preventing alcohol and other drug use by 500 high risk middle school students. The project addresses the needs of the student, his family, the school, and community, in a comprehensive approach to prevention, through the following:

Student objective: Decrease the use of alcohol and other drugs in participating students at a .05 level of significance.

Student activity: Provide individual and small group counseling to identified students.
Assign and monitor progress of identified students in interventions.

School objective: Increase knowledge and skill levels of educators to implement interventions to reduce risk factors, as measured by pre/postassessment.

School activity: Train staff in use of computer management system to identify and intervene with at-risk students.

Family objective: Increase parent knowledge of risk and protective factors and improve family management skills, as measured by pre/post assessment.

Family activity: Provide education, support, and referral services for parents of identified high-risk students.

Project Design and Methods

Describe the process of program services as part of the overall design and describe individual program components more completely if necessary. Example:

A data-gathering system involving students, parents, school personnel, and community resources to identify students who need help is
being developed.

- A data base of all students in the district identifying the lower
  quadrant based on academics, low test scores, and students
  exhibiting at-risk behaviors is being developed.
- A referral form for teachers who have identified a problem
  with a student and a procedure for handling referrals and
  tracking disposition of each referral is being developed.
- An information system to let referring teachers know the
  disposition of the referral is being developed.
- A plan for sharing information with parents of students will
  be developed.

Formative and Summative Evaluation

Describe your evaluation plan, linking it to the measurement of
objectives you described. Try to think of an accurate and easily gathered
measure of your success in each area. The evaluation ought to focus upon
two areas: 1) process (Are the steps to achieve outcomes conducive to
program success?) and 2) product (How well is the program accomplishing its specified objectives?). Example:
Teacher knowledge and skills in implementing the computer management system will be measured by locally developed pre/post tests and
observation checklists. Outcome evaluation will be based on significant
changes (improvement at the .05 level) in baseline data gathered from
participant surveys on drug use against which future drug use and
parenting practices of high-risk students' parents will be compared.

Plan of Operation/Budget and Cost-Effectiveness

List general information describing your organization, including the
line of authority and role definitions for project staff. Generally describe
and support the budget requested. Example:
The board of education is responsible for the project and management
operations. The project director will coordinate all program activities
and supervise project staff.
The budget is adequate to complete project activities and is cost-
effective in that . . .

Accomplishments/Capacity and Commitment

List any related accomplishments of your program and how they relate to the present effort. Show commitment to continue activities beyond the funding period. Example:
The district has a history of commitment to addressing the needs of at-risk students and has developed a number of innovative prevention programs, e.g., the STAGES Program, which assists at-risk students in being successful in school despite stressful changes in their lives. This proposal develops an at-risk management system, which complements these existing prevention and identification strategies now in place. This at-risk management system will make a significant impact on reducing student drug use by creating a computerized delivery system for drug abuse prevention and intervention that utilizes the latest research to predict potential abusers and dropouts with an identification system that, in turn, links to some of the most effective interventions in the country. The identification and intervention services will continue after initial funding through . . .

Chapter 18

DEVELOPING HUMAN RESOURCES
FOR PREVENTION

The two sources of support that may be most available to staff in a local school district for dropout prevention, job training, and job placement are funds from a local or area foundation and the use of volunteers. These sources are related in that you may use one to gain access to the other. Typically, the use of volunteers increases your credibility, and this makes you a candidate for foundation support. The use of volunteers will also increase your chances for state and federal funds for substance abuse and gang prevention efforts.

ENLISTING VOLUNTEER SUPPORT

The primary sources for volunteers may be churches and local service clubs. For example,

(*1*) Ask an administrator which administrators in your district are members of Rotary, Kiwanis, Optimists, and so forth.

(*2*) Ask that administrator to give you the name and telephone number of the club member who is most sympathetic to dropouts and similar causes.

(*3*) Write up one page about your project, make copies of it, and give several to the sympathetic club member.

(*4*) Ask the club member to help you contact the program chair so you can make a presentation at their club to ask for volunteers. Make up a second one-page description of what types of volunteer jobs there are, how much time they take, and whom to contact.

(*5*) Ask the program chair what the priority areas are for all the local

Older Students Can Suggest Possible Volunteers.

service clubs—you may find another club that is your best bet for help.

Go through the same process for enlisting help from local churches. Retired people are a good bet and can often suggest other avenues to try.

Once you have a couple of volunteers working, write up what they are doing for you in about two pages and then seek the names of local or area foundations. Probably the best way to do this is to contact the fundraising office of your nearest university and get names and telephone numbers from them.

When you get the contact name, call them and ask if they are interested in your type of project. Usually, the answer is no for X and Y reasons. Tell them a bit about your project and ask them to tell you which area foundations might support you.

Send the candidate foundation a letter indicating who recommended you contact them, along with your two-page description. Tell them you are using volunteers and doing everything you can to be efficient. Ask to meet with them personally. Once you have met with them, ask if you can write a brief proposal and get them to help you follow their procedures.

POLICY RECOMMENDATIONS

Districts should consider using two support services that may be available for assisting at-risk students to obtain job training and job placement. These are local service clubs and businesses. In order to have credibility with them, administrators should become members of the service clubs and participate in their activities.

Chapter 19

THE COCAINE PROBLEM

Although the use of the coca plant has continued for centuries, over the last decade, cocaine has become especially popular. The notoriety and controversy of cocaine addiction, in addition to law enforcement's efforts to stop cocaine dealers, have grabbed the country's attention. The crack epidemic then began in 1985, which led to a doubling of the number of three to five year olds in special education in Miami and Los Angeles.

INTRODUCTION

During the last decade, cocaine has become very popular — not just the use of cocaine but also the notoriety and controversy of its addiction. You constantly view or hear stories of cocaine use through movies, television shows, songs, books, and magazine cover stories. There has been mounting evidence citing the hazards of cocaine, but the number of people using cocaine continues to rise.

Between 1920 and the 1970s, cocaine use was restricted to the elite. The users were "the rich and famous," musicians and film stars. The popular stimulant of choice was amphetamines. In the 1930s, amphetamines were prescribed by physicians as diet pills and "pep pills." But during the 1960s, cocaine became the "champagne" of drugs. In 1974, a survey conducted by the National Institute on Drug Abuse revealed that approximately 5 million Americans had used cocaine at least once. By 1982, that figure had reached 22 million. In 1973, less than 1% of university students responding to a survey on drug use admitted to having tried cocaine. Nine years later in a similar study, 30% of the student population had used the drug. In 1985, a national survey revealed that 17% of American high school seniors had tried cocaine; over one-third of that group had the drug within the previous month (Weiss and Mirin, 1987).

During a conference held by the Los Angeles County Office of Education on Perinatal Substance-Exposed Children on April 28, 1993, Dr. Sanders-Phillips, Associate Professor of Pediatrics at the University of California, Los Angeles, stated that, in 1982, 4.1 million people, twelve years old or older, used cocaine. One to four have substance abuse problems. She felt these numbers were underestimated. She also stated that 60,000 women have drug problems that cut across all economic and cultural barriers (Los Angeles County Office of Education, 1993).

In a hearing before the Committee on the Judiciary, United States Senate, on May 16, 1991, Senator Edward Kennedy reported that there were a quarter of a million pregnant substance abusers in this country, and only 30,000 (one in eight) receive treatment for their addiction. During the same hearing, Senator Christopher Dodd stated that 40% of the births at the Metropolitan Hospital in New York, which is on the edge of Spanish Harlem, were in intensive care and that he assumed a great percentage of those children had been exposed to cocaine or other drugs. He also stated that, in New Haven, Connecticut, which has the highest infant mortality rate of any city of its size in the country, in the midst of a state that has the highest per capita income in the country, 49% of a survey of children born at a low-income clinic had been exposed to cocaine.

Over the past twenty years, drug use in America has increased tremendously. With more people using drugs, there has been a rise in people hospitalized for addiction or who have had to seek medical treatment because of cocaine-related difficulties. During 1985–1987, the first years of the current crack epidemic, children were born to mothers who were drug users. In two of the cities first hit by the crack cocaine epidemic, Miami and Los Angeles, the number of three to five year olds in special education has doubled since 1986 when this epidemic began (U.S. Department of Education, 1991).

Currently, cocaine use is still on the rise, despite the efforts of medical, social, and educational services to educate the American people to the dangers of cocaine use and other drugs—alcohol and tobacco included. One of the reasons cocaine/crack use is still rising is the cost. Crack, a cheaper form of cocaine, has hit the streets and is now even more affordable.

THE HISTORY OF COCAINE

Cocaine is a stimulant derived from the leaves of the coca plant, *Erythroxylum*. The leaves of the plant were ritually chewed by South

American peoples for their stimulant effect thousands of years ago. Coca was believed to be a mystical drug and was used in religious rituals by the Incas in ancient Peru. The plant was believed to be of divine origin, and the Peruvians had several myths to account for its appearance on earth. During the period of Incan rule, coca was felt to be a magical offering from the gods to ensure a safe passage through the Andes. The plant relieved symptoms of altitude sickness, alleviated feelings of hunger and thirst, minimized sensitivity to heat or cold, and increased endurance in physical labor.

Archaeologists have found evidence of coca dating back as far as 2000 B.C. in the Valdivia culture and materials of coca dating back to the Preceramic period along the Peruvian coast dated about 1600 B.C. It is thought that coca has been used in Ecuador for 5,000 years. There is a suggestion that the use of coca was introduced into Ecuador with the Inca conquest, but it is now certain that the chewing of these stimulant leaves is very ancient in Ecuador and that cultivation of the coca plant may have begun on the eastern slopes of the Ecuadorian or Peruvian Andes (Fisher et al., 1987).

Spaniards operating silver mines in Bolivia in the sixteenth century discovered that Indian slave laborers who chewed coca leaves worked longer hours with less food. After the decline of the Incan empire in the fifteenth century, the Spanish conquistadors took over the cultivation and distribution of coca and used it to force the Andean Indians to work under adverse conditions of brutal labor and little food. Eventually, the Spaniards learned how to enjoy the coca themselves and introduced it to Europe. Then, in 1860, an Austrian chemist, Niemann, discovered how to extract cocaine from the coca leaf. Soon after, cocaine was being used by many doctors for personal use and experiments.

S. F. is a brilliant young physician attending a case conference at a metropolitan medical center where he is a resident. He has been on-call for 36 hours and cannot concentrate on the presentation. S. F. is lonely, depressed, and overworked. All he can think about is his fiancee, who is several hundred miles away. He knows that her father will not permit her to marry until he is able to support her, and with his loans and meager salary that could take years. He excuses himself from the conference, takes a needle from the nurses' station, locks himself in a bathroom stall. He fills the syringe with cocaine and plunges the needle into his arm. Within seconds, the young doctor feels a rush of euphoria. His tears dry up; he regains his composure and quickly rejoins the conference. (Spitz and Rosecan, 1987)

The doctor described above was Sigmund Freud in Vienna, 1884. Dr. Freud used cocaine himself, beginning in 1884 as a research experiment.

Freud was an advocate of "Uber Coca," cocaine, as a treatment of alcoholism, morphine addiction, asthma, and gastrointestinal disturbances, in addition to depression. Freud published his landmark paper, entitled "On Coca," where he describes the effects of cocaine as consisting of exhilaration and lasting euphoria and a sense of self-control; longlasting intensive mental or physical work could be performed without fatigue, and the need for food and sleep were completely banished. Freud also noted the drug's ability to relieve pain and, thus, paved the way for the discovery of cocaine as the first local anesthetic. But Freud's reports of cocaine and his belief that cocaine was nonaddicting became controversial by the end of the nineteenth century (Weiss and Mirin, 1987).

In the nineteenth century, a Corsican chemist named Angelo Mariani understood the power of cocaine, and he realized that there was money to be made from this new drug. So in 1863, he produced a mixture of coca leaves and wine, which he called Vin Mariani. This drink was successful and endorsed by kings, queens (Queen Victoria), a pope (Pope Leo XIII), and popular figures such as President Ulysses S. Grant, Thomas Edison, H. G. Wells, Sarah Bernhardt, the Czar of Russia, and Jules Verne.

In 1886, an American chemist named John Styth Pemberton created a new patent medicine that was advertised as a valuable brain tonic and cure for all nervous affections. This patent medicine was later promoted as a soft drink "Coca Cola," the real thing. Americans and Europeans discovered what the South American Indians had known for thousands of years: that the coca leaf could energize them, lift them up, and make them feel good. Today caffeine has replaced the cocaine in Coca Cola, but the beverage still includes the ingredients of the decocainized coca leaves as part of its natural flavors.

There were many reports of cocaine toxicity and addiction. American physicians became increasingly organized, and professional groups and journalists began questioning the addictive properties of cocaine. Popular newspapers wrote about the relationship between cocaine and criminal behavior. Then the movement to restrict the use of cocaine took a racist tone, which resulted in reports of murders by "crazed [black] cocaine takers" and "attacks upon white women of the South . . . as the direct result of the coke-crazed Negro brain." This combination of events led to cocaine being made illegal in 1914 with the Harrison Narcotic Act, the first federal antinarcotics law, which classified cocaine as a drug to be dispensed only by physicians under prescription. From

1914 until 1970, cocaine use "went underground" until it became popular again in the 1970s. In the mid-1980s a formula for a smokable inexpensive cocaine was popularized – crack.

WHAT IS CRACK?

Crack is cocaine. It comes in the form of small "rocks" of a creamy color that are like pieces of rock candy. The term *crack* refers to the crackling sound that is heard when it is smoked. It is different from the cocaine powder in three ways:

- It is smoked rather than sniffed, which leads to a high in less than ten seconds, and the high is more intense, lasting ten to forty minutes. The "fall" after using can be sudden and devastating. To avoid the painful depression that follows the high, crack users often binge. This repetitive behavior leads to dependence and addiction.
- When smoked, the effect is much more powerful than the powder. The drug goes directly from the lungs to the brain.
- Crack seems less expensive because it is sold in small quantities at a low price. Three to four small rocks are sold in a vial for $10 to $20. A binge session could cost as little as fifty dollars, which is considerably less than the thousands of dollars required for freebasing, or injecting, cocaine.

What is most significant about the development of crack is the placement of the most addictive form of cocaine into the hands of a full range of consumers, from all classes (economic) and all backgrounds (ethnicity). The use of cocaine is no longer the "champagne" of the rich and famous but has become a problem of the upper, middle, and lower classes.

You want to know how tough this drug is? When I smoked crack for the first time, I literally fell in love with the drug. I liked the feeling it gave me so much I thought, This is it. I want to marry this drug! (Chatlos, 1987, p. 11)

THE COCAINE DEALERS

The influx of cocaine into the United States as an illegal drug began in the 1920s as the entertainment industry's recreational pastime. In the late 1970s, cocaine began taking over the "recreational drug" industry. Cocaine as an illicit drug has contributed to criminal activities ranging from street crime to international drug trafficking, murder, violence, and political corruption. In 1985 to 1986, there was a sudden increase in murders, and some criminologists believe that this increase might have been caused by drug violence, in particular, cocaine-related activities. For example, New York City had 1,384 deaths in 1985 and 1,461 in 1986; Boston had eighty-seven homicides in 1985 and 106 in 1986 (Shaffer and Jones, 1989). Drug abuse is strange and sometimes not understood by those who are drug-free. However, drug abuse is a common pattern of human behavior.

It is important to remember that cocaine has been in use daily in many Central and South American countries. Yet the natives of these countries do not show or exhibit the addiction or abuse that the European and American people are experiencing. Although coca chewing may become habitual, true addiction, which in some cases may result from the use of pure cocaine, is not seen among the Indians who use coca leaves (Fisher et al., 1987).

Illicit drug trafficking is conservatively estimated to be a $100 billion a year business. Despite numerous efforts by the United States government to stop the overwhelming flow of cocaine into this country, production has increased. New countries such as Venezuela, Paraguay, and Trinidad have become involved in the drug trade business because of its profitability. Attempts to curb the cocaine trade have been unsuccessful. Law enforcement personnel have focused their efforts on eliminating local refineries in Bolivia, Peru, Venezuela, Panama, Argentina, and, in recent years, the United States. When federal drug enforcement officers began to eliminate the drug trafficking coming in through Miami, Florida, new ports of entry emerged in Texas, Arizona, California, and Mexico (Weiss and Mirin, 1987).

Law enforcement agencies also attempted to concentrate their efforts on eliminating the crops of coca leaves in Peru, Ecuador, Bolivia, and Brazil, but this also failed. For example, a group of Peruvian workers who had been paid by the United States to uproot and burn coca bushes were tortured and murdered (Weiss and Mirin, 1987). What law enforcement agencies fail to remember is that, in some South American countries, growing and selling coca leaves is perfectly legal. Natives drink coca leaf tea like Americans drink coffee and Coca Cola—for an energizing lift. The United States encouraged these countries to grow other crops, such as coffee instead of coca leaves, but it has been difficult to convince the farmers and poor nations to change because growing coca is much more profitable (Fisher et al., 1987). The natives along the Amazon River basin have also found a new strain of coca, Epadu, which can flourish in the jungle and can grow to up to 10 feet tall.

THE DRUG ENFORCEMENT AGENTS

The efforts of the United States government to stop the cocaine trade have been hindered because American cocaine users desperately want the drug, and drug manufacturers and traffickers are ultimately profiting. Attempts to restrict illicit drug trade have also lead to civil war. United States drug enforcement agents have been caught between drug lords and war lords. They have become targets between those who would disrupt and those who would maintain the international trafficking of cocaine. One such official was Enrique Camarena Salazar, a thirty-seven-year-old United States drug enforcement agent who had just left the office of the U.S. Consulate in Guadalajara. As Salazar walked away, he was intercepted by four men at gunpoint, shoved into a getaway car that drove away, and he has not been seen since (Shaffer and Jones, 1989).

In 1985, Colombia was suddenly a very dangerous place for Americans. The powerful Colombian cocaine cartel had threatened to kill five American citizens, including the children of American diplomats, for every alleged drug trafficker extradited. This threat sparked the evacuation of all the children and spouses of United States government personnel. The cocaine kingpins seemed as powerful as the Colombian government.

Colombia's biggest drug lords, Pablo Escobar (the son of a school teacher) and the Ochoa family, have surrendered and gone to jail, claiming they've retired. The world's most important drug bank, the notorious BCCI (Bank of Credit and Commerce International) has largely gone out of business.

General Manuel Antonio Noriega, who turned Panama into a narcotics way station, stood trial in Miami on drug conspiracy charges and was convicted. This sounds like a big victory in the "war on drugs," but the Medellin cartel has regrouped under younger, more sophisticated, and more dangerous leadership. The other problem is that there are other smaller, yet powerful, cartels in Bogota and Cali, two smaller cities in Colombia.

Drugs for war is another reason drug use in America has not ceased. There have been incidents where government officials may have swept information "under the rug" about drugs coming into the United States. One such incident was the Iran-Contra affair. It is suspected that the airplanes that airlifted weapons to the Contra rebels may have been used to return cocaine cargo that was then sold at handsome profits; these profits could have then been used to further subsidize the purchase of weapons. No one knows the full extent to which our government officials could not "just say no" to cocaine.

Chapter 20

DRUG-EXPOSED BABIES

The number of babies exposed to cocaine and other drugs is growing and doubling each year in major cities. Newborns become boarder babies as courts decide parental responsibility and custody. The characteristics of drug-exposed infants and preschoolers are described, as well as the environments most likely to provide positive outcomes for drug-exposed children.

WOMEN AND COCAINE

People take cocaine to alter their brain functions and thereby alter their mood and mental state. The positive effects of cocaine are all a direct result of cocaine-induced biochemical changes in brain activity. The positive effects of cocaine usually include a generalized state of euphoria in a combination of increased energy, confidence, mental alertness, and sexual arousal. Many people feel more talkative, more involved in their relationships with others, and more playful and spontaneous when high on cocaine. Preexisting shyness, tension, and fatigue may instantly appear.

Women who abuse cocaine, as with men, tend to be those women with underlying depression and low self-esteem; therefore, a drug that can increase self-confidence and mood is very appealing to women in American culture. Just as cocaine makes men feel more masculine, cocaine makes women feel more feminine and sexually less inhibited (Spitz and Rosecan, 1987). Cocaine is also an appetite suppressant, which makes it an appealing drug for a woman who desires to lose weight.

With the added responsibilities of a working woman, some women become trapped in a ''superwoman'' syndrome, struggling to maintain a career, to be a ''good mother,'' and to have a successful marriage or relationship. Spitz and Rosecan (1987) state that ''women in American society are undervalued, underpaid and overstressed.'' At times when women become stressed, they become depressed, which is more common in women than in men (Spitz and Rosecan, 1987). The use of cocaine tends to help some of these women with their responsibilities by giving them the illusion of coping with the sense of failure in a relationship, a job, or parenting skills. Cocaine acts as an antidepressant medication for many women. It gives them that extra energy (the ''high'') to cope with their daily routine. But, by increasing the use of cocaine, the euphoric ''high'' effects tend to decrease. In an attempt to regain the ''high'' and make it last, the woman increases her use of the drug even more. Ongoing cocaine use serves to affirm the sense of inadequacy the woman is already feeling, and the depression gets worse. A woman's world begins to crumble; she is unable to function at work and thus, loses her job. Her interest in sex decreases, her marriage or relationship breaks down, and her skills as a mother erode as well. This is usually the last function to fail in a woman (Spitz and Rosecan, 1987).

Women who start using drugs do not expect to become addicted. Dr. Sanders-Phillips and Spitz and Rosecan have each stated that many women initially use drugs because of spousal or male inducement. Spitz and Rosecan found, in a 1984 telephone survey of 165 women cocaine users, that 87% had been introduced to cocaine by men, and 65% were continuing to receive it as gifts, thus, becoming dependent on these men for cocaine (Los Angeles County Office of Education, 1993; Spitz and Rosecan, 1987).

As stated earlier, many women tend to become cocaine abusers because of their demanding role as a woman. Other women use cocaine to relieve the stress of being a successful working mother or to ease the pain of poverty. Shirley Davis, Director of Maternal Education for the City of St. Petersburg, Florida, reaffirms Dr. Sander-Phillips' statements that the number of women who use cocaine cuts across economic and cultural barriers. She also stated that, of the 60 million women of childbearing age, 5 million of these women use crack cocaine. Dr. Lisa Goldstein, UCLA Medical Center, went on to say that, of these women who are using cocaine, 15.4 million are Caucasian and 14.1 million African-American (Los Angeles County Office of Education, 1993).

WHY DO PREGNANT WOMEN USE COCAINE?

Pregnant women use cocaine for the same reasons that men or other women do. They want to experience a "high" that will briefly take their troubles away. The pregnancy may be unplanned or unwanted. Most women who use drugs or alcohol during pregnancy have well-established addictions before they become pregnant. Sometimes, in the early stages of pregnancy, women may not know they are pregnant. Some women live in abusive relationships; others are burdened by family problems and demands. They may be struggling to care for other children. Other women may be undereducated, unemployed, and living in poverty or on the edge of it. Villarreal et al. (1991) state that pregnant women who use dangerous substances are not deliberately trying to harm their fetuses. Many of these women are aware of how dangerous substance abuse is to their fetuses, but they are simply unable to stop using. The fact that they are pregnant should be (but isn't) motivation enough to get treatment and into a recovery program.

When a pregnant woman uses a chemical substance such as cocaine, the substance crosses the placental barrier and enters the fetal bloodstream. When a women smokes crack, she will experience constriction of blood flow to the placenta, and the fetus suffers constricted blood flow to its brain. Also, cocaine has the ability to cause fetal hypoxia (oxygen deprivation). The effects of this transplacental crossing can be mild. Although scientists know that cocaine can penetrate the placental barrier, they have had difficulty measuring the precise amounts that get through. A fetus's development may be accelerated or depressed for a short period of time. Depending on what stage the pregnancy is in and how frequently the mother is using drugs, the effects can also be severe and longlasting. For example, in a report done by Kathy A. Fackelmann (1991a), she states that, during the embryonic stage, the embryo starts to develop (arms, legs, toes, heart, lungs, brain, etc.), and if cocaine is used by the mother during this stage, the embryo may have malformations. During the fetal stage of development, Fackelmann goes on to say that the chemicals in the mother's bloodstream do not cause malformation but may induce brain damage and growth impairments. Most frightening of all, the fetus can also suffer many strokes while in the womb of an addicted woman. Either way, the infant suffers.

There seem to be many deciding factors that can impact the health of the fetus, and the pregnant woman always has the final decision. To review, if a pregnant woman is a polydrug user (a woman who uses cocaine, alcohol, and marijuana) or has had inadequate prenatal nutrition during her pregnancy, she is most likely going to give birth to a child who will suffer slow growth and small size. Further difficulties can include immaturity in the lungs, prematurity, newborn drug withdrawal, seizures, irritability, feeding problems, brain damage, developmental delay malformations of major organs (heart, kidney, brain), and sudden infant death syndrome, also known as SIDS (Los Angeles County Office of Education, 1993; Fackelmann, 1989; Waller, 1993). Yet, with all these risk factors to their unborn babies, the women continue the abuse of drugs.

Now, let's not forget about the fathers of the unborn babies. There is soft evidence that cocaine may "piggyback" on the male sperm into the female egg. As stated by Dr. Lisa Goldstein and reported by C. Ezzel in *Science News*, tiny specks of cocaine can attach to specific sites on human sperm. In a laboratory experiment done by Ricardo A. Yazigi of Temple University School of Medicine in Philadelphia, it was found that a dangerous drug could piggyback its way into a new embryo by hitching a ride on the fertilizing sperm and perhaps harming the embryo's development (Los Angeles County Office of Education, 1993; Ezzel, 1991). It seems apparent that medical scientists have realized that women are not the only responsible parties in the healthy conception and development of the unborn babies.

DRUG-EXPOSED BABIES

The number of cocaine-exposed babies is growing and doubling each year in major cities. These babies have not only been exposed to cocaine, but it is also highly possible that they have been exposed to marijuana, alcohol, tobacco, and AIDS (mothers trade sex for crack cocaine). In the United States, the number of cocaine-exposed infants is as high as 200,000. This number may also be incorrect because inner-city hospitals are the only ones that require pregnant women to be tested for drug abuse when delivering. Private hospitals do not require such testing, and, therefore, the exact number of drug-exposed infants is not known.

The problem of drug-exposed infants born in the United States is not only the problem of cities, but also has reached the suburbs and rural towns. The impact on hospital pediatric wards is overwhelming. Hospital storage rooms are now being used for "storing babies." The newborns become "boarder babies"; they live in the hospital, usually one to two months and wait for the social worker to conduct and conclude the investigation of the natural mother and her home environment. The case workers will decide which babies can go home with mom and which babies go into foster care.

Newborns who have been exposed to drugs prenatally were given a test on the ability to stay alert. These infants scored poorly on the test compared to infants who were not exposed to drugs during pregnancy. These babies had attention and orientation problems and were less likely to respond to a human voice or face. Fackelmann also reported that cocaine-exposed infants are irritable, or they become so overwhelmed that they shut down or go into a deep sleep (Fackelmann, 1989). In Revkin's (1989) article, he also reports how Dr. Ira Chasnoff of Northwestern Memorial Hospital in Chicago found that infants who were prenatally exposed to cocaine showed an eight- to ten-week period of extremely disturbed behavior. The tragedy of this, Chasnoff says, is "that's exactly when the newborn infant begins to interact with its mother, begins to bond, to have a relationship with its environment" (Revkin, 1989). Cocaine-exposed babies spend all of their time crying, being irritable, or in a deep sleep. Just picking the babies up can set them off crying or shaking. These infants tend to reject intimate contact. Trying to make eye contact with a cocaine-exposed infant will cause a behavior called gaze aversion. This happens when you make eye contact with the baby, it gets overloaded, and the baby shuts down and closes its eyes. It's like the baby doesn't want to deal with its cruel introduction to life.

THE FIRST YEARS

At the time a child with prenatal drug or alcohol exposure is born and during the first several years of life, it cannot be determined what the developmental outcomes of a child will be with certainty. As the child grows and reaches school age, he or she may develop problems that were not originally anticipated. But, with appropriate early interventions and prognoses, the child may "catch up" and accomplish much more than was originally expected. The key is early intervention.

Infants who have been drug-exposed have a variety of problems as they grow and develop. They require special attention in many areas. These children present a challenge to their parents or caregivers (a child's primary support person such as a parent, foster parent, grandparent, aunt, uncle, cousin, or adult sibling). The simple task of taking care of the infant, such as picking the baby up, changing its diapers, feeding, or putting it down to sleep, can be a big ordeal (Villarreal et al., 1991).

The babies become irritable because they are being overstimulated by the simple caregiving tasks. The stimulation of their environment is too powerful. They are raw and sensitive because they have not developed as fully or in the same manner as children without chemical exposure, and they do not know how to screen out all the painful distractions (Griffith, 1992).

A "normal" baby can be gently bounced while a grandmother smiles and coos at it. The baby will look at the grandmother's face, seem fascinated and involved, and around age two weeks may even start smiling in response to her loving attention. But, for a baby who has been chemically exposed, the response will be quite different. If the baby is held dangling out in front of its grandmother, the lack of boundaries around the baby will be frightening. If the grandmother bounces the baby gently, the sensation is painfully irritating to the infant. When she looks into the baby's eyes, the baby cannot make sense of the visual patterns in front of its face. The baby screams, becomes rigid, closes its eyes, and turns away from her (Waller, 1993).

Crack-affected infants do not like being touched or looked at. They do not cuddle and often fail to bond with a caregiver. Failure to bond is an important indicator that the child may have great difficulty forming relationships in the future. Developmental theorists have emphasized the importance of an infant's ability to attach to the mother or another primary caregiver. Some have suggested that this attachment behavior is an inherited characteristic of the human species, which is necessary for survival (Villarreal et al., 1991; Waller, 1993).

One of the most important interventions for infants with chemical exposure is careful training of the caregivers. Caregivers need to know what to expect from the child, how to read his or her signals, and how best to respond. By carefully tending to the child's signals, they can help the neurologically immature child become tolerant of a variety of stimulation (touch, vocalization, and visual stimuli).

In a project done by Dan R. Griffith with a group of drug-exposed babies, it was found that infants who were exposed to cocaine and/or other drugs prenatally showed very few differences from a control group's average scores of development at ages three, six, twelve, eighteen, and twenty-four months. By age three, there were no differences in the overall performances of the cocaine/polydrug-exposed children and the drug-free children. These particular drug-exposed children's postnatal care was monitored. Their mothers received good prenatal care and nutrition. The children had good postnatal nutrition and health care; received regular screening, diagnosis, and treatment for any medical or developmental problems; and were in stable caretaking environments. With early intervention, the children who had once been exposed to drugs seemed completely normal with regard to intellectual, social, emotional, and behavioral development through age three (Griffith, 1992).

PRESCHOOL

Preschoolers who have been drug-exposed prenatally are often hyperactive, late in developing language, and late in walking. They are self-absorbed, impulsive, unaware of others, and unable to focus attention for any length of time. They are often isolated because other children do not trust their unpredictable behavior. The toddlers do not understand cause-and-effect relationships. They do not feel remorse for hurting others, and they do not seem to develop a conscience. Their play is random, disorganized, and pointless. Cocaine-exposed children seem unable to engage in free play. They scatter and bat toys, pick toys up and put them down without purpose, and seem uninvolved. The problem is not that the cocaine-exposed children are brain-damaged and can't learn at all, it's that they can't learn in the typical classroom environment. Given the proper supportive, structured environment—with a low adult/child ratio, strong emotional support, and conscious efforts by teachers to form emotionally satisfying attachments with children—the children respond. Gradually, they seem to do better in a more typical classroom (Rist, 1990).

Programs have been developed to help these preschoolers, such as "Therapeutic Nursery Programs." Therapeutic nurseries are being used to respond to the needs of preschool-age children who have been prenatally drug-exposed. These nursery programs not only serve children who have been prenatally exposed to drugs, but also children who are at risk of being physically injured, such as children from homes where there is domestic violence, children who are emotionally unstable because of the numerous foster homes they have been placed in, children of poverty, children who are medically fragile, and children who have developmental delays or learning problems.

The therapeutic nurseries are staffed with individuals who have been specially trained in observation and assessment. The therapeutic nursery recognizes that the children will face particular challenges developing the social, academic, and emotional skills necessary to succeed in school and society. The staff of the therapeutic nursery are able to evaluate a child's behavior and select the appropriate therapeutic response to help the child develop needed skills and capabilities (Los Angeles County Office of Education, 1993).

The most important aspect of the therapeutic nursery is the child/staff ratio. It must be kept very low for the program to succeed. Children appropriate for such programs need considerable individual attention and generally do not share attention well. By receiving intensive individual time with staff, a child is less compelled to engage in problematic behaviors to attract the attention he or she wants and needs (Villarreal et al., 1991).

The therapeutic nursery also works with the parents of the children. The program is located near the families it seeks to serve. Scheduling is flexible to some extent: the parents of the children are often disorganized and are not able to abide by the strict drop-off and pick-up times. Dietary guidelines that are set forth are unlikely to be followed by these parents. While staff will want to establish guidelines and set limits with parents, this must be done in a patient, nonthreatening manner. The therapeutic nursery also must establish a sense of collaboration with parents and family. Parent training programs are offered on a regular basis. Some nurseries are co-located with a drug treatment and alcohol recovery facility. The parent may also participate in the nursery's regular daily schedule to learn from the staff how to care for his or her child and how to respond to the various behaviors the child may be exhibiting.

A child with substance exposure needs a program that can tolerate and adapt to the possible disorganization and chaos of the parents. It is important to make every effort to keep the family together and make healthy decisions for every member's well-being. According to Shirley Davis, the therapeutic nursery is a concept worth supporting and has the potential to assist children and their families in powerful ways. There are many indications in research that early interventions help numerous children who have been drug-exposed catch up on development and skills. The therapeutic nursery approach helps maximize the child's chances of being integrated into a regular school program by kindergarten or first grade. It is with this goal in mind that therapeutic programs are recommended at early ages for children who experience considerable effects of prenatal drug or alcohol exposure (Los Angeles County Office of Education, 1993).

The cost of providing therapeutic nursery programs are bound to be high. But waiting to identify and treat drug-exposed children when they enroll in kindergarten is a mistake that could add substantially to the overall cost of educating the child in a regular public school. The aggression and withdrawal characteristics of drug-exposed children begin to develop immediately after birth. In a chaotic, nonsupportive home environment, these types of behavior are necessary coping mechanisms for crack babies. Over time, such behavior becomes firmly entrenched and increasingly difficult to change. Working with these children before these problems become ingrained is critical. The children will have difficulty adapting to a normal school environment later. The kind of educational environment that cocaine-exposed children need is intensive. Therefore, early intervention is the key to success.

There are therapeutic nurseries that are currently servicing drug-exposed children and their families. The Salvin Special Education Center in Los Angeles works with children ages three to five who have experienced prenatal exposure to drugs. Approximately half of their students have been able to transfer to regular school classes, with ongoing assistance of special tutoring and counseling. California also has two therapeutic programs in Los Angeles: UCLA Infant and Family Services Project and Scott Newman Center. In Oakland, there are two other therapeutic programs available: Healthy Infant Program at the Highland Hospital and Madela House.

The Chicago-based NAPARE group (National Association for Perinatal Addiction Research and Education) has followed 300 babies exposed to cocaine before birth who have received intensive interventions. Looking at ninety of the children when they reached the age of three, they found that 90% demonstrated normal intelligence, 70% had no significant behavioral problems, and 60% did not require speech therapy. The therapeutic nursery program available in Chicago, Illinois, is the Perinatal Center for Chemical Dependence.

In St. Petersburg, Florida, the Child Development and Family Guidance Center of Operation PAR has provided a nurturing environment for drug-exposed children in a therapeutic setting. Shirley Davis, Director of Maternal Education in St. Petersburg, Florida, states that what is needed is early intervention. With intervention, these drug-exposed children can be successful if there are high expectations for their success and the successful rehabilitation of their mothers (Los Angeles County Office of Education, 1993). Miami, Florida, also has Partnerships to Empower Parents, which assists drug-affected families in assessing and developing support networks.

New York City also has a special education preschool program for children at risk for development difficulties. Three such programs are Comprehensive Services to Drug and HIV Exposed Children and Families (Children's Hospital PACT Program), Special Prenatal Program and AIDS Initiative Programs (Harlem Hospital), and Pregnant Addicts and Addicted Mothers Program Center for Comprehensive Health Practice (New York Medical College). Discussion with preschool teachers in these settings indicates that many of the children who receive intensive services gain skills and catch up in areas that were known to be weak at the onset. These New York preschool programs include group activities where caregivers receive parent education, learn about their individual child's development, and are given instruction on how to support their child's learning needs in the home. The children who are receiving this combination of school- and home-based development services are showing the most improvement (Villarreal et al., 1991).

Chapter 21

DRUG-EXPOSED CHILDREN IN ELEMENTARY SCHOOL

Serving drug-exposed children in elementary school may mean keeping them in the regular classroom. Often, their needs can be met in a mainstreamed setting, and special education programs may already be filled to capacity. There are classroom accommodations that teachers already know how to do that often help drug-exposed children, i.e., the use of learning styles, classroom structure, and behavior management techniques. Suggestions for the problem of drug-exposed children directed especially to educators are included.

CHILDREN IN THE ELEMENTARY SCHOOL

We just enrolled a new boy in kindergarten today. The kindergarten teacher couldn't do a thing with him. He was all over the classroom, banging into the furniture, knocking things down, hitting the other children, and the teacher could not hold on to him when she would catch him. It took three adults to finally restrain him. We had to call his grandmother to come and pick him up and take him home for the rest of the day. – Principal

It was this story, overheard in a college classroom and told by a classmate, that ignited my curiosity about the drug-exposed children coming into the elementary schools. I listened to my classmate as she told her story about her first day as a principal. She felt she was not prepared to handle these "crack kids" on a daily basis. But my deepest concern was for the teacher: What is she going to do tomorrow when he comes back? Will they send the boy home again? Will this be a daily pattern? What is the school going to do? How many more of these "crack kids" are out there? Will they only be in the cities?

The news media has warned the public of the current drug problem in our country. The children exposed to drugs prenatally have been sensationalized by the media by showing the extreme cases of babies wire-laden, tiny, premature, trembling, and screaming uncontrollably. The older children have been described as ''crack kids,'' unable to learn, unable to love, hyperactive, hyperaggressive, and without a conscience. The media has made the public aware of the growing problem of cocaine use, but the picture they draw for the public of the children exposed to cocaine has not been correct.

The media has made the assumption that all cocaine-exposed children are severely affected; that little can be done for them; and that all the medical, behavioral, and learning problems exhibited by these children are caused directly by their exposure to cocaine. They have not considered other factors that may have caused these children's learning and behavioral disabilities. Considerations need to be made of the child's home environment, as well as prenatal exposure to other drugs such as marijuana, alcohol, and tobacco. We hear many stories of drug trafficking, politicians involved in the trafficking, police enforcement cover-ups, adults selling and using drugs, and children who are also dealing drugs to make fast money. But the current problem that educators are facing today are the children who have been drug-exposed and are now entering the regular classrooms.

The first response of educators would be to put these ''crack kids'' in special education programs because they are children who are hard to control, have short attention spans, have difficulty learning, are impulsive, exhibit aggressive behavior, and have little chance of learning. But this is not the case with the majority of ''crack kids.'' Special education programs are already at maximum capacity, and budget cuts are depleting resources. So the majority of the crack-exposed children will be ''mainstreamed'' in the regular classroom.

Teachers, in reality, will not know if a student has had prenatal exposure to crack cocaine. This is confidential information that is generally not in a student's record unless parents release the information; therefore, the teacher will have nothing more to go on than the child's individual behavior. Each child is an individual and deals with challenges in different ways. Educators cannot know, without assessing the individual child properly and carefully, what the child's particular strengths and challenges are likely to be. One of the most important things a teacher can do is document the student's behavior. Then the teacher can take the steps to assess the child's development and social

Drug and Alcohol Exposed Children Will Usually Be Placed in a Regular Classroom and Will Look Like the Other Children.

and learning capabilities and to develop strategies to respond to the child's particular areas of difficulties and enhance areas of strengths and capabilities. It would be helpful if the most severely affected children with prenatal chemical exposure could be identified before they reach kindergarten and for them to participate in special education programs, but this is not always the case. Because schools do not have control of the home environment of the children before they enter the school, it cannot be determined how many or which children will need special programs when they enter the regular classroom. This cannot be done until the classroom teacher has time to relate to the child. The greater portion of children born with drug or alcohol exposure will be in the regular classroom and if early intervention (hopefully at birth or pre-school) has not taken place, then the classroom teacher will probably know right away that such children need special assistance.

HOW TO HELP "CRACK KIDS" IN A REGULAR CLASSROOM

There is uncertainty about the numbers of crack babies being born in our communities. But we do know that the number of drug-exposed children coming into school systems is increasing. Untreated, these children will find it difficult to function in a regular classroom setting; therefore, schools need to prepare for them by providing structured, supportive learning environments for these children to succeed in the regular classroom. Educators who have worked with children for a long time have worked with children who have poor impulse control, who have difficulty learning to read, who misbehave, and who fight with other children. Competent professionals in child services learned long ago that such children need individual attention and individualized strategies in response to the difficulties they face. When children demonstrate problems, they are referred to a developmental specialist to evaluate the need for an Individualized Educational Program (IEP) and to work with family and school to develop a program appropriate to the particular strengths and challenges of the child. This does not mean however, that the child will be placed in a special education class for the entire school day but, rather, that s/he will receive services that will help the child with a particular learning disability.

It is important that children who fit the "profile" of a child with drug exposure not automatically be considered to have significant limitations in his or her potential to learn. The goal is not to place the children in

Children Receiving Needed Services Can Function with the Other Children.

special education class for the entire school day, but to get help for the children in the specific areas needed and to keep them in the regular classroom for the majority of the day where the children can relate with their peers. Teachers need to be aware that, most likely, they already have the skills to work with children who have been drug-exposed.

Drug-exposed is a term that refers to a medical condition, and it has no place in the educational arena. The term will more likely be a label that will handicap a child unfairly. It is possible that drug exposure is not even the basis of the problem. Children born drug-exposed can learn and can contribute to their school and their community. It is better to use diagnostic labels that describe a specific attention disorder or learning problem, such as limited audio recall, that will help the child receive the kind of services he or she can benefit from. All children can learn, and they learn in different ways. Everything they see, hear, touch, and smell provides them with information that they then use in their own unique way. Children with prenatal drug exposure are more likely to have learning difficulties and need a variety of teaching techniques to successfully learn the important concepts of their education. It will be essential, however, for the teacher to be flexible and willing to use a variety of teaching techniques and strategies that will benefit the children. If we know how a particular child learns (learning styles) and if we teach that child in the way he or she can best process the information, there will be many students who will be successful in their educational experience.

LEARNING STYLES

Learning styles are the cognitive, conceptual, affective, and behavioral patterns that are typical, consistent, and stable processes that people use in their learning. To put it in uncomplicated terms, these are the ways people handle new situations and information and apply their experiences and knowledge. There are a variety of learning styles. Children may have a single, dominant style of learning, or they may learn through a variety of different styles. Some of the most common styles are: visual learner, auditory learner, kinesthetic learner, global learner, and analytic learner.

Children with drug and alcohol exposure and other children at risk for school difficulties may present a number of problematic behaviors. Each child is unique. Students with prenatal chemical exposure will benefit from a learning environment that is consistent and structured. When teachers suspect a problem of a serious nature, they need to consult their school-based assessment team to set up an Individual Educational Program.

First, the teacher needs to recognize that the at-risk child (includes prenatally drug-exposed children) will probably have one or more of the following traits as described by Villarreal et al. (1991):

- is easily distracted
- has limited problem-solving skills
- takes longer than other children to complete tasks
- is easily stimulated by other children or events inside or outside the classroom
- develops interactive and representational play skills later than other children
- has difficulty understanding instructions or responding to commands
- has a limited range of facial expressions
- exhibits problems with emotional attachments
- shows poor impulse control
- is delayed in expressive and/or receptive language
- exhibits gross motor or fine motor coordination that is not as developed as other children; may be awkward or clumsy

There are techniques and strategies to help children with learning needs. These techniques and strategies have not been newly designed for drug exposed children but have been used by teachers for many years to help children with learning difficulties (Guild and McKinney, n.d.).

First, there is the visual learner, who uses a sensory learning style. These children learn by seeing things and describe information and experiences in visual terms. The teaching strategies to use with a visual learner are to use visual cues in questions and discussions and to demonstrate new tasks. Use visual aids such as videos, films, diagrams, visual computer learning programs, illustrated books, and photographs.

The next learning style results in the auditory learner and is also a sensory learning style. This child learns by hearing things and describes information and experiences in auditory terms. (These children will probably have to read aloud to themselves in order to comprehend better.) Strategies to help these children make sure they hear instructions or information about the learning that is to take place. Use auditory cues in questions and discussions. Another strategy to help auditory learners would be to use audio-oriented materials such as cassette tapes of stories, films, or videos with sound, music, and computer learning programs with sound, voice instruction, and feedback.

There is also another sensory learning style, which is used by the kinesthetic learner. These students learn by touching and feeling things and by using descriptions of information and experiences in kinesthetic terms. These children can be helped to learn by providing hands-on experiences in learning activities. Use kinesthetic cues in questions and discussions. The kinesthetic learner can also be helped by providing hands-on materials with a variety of textures and by providing the learner with activities that allow movement, building, sculpting, and role-play.

Then there is the global learner, who uses a cognitive learning style. This child uses a global approach; he or she needs to see the whole picture before breaking it into parts. This student can be helped by using cues related to the larger task before presenting details of the work. Use whole-language techniques that combine reading, writing, and speaking. These children can work with a variety of materials and approaches. Global learners need regular feedback and do best with structured activities.

The last learning style is used by the analytic learner. This kind of learning is also cognitive. The child uses an analytic approach for learning; in other words, he or she needs pieces of the whole and builds upon the pieces to put the whole together. These children need details; then they can put them together in a complete project. Some cues to use should be related to the development of the larger concept. A variety of teaching materials that can be used includes: books and written material, films, videos, and computer programs that provide direct feedback. Drug-exposed children are less likely to learn in the analytical style often emphasized in school systems (Villarreal et al. 1991).

Now, how does the teacher make sure she is teaching to all her students in all the teaching styles that her students need? The teacher will need to have the ability to work with a variety of teaching styles. The teacher will have to find ways to adapt and modify lessons to provide a variety of instructional techniques. The teacher will need to provide a classroom that establishes an environment that respects a variety of learning styles and works for everyone. Villarreal et al. (1991) also contribute six suggestions for instruction of children at risk for school failure:

(*1*) Help create a positive environment in class, one in which students help one another.

(*2*) Make the content personal.

(3) Present learning in a global way.
(4) Make connections that highlight the relevance of the lesson.
(5) Provide a context for learning and a rationale for the lesson.
(6) Provide structure. Be clear in expectations and directions. Be organized.

Eileen-Marie Moore, Resource District Counselor at San Diego City Schools, presented suggestions for working with prenatally drug-exposed children who exhibited difficulties with certain learning behaviors (Los Angeles County Office of Education, 1993). The following is a list of learning behaviors and teaching strategies to use in the classroom:

Learning Behavior	Teaching Strategy
1. Overstimulated	• Visual stimulation can be people alleviated by smaller group movements. • Center with soothing music. • Reduce interruptions, excitement, and noise. • Provide support and emotional reassurance.
2. Poor vision scanning	• Limit the number of objects around the child's work area.
3. Trial and error	• Establish classroom routines with minimal numbers of transitions. • Model alternative strategies. • Demonstrate, be clear.
4. Preservative behavior/ gives up easily	• Direct the child to watch another child who is using a successful strategy. • Recognize and consistently praise child's attempts.
5. "Sporadic mastery" (masters then forgets)	• Be patient and reassure. • Ask child to verbalize steps. • Talk child through the tasks.
6. Unable to take turns	• Provide child with many opportunities to take turns with peers. • Model taking turns.

Learning Behavior	Teaching Strategy
7. Unable to sit still	• Reinforce behavior you want. • Draw attention to the children who are behaving appropriately.
8. Nonresponsive/shutdown (body folds inward)	• Use one-minute removal (time out), no longer. • Protect child from overstimulation.
9. Can't handle transition	• Alert child routinely that activity will soon be over. • Talk about the next activity. • Allow adequate time for the transition. • Use pauses. • Guide children through the transition.
10. May not learn incidentally	• Develop a pattern the children can depend on. • Bullseye the homework written on the board.
11. Overwhelmed by whole page assignments	• Reduce page or numbers to be done.

Eileen-Marie Moore also suggested four teaching strategies to use when children who have been prenatally exposed to drugs exhibited learning behaviors connected to social/emotional factors. For example, she suggested that, when a child is showing lack of trust, usually because the child has had too many homes (caretakers) and schools, provide the student with opportunities for contact, mutual but appropriate touch, and smile frequently. Moore also suggested that, when a child ignores your cues, address the child by name, elicit eye contact, and touch appropriately before giving the child a command. She also suggested the teacher should move close to the child, and help the child read his/her facial cues. Also one might provide the child with explicitly consistent limits of behavior and frequently verbalize the expected behaviors.

Moore also suggested that, when a child shows a restricted range of emotions, the teacher may try using books or pictures to explore and help the child express a range of feelings. The teacher or a small group (as an activity) can model a full range of emotions for the child. The last suggestion that Moore had was that, when a child exhibits inappropriate behavior such as hitting, pushing, biting, swearing, and negative remarks, the teacher should, first of all, recognize the child's needs. Then the teacher should find a way for the child to express his or her feelings. The teacher should verbalize expected behavior and redirect the behavior. The teacher needs to remove the child from the situation and help the child work through his or her feelings. The teacher can also help the child by providing him or her with appropriate language to use with peers. The teacher should set consistent limits and provide talk time for the students as well (Los Angeles County Office of Education, 1993).

ATTENTION DEFICIT HYPERACTIVITY DISORDER

Although there is no common profile for children who have been drug-exposed, one common characteristic that has been dominant in almost all drug-exposed children is Attention Deficit Hyperactivity Disorder (ADHD). These children are overactive, impulsive, out of their seats, talk out and act out, but are less hyperactive at home. ADHD is not new. Children who have not been exposed to drugs have exhibited ADHD in the classroom. There are many services to help these children: medical, social, and educational. The key symptom of hyperactivity is not the high activity level, but the primary sign is short attention span and poor impulse control. These are two behaviors that cocaine-exposed children are exhibiting. Therefore, the interest in ADHD is soaring, along with the number of children prenatally exposed to drugs.

The controversy, however, is the treatment for ADHD. Most experts agree that a multimodality approach to treatment of the disorder aimed at assisting the child medically, psychologically, educationally, and behaviorally is often needed. This requires the efforts of many professionals. Currently, children with mild symptoms of ADHD can be managed by parent counseling, behavior modification, and special education. But, when the disorder is serious, medication enters the picture. The medication or drugs used are Ritalin, Cylert, and Dexedrine. These drugs do not slow children down, but, instead, they stimulate the central nervous system, putting it back "in tune," allowing the child to pay attention and complete assignments. These medications do involve some risk, but they are less dangerous than most prescription drugs. Side effects are usually limited and temporary (Rosemond, 1989), but to treat drug-exposed children with more drugs to control what the previous drug exposure did seems a bit contradictory.

Children with prenatal drug-exposure are at risk for academic difficulties and school failure. Recent research indicates that all children can learn and that, when teaching strategies take a child's learning style into consideration, most children do learn. The successes of these children depend on the teacher's ability to make a commitment to the students and the teacher's attitude towards the child's learning potential.

CHILDREN WHO HAVE BEEN "EXPOSED" TO DRUGS

The American dream: the beautiful home, the fast sports car, stylish clothes, and plenty of money to spend on anything that comes your way. This dream, in today's economy, has remained just a dream for the majority of Americans. College graduates are finding it difficult to find jobs. People are losing their homes. And the only future for the poor seems to be more poverty. So what can we offer young kids today who cannot see progress in their future?

Children in the inner cities are being falsely lured to quick success by the financial opportunities presented by the growing problem of drugs in their neighborhoods and the fall of the economy. Only a few escape. The rest are joining gangs or starting their own business—drugs. Many children living in the inner cities are barraged with the message that selling drugs is an easy road to riches. The children are finding illegal employment opportunities in the highly profitable, rapidly growing, multinational drug trade. These sixteen-year-old children are making $20,000 a week selling drugs for drug traffickers. To these children, the American way is just a myth (Williams, 1989).

Those who recruit teenagers are following a tradition that dates back almost twenty years and that was the direct effect of the harsh "Rockefeller laws," which mandated a prison term for anyone over eighteen in possession of an illegal drug. This led drug dealers to use kids as runners to avoid the impact of the law. They used these children because they were easy to frighten and control. The most tragic victims of the drug laws are children. Many have been killed as innocent bystanders in gun battles among traffickers.

Equally tragic are the children of Medellin, Colombia, which housed the largest and most powerful drug cartel. These children, young teenagers, are taking the law into their own hands to clean up their city. They have formed their own militia. These vigilantes, as young as fifteen, are "putting people to bed" —killing criminals and drug dealers in their communities. They want to rid their streets of violent crimes. The older members of the city feel that what the children are doing is helping to "clean up" their town. They aren't stealing or selling drugs. They are eliminating the bad element in the town. The militia members claim killing is not their main method of social cleaning. They claim to start with dialogue. The person is warned. Then if they don't leave the town or fix themselves up, they are eliminated. One young Colombian girl stated that, at first, she felt bad because the victim is also a human being who has a family. "But there are people who just don't . . . get it. Some people just don't understand dialogue. So, they are put to bed" (Benesch, 1992).

Then, there are the children who are taking the drugs—children without hope for their future. We need to give these kids more than a slogan—"just say no" isn't working. These children are getting mixed messages from the tobacco and alcohol trade. These substances are equally hazardous to your health, killing thousands of people every year, but they are legal. So let's stop the slogans because the present system is not working. These children need a brighter tomorrow, a sense of purpose, and a chance at opportunity.

WHAT DO WE DO?

It is clear that the number of babies being born chemically exposed to drugs such as cocaine is growing at a tremendous rate. If the drug exposure were to stop now, we would be dealing with the afteraffects for fifty to seventy-five years. In the year 2000, if the current drug epidemic continues to grow at the same rate, there will be 4 million drug-exposed children. Cocaine and other drugs are everywhere: cities, suburbs, and rural areas. No school or community has been immunized against this disease. So we must be prepared.

WHERE DO WE START?

One suggestion is to get tough with the mothers of these infants. Jail pregnant women who use drugs or confine them somewhere until they deliver their babies. In Butte County, California, Michael Ramsey, District Attorney, decided that hospitals would start screening all newborns exhibiting symptoms of drug exposure. Any positive test results might then be used as evidence to prosecute the mothers for illegal drug use—a misdemeanor that carries a mandatory sentence of ninety days. The woman's other option would be to enter a drug treatment program (LaCroix, 1989). In either case, drug treatment or jail confinement, the infant loses. The mother would be jailed for ninety days, and the child would be placed in foster care. Or, if the woman enters a drug treatment program, she can be prosecuted for using illegal drugs, and, again, the infant can be put in foster care during the most crucial time of its early life.

There are many states (California, Illinois, Florida, and others) trying to convict women for taking illegal drugs during pregnancy. In August 1989, in Florida, a grand jury convicted a woman for delivering a controlled substance to a minor—in this case through the umbilical cord. Her sentence was a year of house arrest in a drug treatment center and fourteen years' probation.

Judith Rosen, a founder of California Advocates for Pregnant Women, questions the legality and ethics of inviting criminal justice authorities to force a doctor's orders upon a woman. Are we, as women, to have perfect babies and be subject to prosecution if we don't (LaCroix, 1989)? The threat of punishment or incarceration will serve only to prevent women from getting vital prenatal care. And the prospect of going to jail will not make crack-smoking women quit their drug habit. These cases are attacks on women, and if states can create prenatal police patrols for cocaine use, then where will they draw the line (Sachs, 1989)? For some women (e.g., teachers), just standing on their feet all day is harmful. Will they be arrested, too?

Treating drug-using pregnant women may be an answer to slow or halt the increase of crack-exposed births. The problem is that providing drug treatment programs is expensive. Another problem is the lack of medical facilities to help pregnant women with drug problems. In California, there are five full-time drug treatment programs that accept pregnant women, and waiting lists are up to six months long. Most centers specialize in treating men.

The timing of intervention is critical. A woman's sense of success as a mother and woman will help her in preventing drug abuse. Not all women who are drug addicted are unfit to raise their children. What they need is job training, occupational opportunities, crisis interventions, and parenting skills. In California, there is a center to help women and their babies. The UCLA Infant and Family Service Project provides child assessment for newborns to two year olds and parent education for medically fragile children with substance exposure.

SCHOOLS—READY OR NOT, HERE THEY COME

There is no clear picture regarding how many children in our schools today have been prenatally exposed to drugs. What is certain is that the number of children needing special services is increasing and has more than doubled within the past two to three years. Schools need to be ready to provide the structure and the supportive learning environment that these children will need to succeed. State and local health department administrators need to be contacted to form alliances with child protective services. These agencies can help as early warning systems and allies. If these agencies keep accurate records of the babies being born drug-exposed, they can give the schools an estimate of how many children will be enrolling in kindergarten in a few years. The child protective services can also help identify those children who might need special education services.

Providing the low teacher/child ratio cocaine-exposed children need in the classroom will be expensive. There is a need to begin lobbying for funds to serve the needs of these children. The schools should put drug education and prevention programs in place if they aren't already. In some cases, the message needs to be blunt in order to get the message across. ''Drugs and parenthood do not mix.'' The drug-exposed children will need an environment in the schools that is stable and secure. The children need consistency; moving them around from room to room causes them confusion. Teachers will need to develop warm and strong relationships with the children. Difficult as it may be, teachers will need to be encouraged to develop ''favorites'' when working with drug-exposed children who have trouble forming attachments to other people.

CONCLUSION

I, Diva Abel Vasquez, went into this topic with very little knowledge and many, many questions. I knew only what I saw on television, read quickly in a magazine, or through stories I had overheard. In other words, I was very ignorant about the problem of children who have been prenatally drug-exposed. I had always been interested in the topic but never took time to find out the facts. I know now that children with prenatal drug or alcohol exposure are at risk for academic difficulties and school failure. All children can learn; when teaching strategies take a child's learning style into consideration, most children can experience academic success.

The success of these children depends on the ability of the individual teachers and entire school systems to make commitment to students. Teachers will need to meet with parents or caregivers at the beginning of the school year and discuss the children's learning styles, strengths, and competencies. Parents and caregivers can be very insightful about these areas. The teacher must let the student know how valuable they (the student) are and how much the teacher believes in their ability to learn; think positively. The teacher will need to create an environment of excitement, where learning—and teaching—can be fun. But, most important for the teacher, there should be sharing of ideas of success and failure with other teachers and classroom aides.

Each child has the potential to learn. The failure of that child is also the school's failure, and the school must not let the child fail. We must not let crack take our children. Crack has just begun to do its deadly work, producing thousands of helpless babies each year. We, as people, parents, and educators, must lead our society and take action against these drugs and, ultimately, help these innocent children redeem their lives.

A variety of strategies have been presented for identifying students at risk and for offering them improved instruction and services. Our aim has been to identify the most promising efforts now operating throughout the country and to describe them for you. We have developed a step-by-step process for implementing these strategies, and each step is a chapter in this book. In order to make the entire effort really feasible, we have designed and implemented software to identify students who need help, to place them in effective interventions, and, finally, to evaluate the interventions to see if they are working. We trust that you will find personal satisfaction and renewal in your efforts to help our nation's young people who need our assistance.

SAFE, DISCIPLINED, AND DRUG-FREE SCHOOLS[8]

This document was prepared by the Goal 6 Work Group, Office of Education Research and Improvement, U.S. Department of Education, February 1993 (NYGIC Document Number D0169).

U.S. Department of Education
Richard W. Riley
Secretary

Office of Educational Research and Improvement
Emerson J. Elliott
Acting Assistant Secretary

Fund for the Improvement and Reform of Schools and Teaching
Janice K. Anderson
Interim Director

Library Programs
Ray Fry
Director

National Center for Education Statistics
Emerson J. Elliott
Commissioner

Office of Research
Joseph C. Conaty
Acting Director

Programs for the Improvement of Practice
Eve M. Bither
Director

OERI Goal 6 Work Group
Diane Aleem, Cochair
Oliver Moles, Cochair
Nancy Cavanaugh
Kathryn Chandler
Vonnie Clement
John Grymes

OERI Work Group Coordinator
Hunter Moorman

[8]This document is a reproduction of an original document published under the title shown. It has been reproduced and distributed by the National Youth Gang Information Center (NYGIC) with the permission of the publishing agency and copyright holder. Some material in the original may have been omitted for the sake of brevity, relevance, and suitability for reproduction. Some graphics may have been rendered in tabular format for greater accessibility. NYGIC bears sole responsibility for the faithfulness of the reproduction of the original. Points of view or opinions expressed in the document are those of the authors and do not necessarily represent the official position or policies of the U.S. Department of Education.

FOREWORD

In determining sound educational practices for their schools and communities, policymakers, educators, and parents must often find their way through a maze of conventions, recommendations, and theories. Sometimes new research seems to conflict with established practice, with older research, or even with other current research. But does education research allow us to say anything with confidence about what works? In fact, while substantial gaps remain, we do know a great deal about what is effective in education.

In 1989, the President and the nation's 50 governors held an historic education summit that culminated in the adoption of six National Education Goals. These six broad Goals serve as a framework for much of the current reform movement. In order to help all those who are critical to its success — from parents to national policymakers — the Office of Educational Research and Improvement (OERI) has produced Reaching the Goals, a series of publications describing what we know from research on individual Goals, as well as the limits of that knowledge.

Each publication is the result of a deliberate process guided by work groups composed of talented individuals from various programs and offices within OERI, including the National Center for Education Statistics, the Office of Research, Programs for the Improvement of Practice, Fund for the Improvement and Reform of Schools and Teaching, and Library Programs. Each task force was charged with assessing the state of research for a particular Goal and developing a research and dissemination agenda for OERI. Lengthier technical documents which formed the basis for these publications and include all relevant research citations, are available from OERI.

If we are to succeed in improving education and training to meet our ambitious National Education Goals, research must inform and encourage the development of sound policies and practices. By making available in a clear and understandable format the best research we have, these publications can be invaluable to those who are serious about reform.

ACKNOWLEDGEMENTS

This report was prepared by the OERI Goal 6 Work Group, cochaired by Diane Aleem and Oliver Moles, from the group's technical report on the same subject. The Work Group shared the overall task of collecting information and structuring the technical report. Oliver Moles and Diane Aleem, with Vonnie Clement, wrote most sections of the technical report. Brian Rowan, of the University of Michigan, drafted the research section on the role of school climate and organization. Walter Doyle, of the University of Arizona, drafted the research section on classroom organization and management.

Under contract to OERI, Donald L. Hymes developed the initial draft of the publication from the technical report, the cochairs prepared the text, and Jacquelyn Zimmermann edited it.

Theodor Rebarber and Jeanette Randolph, Office of the Assistant Secretary, provided extensive review and comments and facilitated decision making within OERI. Many other OERI staff members made important contributions, too numerous to mention, at every stage of the Work Group's efforts.

Many others reviewed the documents and made helpful suggestions at various stages. They include Mary Frase, William Modzeleski, and Kimmon Richards within the U.S. Department of Education, and Gilbert Botvin, James Breiling, William Bukowski, Daniel Duke, Gerardo Gonzalez, Denise Gottfredson, William Hansen, J. Robert Hendricks, Edward Jonas, Fred Newmann, William Pink, and Ronald Stephens from outside the agency.

The Reaching the Goals series was developed under the leadership of Diane Ravitch while she was Assistant Secretary of the Office of Educational Research and Improvement and Counselor to the Secretary.

EXECUTIVE SUMMARY

The sixth National Education Goal states, ''By the year 2000, every school in America will be free of drugs and violence and will offer a disciplined environment conducive to learning.'' Surveys within the last 5 years show, however, that we are far from that goal. While the use of alcohol and other drugs among America's youth has declined in recent years, it is unacceptably high, and in a large percentage of our schools, violence, misbehavior, and a lack of engagement in learning interfere seriously with the education process.

Efforts to improve this situation have increased during the past decade, and the effectiveness of some of these efforts has been researched. This report is designed to share information with policymakers about both effective and ineffective approaches, as well as about those for which little research exists, so as to guide the development of programs that can succeed in realizing Goal 6.

A disciplined environment has been a cherished goal of educators even before the problems of drugs and violence disrupted schools. Maintaining a ''disciplined environment conducive to learning'' does not necessarily mean adopting tough policies to keep students silent in their seats. Rather, it means principals and teachers working together to develop appropriate curricula and instructional techniques in support of one overriding goal—to improve students' academic performance. The key here is to create an atmosphere in which students and teachers are engaged in learning and where misbehavior is dealt with quickly, firmly, and fairly. Most important, a learning environment requires an ethic of caring that shapes staff-student relationships. Changes in classroom organization and management may also be necessary to effectively maintain such an atmosphere. In some cases, these changes involve alternative settings where disruptive students receive special attention, counseling, and remediation.

Drug use prevention has shifted within the last 8 years from simplistic one-dimensional approaches to comprehensive programs. Studies show that many of the factors that put children at risk to become drug users are related, as are the protective factors that can possibly minimize the risks of drug use, violence, and disruptive behavior. It is also obvious that, since decisions about drug use are formulated by many in early adolescence, prevention programs must start in elementary school.

Successful drug use prevention programs combine the teaching of resistance skills with correcting students' often erroneous perceptions about the prevalence and acceptability of drugs among their peers. Some programs using student leaders have been more successful than those led by adults only, and prevention is sustained longer when a "booster" course is given on a regular basis. The most promising strategy is comprehensive—encompassing peer groups, families, schools, media, community organizations including religious and law enforcement groups, and a wide variety of approaches that provide information, develop life skills, use peer facilitators, and change community policies and norms.

In the area of violence reduction, solid research on the effects of different strategies is sparse. However, according to available evidence, coordinated school and community efforts seem promising. Within schools it seems clear that the best way to reduce youth violence is by creating an atmosphere that encourages students to focus their energies on learning. Firm, fair, and consistently applied student behavior standards play a part here, as does an ethic of caring for students by staff.

As teachers and principals in our nation's schools strive to attain Goal 6 in the next decade, research will provide more insight into the causes of drug use and violence afflicting so many of our young people, and the means of preventing them. While the roots of these ills may be deep in society, the schools can be very well positioned to reduce their incidence and their effects on learning. Armed with an understanding of the complex linkages among the factors that put children at risk, focusing on the related protective factors that may shelter children from these risks, and drawing on strong family and community involvement, our schools can become the healthy learning environments that are a strong defense against drug use and violence.

REVIEW OF RESEARCH ON WAYS TO ATTAIN GOAL 6

Introduction

Goal 6 states: "By the year 2000, every school in America will be free of drugs and violence and will offer a disciplined environment conducive to learning." While the use of alcohol and other drugs has declined in recent years, the current situation in many of our schools is still far from this goal.

Studies reveal the following profile:

• Seventy percent of public school students and 52 percent of private school students aged 12 through 19 reported in 1989 that drugs are available at their school;

- Nearly 13 percent of 8th-graders, 23 percent of 10th-graders, and 30 percent of 12th-graders had five or more drinks in a row in a 2-week period during the 1990-91 school year;
- At least 71 persons were killed with guns at school in the period 1986 − 90; and
- Nationwide, 44 percent of teachers reported in 1991 that student misbehavior interfered substantially with their teaching.

There is no question that safety and order are essential if learning is to take place. Yet the problems of drug use, violence, or discipline confront students and educators to some extent every day in virtually every school in the nation. Schools must address this crisis aggressively if they are to provide the quality of education that a healthy and prosperous nation requires.

Goal 6 covers three distinct problem areas, each with unique challenges. A disciplined environment conducive to learning must be provided by all schools. The other two, drugs and violence, are problems of society and schools alike. While these two problems are different, they are also related. Drug use is often linked to misbehavior in school, poor academic performance, dropping out, delinquency, and teenage pregnancy. Violence often plays a role in drug transactions and in getting money to buy drugs. The easy access to guns makes their use to settle turf battles and personal disputes increasingly commonplace. Children who see violence and drug use around them may resort to the same high-risk behavior and means of handling conflicts in school.

Drug use and violence are also linked by their origins and can be encouraged or discouraged by various characteristics of the person, family, community, and school. Some of the common risk factors include poverty, high-crime neighborhoods, and ineffective schools. A high level of family conflict increases the likelihood of drug use and delinquency, as does a lack of positive parent-child attachments. Protective factors include effective parenting, positive relationships to competent adults, and personal skills in various fields.

Regardless of students' personal histories, however, the mission of America's schools is to educate and prepare all of them for a productive life. Schools impart knowledge and skills, transmit values, and help youth strive for success in learning in order to reach their life goals. With that role in mind, this report examines several aspects of schools and classrooms, their relationship to the community at large, and their effect on achieving Goal 6. The following topics are considered:

Classrooms

- Curricula and instructional techniques for preventing drug use and violence; and
- Organization and management for establishing and maintaining order.

Schools

- Number of students in each school;
- School climate or culture, which is the beliefs, values, and attitudes of staff and students regarding schools and learning;
- Goals emphasized, such as academic achievement or control of students;
- Persons and issues involved in leadership and decision making;
- Establishing procedures, and enforcing policies and rules; and
- Specialized roles and programs such as alternative schools.

School-Community Relationships

- School-community connections, for example coordinated drug use prevention and violence reduction activities; and
- Federal, state, and district education policies on drug use and discipline.

Finally, the three objectives under Goal 6 seek firm and fair school drug policies, comprehensive K – 12 drug use prevention programs in schools, and community support for making schools safe and drug free. In response to federal regulations, most schools have certified that they have developed drug policies and comprehensive K – 12 drug education and use prevention programs. We recognize that schools and school districts may choose additional strategies to attain Goal 6. This report examines many types of strategies.

Background

In this section the three Goal 6 topics – disciplined school environments, drug use, and violence – are treated in terms of the specific nature and extent of the problem. Because of its overarching importance, the topic of disciplined environments is reviewed first.

Disciplined School Environments

A "disciplined environment conducive to learning" refers to more than controlling misbehavior. It comprises maximizing intellectual and personal development as well as minimizing disruptions. A disciplined environment should ultimately help more students graduate from high school, the aim of Goal 2.

A "disciplined environment" relies not only on student behavior but especially on school organization and climate, classroom organization and management, and specific discipline policies and practices. When teachers can teach without interruptions and display real interest in their students, and when students and staff attend school regularly and are engaged in their work, then young people should also be less inclined to drop out of school.

From the teachers' perspective, 44 percent surveyed nationwide in 1991 reported that student misbehavior interfered to a considerable extent with their teaching. And in 1986, 29 percent said they had seriously considered leaving teaching because of student misbehavior.

From the students' point of view, on the other hand, between 63 and 80 percent of eighth-graders felt that teachers are interested in them, really listen, praise their efforts, and teach well. All of these indicate that for most students, their teachers are working hard to provide a disciplined classroom environment.

While responses were similar across racial, gender, and ethnic lines, low-achieving students and frequent absentees had less positive attitudes toward their teachers. Such students are more alienated and need special efforts to engage them in learning.

Student absenteeism and tardiness have long signified less student involvement in learning. Yet teacher absenteeism and lack of involvement are seen by some principals as major problems at their schools, most often in urban and secondary schools.

Drugs and Schools

While important regional, racial, and economic differences exist regarding use preference, drug use affects all segments of the population. It has become increasingly evident over the past two decades that the use of alcohol and other drugs creates serious educational, social, and psychological problems for many preadolescents as well as adolescents. Tobacco is also included as a drug in this report due to its addictive nature, its long-term health risks, and the inclination of some young smokers to then try other drugs.

A 1990–91 survey shows an encouraging decline in the use of certain illicit substances. However, both the level of use and age of users are still very disturbing. Survey findings indicate that in 1991, a majority of adolescent students had tried alcohol—54 percent of 8th-graders and 72 percent of 10th-graders. Additionally, 78 percent of 12th-graders tried alcohol. Fourteen percent of 8th-graders, 21 percent of 10th-graders, and 28 percent of 12th-graders smoked cigarettes during the previous 30 days in the 1990-91 school year. Marijuana use is dropping but still 14 percent of seniors used it during the same period. Research shows that the younger children are when they start using tobacco, alcohol, and marijuana the more likely they are to progress from casual to regular use, and go on to use marijuana, crack, cocaine, and heroin.

Moreover, the use of alcohol and other drugs is often initiated, and attitudes and beliefs about it formed at ages 10–16. The startling result of a 1989 study reflects that 70 percent of public school students and 52 percent of private school students aged 12 through 19 reported that drugs are easily available at their school. Sixty percent in elementary school, and 68 percent in secondary school believed drugs are easily obtained on their campuses. While efforts have been under way for over 20 years to prevent drug problems from occurring at all, research clearly indicates that more attention must now be given to the elementary years.

Early intervention is essential for protecting youth from acquiring harmful habits. It would also alleviate the enormous cost of drug use to education. Poor school performance, misbehavior, truancy, dropping out, delinquency, teenage pregnancy, and suicide are all associated with drug use, and impact the delivery of educational services. Thus educators in public and private elementary and secondary schools, whose primary responsibility should be the education of our youth, must instead spend an inordinate amount of their time and resources dealing with the many consequences and correlates of student drug and alcohol use.

Violence in Schools

Criminal violence in schools is a shocking but rather uncommon event. In a 1991 national survey, 2 percent of teachers at all levels reported being physically attacked, and 8 percent threatened with bodily harm in a 12-month period. Up to 23 percent of eighth grade students admitted being involved in fights with another student in the previous semester, and 12 percent expressed fear for their own safety in school. Serious discipline problems are more common. Nineteen percent of the teachers said they had been verbally abused by a student in the previous 4 weeks.

Repeated antisocial behavior among preadolescents, such as fighting and similarly disruptive activity, is considered likely to lead to later delinquency. Adolescents from lower socioeconomic levels commit more serious assaults in the community than those from higher levels. Communities with higher crime rates and gang warfare can expect more violence in their schools than those with less crime in their neighborhoods. Family factors directly related to serious offenses include lack of parental supervision, indifference or rejection, and criminal behavior of parents.

A large national study in 1976 that helped launch the investigation of crime in schools showed that junior (vs. senior) high schools, and schools with more male students, larger environments, and larger classes experienced more violence, as did those schools lacking strict and fair administration of discipline.

Student attitudes also seem to foster violence. It has been shown to be more prevalent where students (1) felt their classes did not teach them what they wanted to learn; (2) did not consider their grades important; (3) did not plan to go to college; and (4) felt they had no influence over their own lives.

It is evident, therefore, that personal, family, school, and community factors all contribute to violence in schools. Efforts to reduce discipline problems and violence in schools need to consider these multiple sources of the problem.

Research: How Does It Help Us Meet the Goal?

We now turn to research on how to meet Goal 6 through school-based programs and practices that address the unacceptable level of youth drug use and violence. Since a disciplined environment is essential for implementing such practices, we first review research on that topic, and follow with the research on drug use and violence prevention.

Disciplined School Environments

A disciplined environment is a worthwhile goal for every school. Even the most trouble-free and high-achieving environment needs continued reinforcement, and children and teachers need support to remain focused on their tasks. This is all the more important, and certainly more difficult, in an atmosphere of violence and defiance. Two broad areas related to disciplined environments are discussed here: school climate and organization, and classroom organization and management. Each includes discipline policy and practice issues.

The Role of School Climate and Organization

It is common wisdom that discipline and learning go hand in hand. Learning requires a pattern of behavior that includes regular attendance in class, active engagement in lessons, and completion of class and homework assignments. A school's climate influences the extent to which this pattern is developed. Research over the past decade has uncovered important differences in climate from school to school that cannot be attributed solely to differences in students' social background. Among the factors that affect school climate, three are especially important:

- Goals: A strong emphasis on the school's academic mission;
- Rules and procedures: Clear discipline standards that are firmly, fairly, and consistently enforced; and
- Staff/student relationships: An ethic of caring that guides interpersonal relationships in the school.

While each one of these factors can affect student behavior and learning, when they occur in combination they constitute a powerful school ''ethos'' or culture – a coherent force that makes students work harder, minimizes disruption, and leads to increased student achievement.

Researchers often find that schools with such cultures are identifiable by the positive attitudes of students and teachers. For example, in schools that emphasize academics, students care more about getting good grades, are more interested in their coursework, and, in secondary schools, do more homework and take more academic courses. Teachers in these schools have a higher sense of teaching mastery, hold higher expectations for their students, are more committed to the continuous improvement of instruction, and derive more enjoyment and satisfaction from their work. Not surprisingly, they report less absenteeism.

In schools with clear discipline standards, students and teachers feel safe and they have a clear understanding of school rules. Furthermore, students feel the rules are fair. Teachers say they treat all students equally, they can turn to counselors for advice to deal with misbehaving students, and they get up-to-date information about problem students from the administration.

In schools with a strong ethic of caring, students feel their teachers like them. They tell researchers that their teachers are good and care about them, and that they value their teachers' opinions. At the same time, teachers report knowing more students in the school, including those who are not in their classes, and report higher levels of staff cooperation and support.

Researchers and policy analysts have suggested that schools can create disciplined environments conducive to learning by implementing changes in the following three areas:

Changes in curricular standards and organization. The first goal is to bring more focus to the school curriculum. At the elementary level, this means establishing clear instructional objectives, aligning materials and tests to these objectives, and monitoring student progress frequently. In secondary schools, studies have shown that raising graduation requirements spurs students to take more academic courses. Whether higher standards also result in more course failure, which is itself linked to adolescent problem behavior, is an open question. In addition, while competency tests sharpen the focus of the high school curriculum, the effects of state and district policies governing course requirements and competency testing remain unclear.

Systems of academic tracking and ability grouping dilute the mission of the school, especially for low-achieving students. In such systems, low achievers are exposed to less rigorous courses and their teachers have lower expectations for their success. Furthermore, students in low-ability groups are more likely to misbehave, and middle and high schools with less tracking and ability grouping seem to have fewer discipline problems.

Changes in school organization. In this second area recommended for change, researchers have focused on studying the size of schools and classes, assuming that smaller educational settings may improve relationships among teachers and students. Research confirms that smaller schools indeed foster better discipline.

The shift from a single teacher for most subjects in elementary schools to departmentalized classes in secondary schools represents a significant difference for school climate. Departmentalization results in teachers having many more students which, in turn, discourages personal relationships among students and teachers. In contrast, self-contained classrooms in middle schools have fewer students, permitting more opportunities for student-teacher relationships. Other research has shown that middle schools with self-contained classrooms or team-teaching arrangements have fewer discipline problems and higher academic achievement.

In schools with disciplined environments, the teachers' work extends beyond the classroom. Their participation in extracurricular activities leads to positive and more personal relationships with students. There are fewer disruptions when teachers themselves take the responsibility for discipline in the hallways as well as in the classrooms.

Seriously disruptive students are being educated to an increasing degree in alternative settings, either in separate rooms or separate schools. Several studies of alternative schools show greater satisfaction on the part of students, more positive attitudes, and better behavior than before. One study of 18 alternative high schools found that student behavior was rarely a problem. The authors suggest this may be due to the schools' relatively small size, easier interaction between staff and students, and a lack of conflicting expectations.

When very close control was introduced as part of one alternative program, however, delinquent behavior increased. And according to labeling theory, putting "troublesome" youth into separate programs could stigmatize them, making improvement more difficult. Therefore, while alternative schools appear promising, program structure seems to have significant effects on students.

In general, smaller schools, self-contained classrooms, and an extended role for teachers all promote better discipline, probably through more personalized relationships with teachers which convey a greater sense of caring.

Changes in school management. In the final area where researchers found change fruitful for developing a disciplined environment, leadership by principals is clearly critical. While less effective principals devote more time to routine administrative tasks, effective principals attend more to instructional leadership by highlighting instructional goals and priorities. They take an active role in promoting school discipline; set firm and fair standards, and ensure that they are consistently enforced; and pay more attention to interpersonal relations in the school.

Principals alone, however, cannot shape the school environment. Research repeatedly finds that schools with disciplined environments are distinguished by teacher participation in decision making.

School management of discipline has commonly included the development of student discipline codes, due process in suspensions, the use of suspension, and in-school alternatives to suspension. Each of these is reviewed below.

Regarding discipline codes, a recent report by the New Jersey Education Commissioner, for example, recommended that districts develop policies to

330 APPENDIX A

protect students and staff from disruptive behavior, promote pride and respect for persons and property, and hold students accountable without being oppressive or unfair. It inferred that a good discipline policy contributes to feelings of self-worth and high morale. Another study of school districts elsewhere came to the same conclusion, but neither study measured the actual effects of discipline policies on students.

In developing discipline codes, the rights of students, expectations about student conduct, prohibitions, sanctions, and disciplinary procedures need to be considered. And support for the policies is best secured by involving staff in their development. Student involvement in developing discipline codes, however, is not so clearly necessary for reducing violence.

The practice of due process received bad press after the Supreme Court ruled in 1975 that even in suspensions of less than 10 days school officials must justify the suspension and hear the student's side of the story. While a surge in lawsuits against schools was anticipated for non-compliance, it did not materialize. The fears that such due process procedures would impose excessive hardship on school administrators were unfounded: a national survey of secondary school principals showed that only 3 percent considered these procedures a burden. In fact, many principals invite parents to hearings, allow third-party evidence, and establish an appeals process. As noted above, fairness such as this is an essential element in deterring misbehavior.

Suspension itself, however, has not been a successful discipline measure. While it temporarily rids the school of misbehaving youth, suspension also deprives those students of instructional time, and discharges them into the community, often without supervision. In many cases, suspension reinforces truants' desire for free time, rather than helping to improve their behavior. This is not an insignificant problem since more than 1 million students were suspended from school in 1990–91. Rates were higher in secondary schools, in those with a large student population, and in areas with high concentrations of low-income families. And equally as troubling, statistics show that suspensions are applied more frequently against minority students.

Short-term in-school alternatives to suspension are used even more widely than suspension: 1.4 million students were sent to such programs in 1990–91. These programs exist in 75 percent of all schools, and they range from total isolation to academic remediation and counseling outside the classroom. Early studies showed a drop in suspension rates after in-school alternatives were introduced, but now it appears that in-school suspension is being used merely as a punishment for less serious offenses, and that it has lost its effectiveness as a deterrent. One reason may be that most of the alternatives do not include academic tutoring or counseling, which should help re-engage students with learning.

The research on school management suggests that leadership, and planning by principals and teachers together to reach instructional and disciplinary goals constitute a more effective strategy than the common approaches of suspension or its in-school alternatives.

Remaining Questions Regarding School Climate and Organization

The studies reviewed here tend to examine school curriculum, organization, and management as separate fields rather than as related components of a complex structure. It is unlikely, however, that a disciplined environment results from change in any one of these discrete areas alone. Instead, it probably requires a multiyear, multidimensional approach to change that involves concurrent attention to school curriculum and instruction, organization, governance, and social relations.

Questions also remain about how the administrative contexts of schooling affect the chances that large numbers of schools will be able to develop disciplined environments conducive to learning. The regulation of public schools by district, state, and federal authorities may handicap them in achieving a positive school climate. It is the case, however, that some public schools have managed to do it despite tight regulations or mandates in such areas as personnel and special programs. Studies of these successful schools would be useful.

The Role of Classroom Organization and Management

Research on the role of classroom organization and management focuses on structures and processes, and especially on actions taken by teachers, that promote order and student involvement which, in turn, help students attain curriculum objectives.

This research has some limitations. First, with few exceptions, it has focused on elementary school classrooms. Therefore caution is necessary in applying the findings to high schools. Second, since few studies have been done on severely disrupted classrooms, it is not clear how much of the information can be applied in classrooms with serious or frequent disruptions. Finally, the bulk of this research has been done on the process of social organization in the classroom. Its audience is teachers rather than policymakers, and its implications for policy are not always clear.

Establishing and maintaining order. In classroom management, "order" does not necessarily mean silence or rigid compliance with externally imposed rules at all times. Rather, it is defined as reasonable cooperation by a class in the program of instruction which may require movement, conversation, and noise. Cooperation is an agreement between teachers and students, and does not rely on directions from higher administrative levels.

Teachers achieve and maintain order by introducing, monitoring, and guiding complex action systems that organize their students to accomplish curriculum tasks. Success depends on how well teachers understand these action systems, and how effectively they can adjust them in a timely and appropriate manner when circumstances warrant it.

Successful managers introduce rules, procedures, and routines, preferably at the beginning of the year, to increase the efficiency and predictability of classroom events. A key to their success is monitoring. Teachers must be aware of what is going on in their classroom, and must be able to attend to two or more incidents at the same time. The concept of monitoring—what teachers watch when scanning a room—has at least three dimensions:

- Teachers watch groups, remaining aware of the entire room and how well the total activity is going;
- Teachers watch conduct or behavior, paying particular attention to students' deviations from the intended program of action in order to stop them early; and
- Teachers monitor the pace, rhythm, and duration of classroom events.

Classroom arrangements and teaching styles. The physical characteristics of a classroom, including the closeness of students, the arrangement of desks, and the design of the building (open space or self-contained) have an impact on students' behavior, and the teacher's ability to control it. In general, the more loosely structured the setting, the more likely inappropriate behavior will occur. Similarly, the greater the amount of student activity choice and mobility; the greater the need for overt management and control by the teacher.

Demands on teachers in managing their classrooms change according to the nature of classroom activities. In general, where student involvement is highest—in teacher-led small groups—misbehavior is rare. Conversely, student participation is lowest and misbehavior is common during pupil presentations. Between these extremes, participation is higher in whole-class recitation, tests, and teacher presentations than in supervised study, independent seatwork, and student-led small groups.

Highly structured forms of cooperative learning have been shown to increase student achievement levels as measured by standardized tests, but only if the activities incorporate both group goals and individual accountability. This finding should not be generalized to include all forms of small group instruction, as these are not necessarily forms of ''cooperative learning.'' In fact, small group instruction is often a problem from the perspectives of management, curriculum, and student learning. Poorly designed tasks can shift students' attention from content to procedural matters. There is often an emphasis on drill and practice rather than on problem solving, making students passive rather than active learners.

Curriculum and classroom order. The complexity of work assigned to students has a direct effect on order. When academic work is routine and familiar to the students, like spelling tests or regular worksheet exercises, the flow of classroom activity is usually smooth and well-paced. When the work is problem centered—when students are required to interpret situations and make decisions to accomplish tasks, such as with word problems or essays—the flow of activity becomes slow and uneven. Since this is contrary to the assumption that challenging assignments automatically engage students in their work, teachers must be aware that managing higher order tasks requires exceptional management skill.

The tension between the need for classroom order and the need for the freedom to explore and solve problems is a core issue in a disciplined educational environment. Clearly, school policies that define order as silence and conformity can force a teacher to emphasize drill and practice, and preclude valued curriculum experiences. Schools must recognize the demands of loosely structured settings and open-ended tasks, and provide teachers the support they need to solve the problems these patterns can generate.

It is axiomatic that teacher expectations have a significant effect on student achievement. Low expectations are associated with lower achievement. If a teacher is convinced that certain students are low achievers and gives them only easy tasks, avoids calling on them, and prompts them excessively, they will probably become more passive and avoid academic work. But higher expectations themselves are not enough. They must be backed up with deliberate efforts to help the student learn. Then as students experience success, their perceptions of the school and of themselves as learners improve. These positive attitudes contribute to a more disciplined environment.

Dealing with misbehavior. Misbehavior is defined as any disruption in the primary program of activity in a classroom. It usually affects the level of attention, crowd control, and productivity. In many cases misbehavior is public—visible to a significant portion of a class—and contagious—capable of spreading rapidly among classmates. As already noted, misbehavior is more common in situations where students are easily distracted from academic work, and where class activities are frequently interrupted.

Teachers usually feel compelled to interrupt the whole class to stop misbehavior. But in calling attention to potentially disruptive behavior, this approach risks sidetracking the class even further from its primary activity, thus undermining rather than ensuring classroom order. A more effective response to misbehavior is to use a variety of unobtrusive nonverbal signals—gestures, direct eye contact, or proximity. If verbal reprimands seem necessary, "Shh," "Wait," "Stop," or "No" are appropriate. This approach, used at the onset of misbehavior, is likely to cause no additional disruption.

There are a number of commercial discipline models, but, aside from teachers' testimonials, very little is known about their effectiveness in reducing misbehavior. Certainly there is little concrete proof of the exaggerated claims of benefits often made by the promoters of these systems.

Behavior modification techniques, involving privileges, soft verbal reprimands, and other reinforcements for appropriate behavior, have been widely recommended for their proven success as tools for helping teachers work with problem students. In many settings, however, the practicality of implementing them is at issue. Also at issue is the detrimental effect that heavy reliance on rewarding students for good behavior or academic performance can have in the long run on inherent motivation. For these reasons, more attention has been given recently to social skills and coping strategies which are less cumbersome and intrusive than behavior modification.

Corporal punishment is practiced widely, and the Supreme Court has ruled that it is not cruel and unusual punishment. Nevertheless, more than a third of the states ban the practice in their public schools. Supporters of corporal punishment argue that it is effective, inexpensive, quick, and often the only means of maintaining order. Critics, on the other hand, charge that it is used disproportionately against male and minority students, and that it is dehumanizing, physically and psychologically harmful, and sends a message that violence is an acceptable way to handle problems.

In addition, the effectiveness of corporal punishment is questionable since students who are punished may actually gain status among their peers. It also seems to cause resentment and undermine working relationships. Therefore, in view of its potentially negative effects and the lack of systematic evidence of any benefits, corporal punishment might best be avoided as a method for controlling behavior.

Policies and classroom processes. Little research has been done on how state or district policies actually affect what goes on in classrooms. Policies based on research about teaching are often simplistic. They tend to highlight quantity—more time, more courses, more homework—rather than quality and substance. Since quality and substance are central to the issue of achievement, policies need to be focused there.

Certain policies present many potential pitfalls for their enforcement. For example, testing programs that call for rote learning, or mandates to adopt uniform practices to address complex problems, can narrow the curriculum, lower teacher morale, and undermine student motivation. Similarly, classroom discipline codes that require passivity, obedience, and control can sabotage efforts to promote true learning.

Student outcomes is a central issue in policy discussions and research about classroom processes. All too often, the focus is on mandated standardized achievement tests which, for the most part, measure lower level skills. As the focus in the national curriculum debate shifts toward higher order skills, conceptual understanding, problem solving, and self-regulation for all students, research and policymaking must also refocus on the design and management of curriculum tasks with similar objectives. Working toward creating classrooms conducive to this kind of active learning is also important for attaining Goal 3 which is concerned with helping students "learn to use their minds well."

Conclusions Regarding Classroom Organization and Management

Several major implications for policy and practice emerge from the studies of classroom management:

- The beginning of the school year is a critical time for establishing classroom order. Teachers must be supported in achieving a well-run classroom as early as possible. Classroom interruptions and abrupt changes in class enrollments can seriously impede this process.
- The rhythms and patterns of classroom life should be respected. Interruptions during the year should be minimized, and teachers should be warned in advance if schedule changes will affect their classes. This approach tells students that learning is important, and makes the flow of classroom work predictable.
- Teachers need support to learn about approaches for maintaining well-managed classrooms that do not rely on rigid definitions of order. In such classrooms, order promotes the use of a variety of instructional activities to maximize engagement in learning.
- Finally, schoolwide policies and support systems are needed to deal with serious misbehavior. Such policies clarify issues and create a climate for addressing problems. A well-functioning support system means that a teacher is not isolated when confronted with a serious disruption.

Drugs and Schools

The drug use prevention field has evolved toward greater effectiveness. Today, rather than targeting one or two risk factors, such as low self-esteem and poor school achievement, effective programs take into account the multitude of risk factors facing many youth, and put into play a combination of strategies to address them. In this section, we review the research on strategies for defining and addressing the drug problem faced by schools and their communities, and indicate which ones seem to have the most significant impact on the prevention of drug use.

Risk and Protective Factors for Alcohol and Other Drug Use

The widespread availability of legal and illicit drugs puts all adolescents potentially at risk. Yet some are at higher risk than others due to a variety of individual, family, and other environmental factors that seem to influence a child's first use of drugs.

Individual psychological and interpersonal factors. These include needing the approval of others; letting others make one's decisions; being unassertive; having low self-confidence; and showing early aggressive and antisocial behavior, low commitment to school, and poor school performance. One of the strongest predictors of drug use by teens is their association with drug-using peers, as well as their attitude about drugs. Beginning in the early elementary grades, academic failure increases the risk both of drug use and of delinquency. Conversely, some of the protective factors that appear to bolster a child's resistance to drug use are self-confidence; strong social competencies; peers who value achievement and responsible behavior; and clear adult supervision.

Family factors. Tolerance of substance abuse by parents and older siblings can be compounded by a family history of alcoholism, drug use, and mental illness, and poor family management and parenting skills. While parents who abuse drugs are more likely to have drug-abusing children, the question of the relative influence of heredity and environment has not been resolved. It is clear, however, that parents who are considerate and supportive, yet firm in their beliefs, can protect their adolescent children from drug use. And parents who monitor their children's activities carefully and influence their choice of friends are more effective in preventing experimentation with drugs.

Broader environmental factors. These include community norms regarding alcohol and other drugs, and their real or perceived availability; unclear or inconsistently enforced rules and laws; community characteristics like poverty, mobility, and violence; and contradictory messages in the media about drug use. All of these factors present opportunities for delivering inconsistent messages regarding drug use. Since one of the most direct influences on a child's drug use is the number of drug-using friends, it is essential – and proven effective for drug use prevention – to provide children with accurate information about the prevalence and acceptability of drug use among their peers. In particular, the mass media and advertisements affect drug use among young people by targeting them for messages about its attractiveness. These messages can be more power-ful than public service announcements that address drug use as a problem.

The transitions to middle, junior, and senior high school are moves to progressively less protected environments. Schools can compensate for this instability in many ways by guiding and supporting students' daily social and recreational, as well as educational activities, improving their self-concept by recognizing a variety of student accomplishments, and by facilitating a variety of student groupings and interactions. Students who like school and have a close relationship with teachers are more likely to adopt nonuse norms than those who do not.

The strength of religious commitment is also associated with less alcohol and other drug use.

Targeting Multiple Factors

Most drug use prevention strategies or efforts target two risk factors in particular – laws and norms favorable to drug use, and social influences.

Current evidence suggests, however, that an effective strategy must target a broad spectrum of risk and protective factors related to individual vulnerability, inadequate rearing, school achievement, social influences, social skills, and broad social norms.

The challenge for the 1990s is to develop and implement strategies that help youth succeed in staying drug free, in spite of adverse conditions in their families, schools, and communities. Caring and supportive relationships; high expectations for appropriate choices and behavior; and the availability of a variety of opportunities to participate and contribute in meaningful ways: these three protective factors are seen as essential for healthy development across the three domains of family, school, and communities. And strong collaborations among these groups are required to achieve healthy development in our youth.

Within the family. Parents can nurture a close bond with their child throughout childhood and adolescence; create expectations for their child's success; provide human warmth, clear rules, and discipline; instill beliefs that provide stability and meaning to their child's life, especially in times of hardship and adversity; and treat their child as a valued, contributing member of the family.

Within the school. Teachers can acknowledge their role not only as instructors, but as caregivers. They can be confidants and positive role models for students. They can also encourage relationships with caring peers and friends through, for example, peer programs and cooperative learning strategies. Successful schools – those with low levels of delinquency and misbehavior, and high levels of attendance and academic attainment – make available a variety of opportunities that engage students' interest and desire to succeed. Students are expected to be actively engaged in problem solving, decision making, planning, goal setting, and helping others.

Within the community. The community can coordinate its available resources in the areas of health and child care, housing, education, job training, employment, and recreation to address the needs of children and families. The community can also view prevention of drug use as a shared value and responsibility, and establish norms accordingly. By providing young people with opportunities to be meaningful participants and contributors in community life, the community gives evidence that it values them as resources.

Prevention Strategies

Primary prevention strategies are defined as activities that deter youth from using alcohol and drugs by helping them develop mature positive attitudes, values, behaviors, skills, and lifestyles. Following are common interventions and a brief comment on what research indicates about their impact.

Laws and regulations. Evidence suggests that laws and regulations can play a supportive role in controlling alcohol use provided these laws are clearly communicated, supported by the community, and equitably enforced. For example, a decline in drinking has been due partly to the enactment of laws raising the legal drinking age to 21. This has resulted in reducing alcohol-related traffic deaths as well as reinforcing the control of alcohol use.

School policies. Almost all public school districts and private schools address drug use in their overall disciplinary policies. Most of these policies have changed significantly since 1986 with the passage of the Drug-Free Schools and Communities Act. Another influence on local policy came from the new guidelines tying federal funds to establishing standards regarding drug use, possession, and sale, as well as to implementing a drug use prevention program in grades K − 12. The systemwide impact of these changes, however, has not been determined.

Since 1986, drug policies have evolved in two distinct directions: (1) the adoption of a strong ''zero tolerance'' approach leading to strong punishments like long-term suspension or expulsion; and (2) the recognition that policy enforcement is not an end in itself but must be combined with rehabilitation. A policy of zero tolerance gives many students a safe haven−an opportunity to say no in a setting where being drug free is the norm and drug use is prohibited. Schools that aggressively involve parents with a zero tolerance approach create a strong partnership which boosts the chances for program success. In fact, extensive parent and community involvement is essential if any new policy is to be effective.

In the case of combining enforcement with rehabilitation, one Arizona school district provides a carefully monitored alternative to suspension, including mandatory intensive counseling, periodic urinalysis, and community service. It gives parents and students a chance to weigh the choice between rehabilitation with a view to a drug-free life and further education, or loss of the opportunity to continue school due to suspension or expulsion.

Information programs. Virtually all prevention programs include an information component to address the consequences of substance use. Information is deemed to be necessary, but not by itself a sufficient component of a prevention program. There is no clear evidence that programs relying on information only or on strategies for arousing fear prevent students from using tobacco, alcohol, or other drugs. A recent report concluded that information-only substance-use education may alter knowledge and attitudes but rarely changes a student's drug-using behavior. Anti-smoking efforts, on the other hand, have been somewhat more successful.

There is also evidence of success from programs that conduct media campaigns. There is some controversy among experts about the wisdom of emphasizing ''designated drivers'' or safe rides and moderate drinking rather than abstinence for those under the legal drinking age. Nevertheless, all of these activities support efforts to reduce automobile crashes, and, according to a 1992 statewide study in Minnesota, there has been some decline over a 3-year period in students riding with friends who have been drinking.

Affective education programs. These programs focus on self-examination, self-esteem, responsible decision making, and values clarification, but seldom relate these general skills to resisting specific drug situations. Most studies show such programs have little effect on reducing tobacco, alcohol, and other drug use. When there is evidence of effectiveness, the benefits appear somewhat more likely for reducing marijuana and tobacco use than alcohol use.

Social influence/resistance strategies. There are two key components of such programs. The first is training in refusal skills, which identifies the sources of pressure and teaches how to counter them. The second is norm setting, which involves correcting the perception that drugs are widely used and accepted by peers. Youth in the experimental stage of drug use tend to grossly overestimate the prevalence and acceptability of drug use among their peers, which sets up internally driven pressures to conform to these assumed peer patterns.

Resistance activities led by students are more effective than those led by teachers, according to some studies. This is partly due to greater consistency in curriculum implementation by peer facilitators.

However, while students who receive resistance training have greater knowledge of the social pressures to use alcohol, and of the methods to resist them, this does not necessarily translate into an ability to say "no." In fact, the research shows that resistance skills training by itself has little effect on the onset of either tobacco, alcohol, or marijuana use. When norm-setting education was studied separately from refusal skills training, it was found to have a greater impact.

Student support and assistance services. Student support and assistance services are defined as nonacademic services provided by the school that work in concert with other prevention program efforts. They include activities such as student support groups, mentoring programs, and drug-free events, and are primarily designed for students who are currently using or abusing alcohol and other drugs, or who are considered at high risk for developing substance-related problems. Unfortunately, the evidence for the effectiveness of student support and assistance programs is limited given the absence of a solid base of research.

Alternative activities and programs. These interventions attempt to prevent drug use by changing parts of the adolescent's environment. They provide positive activities or focus on overcoming deficiencies in basic life skills, low self-worth, and experiences that place adolescents at risk. A limited number of studies have shown that high-intensity programs that empower high-risk youth, like drug abusers and juvenile delinquents, to master new basic life skills are linked to improved behavior and achievement. The impact of such programs on drug use prevention is less evident.

The Importance of Ongoing Prevention Activities

Follow-up studies indicate that the effects of prevention efforts gradually erode and then vanish after 4 or 5 years. A booster strategy can effectively extend initial prevention efforts. For example, a ''booster curriculum'' was designed to reinforce material taught the previous year in a seventh grade substance use prevention program. Since the results were far better than when the booster curriculum was not implemented, it became clear that resistance is maintained at a higher level when students receive periodic, sequential, and meaningful booster sessions. While the ideal duration of prevention programs is not clear, it is obvious that the effects of the powerful factors leading to drug use cannot be eliminated in a few classes during one or two semesters of middle school. These programs must be more intensive and sustained to have a lasting impact. Therefore, interventions beginning in elementary, middle, and junior high schools need to continue through high school.

Future Directions in Drug Use Prevention

Based on testimony from experts in the field, as well as a cross section of students, teachers, school administrators, parents, and community representatives, the National Commission on Drug-Free Schools recommended in 1990 that comprehensive drug education and use prevention programs include the following elements:

- Student surveys to determine the nature and extent of the drug problem, school needs assessments, and resource identification;
- Leadership training for key school officials and staff;
- Clear, consistent school policies, with responses to violations that include alternatives to suspension;
- Training for the entire staff on the effects of drug use, the school's drug policies and policy implementation program, intervention, and referral of students for rehabilitation;
- Assistance programs and support for students from preschool through 12th grade;
- Training for parents to assist them in understanding drug use prevention, and related issues and concerns; and
- Current, factually accurate, age-appropriate, and developmentally oriented curriculum for preschool through 12th grade.

Similarly, a 1992 report of the Government Accounting Office focused on 10 comprehensive community-based drug use prevention programs targeting 10- to 13-year-old high-risk youth in rural and urban settings. While the effectiveness of these programs was not assessed, a number of their promising features were identified by the authors as follows:

- A comprehensive strategy;
- An indirect rather than a direct approach or one labeled ''drug prevention;''

- A focus on empowering young people by teaching them the broad range of skills they need to choose positive, constructive options;
- A participatory approach that requires group cooperation, planning, and coordination to accomplish tasks;
- A culturally relevant approach; and
- Highly structured activities appropriate for younger adolescents aged 9 through 12.

Conclusions Regarding Drug Use Prevention

It appears that the most effective strategies against drug use target both multiple risk and protective factors. They are comprehensive and encompass many social systems-peer groups, families, schools, media, community organizations including religious and law enforcement groups. In addition, they apply a wide variety of approaches that provide information, develop life skills, use peer facilitators, and change community policies and norms. Success is enhanced by community support and the involvement of parents and peers. The teacher also plays a critical role, and thus teacher training in this area is essential.

Despite the progress made over the past decade, however, much work remains to be done on virtually all aspects of this critical issue. Research must continue to determine the effectiveness and long-term impact of various approaches to drug use prevention, and the means of overcoming the barriers to success.

Violence in the Schools

Research on reducing violence in schools is sparse. Nevertheless, we have reliable information about the nature of various threats to school safety, and on the relative effectiveness of some safety-enhancing strategies.

Weapons

Students may bring weapons to school for many reasons: to show off, to protect themselves, to be aggressive, to hold them for others, and even to use in gang or drug-related activity. Although knives are most common, powerful firearms are becoming more readily available. The fact that there are weapons in schools is an indication of their easy access in the community, their presence in many homes, and the apparent widespread attitude that violence is an acceptable way to solve problems.

Various approaches have been tried to keep weapons out of school buildings. Stationary metal detectors at the school entrance and random searches with hand-held detectors are commonplace in some cities. Other schools lock outside doors, search student lockers, and employ campus security patrols. There is no real evidence of how well any of these approaches works, and each has certain shortcomings. Metal detectors have become especially controversial. While they are easy to set up, require little training, and are effective in spotting weapons, they are opposed by some as an invasion of privacy. They also can cause a logjam at the door, and in general create an unwanted image of schools as fortresses. Locked doors can be a hazard in the event of fire, and patrols and searches are time consuming and expensive.

Educators and school security experts know of many practices against weapons that may warrant further study. They include encouraging tips from students, displaying posters condemning guns in schools and listing a hotline telephone number, requiring coats and book bags to be kept in lockers, offering violence prevention courses and peer counseling programs, and responding immediately to trouble with suspension or expulsion. However, expulsion simply transfers the problem to the streets, and is not a realistic long-term solution.

Overall, strategies to keep weapons out of schools have not been tested on a systematic basis. Most of them are attempts to control student behavior rather than to address the factors contributing to the behavior. While control may be important to stabilize threatening situations, such strategies may be less useful in the long run than changing school practices so that students are more engaged in academic work.

Intruders

Many schools are particularly concerned about barring unwanted and potentially dangerous visitors. Some of the methods used to keep out weapons can be used to bar intruders, but their use is controversial and their worth unproven. For example, electromagnetic locks can be installed on exit doors likely to be used by intruders, and be set to open when the fire alarm sounds. New schools or additions can be designed with these security problems in mind.

Supervision by staff members may help secure entrances, and security monitors can be given police powers to remove intruders. Staff and students who stay after school are advised to avoid remote areas, move around in groups, and lock inside doors. However, the effectiveness of any of these precautions, as well as the use of security officers or aides, has not been documented by systematic studies. New programs to bar intruders must be well planned and their intended and unintended results monitored before implementing them permanently.

Fights and Assaults

Incidents like these involve bodily harm or threats, as well as robberies. This is one area where curricular approaches dealing with violence prevention and conflict management have been implemented with some success.

The Violence Prevention Curriculum Project is perhaps the earliest and best known of these. This approach examines anger and how to channel it constructively, while offering alternative means of resolving conflict. A six-city evaluation showed some benefits to self-esteem and reductions in fights and arrests. While there were problems in implementing the study and a follow-up would be desirable, this is a promising program that has also been extended into the community.

In the past decade, several programs have been developed to teach conflict resolution skills to students. Some include peer mediation and staff training. They aim to encourage self-discipline, effective decision making skills, and nonviolent responses to disputes. Interest in this approach is so great that the *Healthy People 2000* report of the U.S. Public Health Service calls for teaching nonviolent conflict resolution skills in half the nation's schools by the end of this decade.

A review of many of these conflict resolution programs concluded that they showed some benefits for the peer mediators, the student body, and the teachers. Success rates of mediation were generally high, student attitudes toward conflict changed, and fewer fights were reported. It should be noted, however, that these and other skills training programs involve changing people's behavior directly. Another promising preventive approach is to change school practices, such as tracking, that set up the conditions leading to student conflicts.

Gangs

Young people may become involved with gangs for various reasons, such as power and prestige, peer pressure, self-preservation, adventure, and money. Like many organizations, gangs have a name and distinguishing features, continuing members, and a territory. But these groups are engaged in criminal activities, and they appear to be spreading from large cities to suburbs, smaller towns, and previously gang-free regions of the country to avoid police and rival gangs, and to expand drug markets.

Without the powers of law enforcement agencies, schools may best try to create a nurturing environment for students where success becomes an attractive alternative to gang activity. There is little research in this area but lots of advice, much of it mirroring those activities designed to deal with drugs and violence. These include training staff about gangs, enforcing procedures to keep out intruders, eliminating gang graffiti and insignias, adopting clear and consistent discipline standards, creating alternative programs for disruptive students, teaching students social skills to help them make wise choices, and maintaining close coordination with the police, other agencies, and parents.

The most extensive research on cities with chronic gang problems indicates that the most effective approach for preventing gang membership combines education and job training opportunities with interagency networking and grassroots participation in agencies serving youth.

Coordination with the Community

A stated objective under Goal 6 is that parents, businesses, and community organizations will work together to make schools "a safe haven for all children." Their work may take a number of forms, including those listed above, to reduce gang problems. A recent review of community-based interventions (mostly without school involvement) concluded, however, that there is little evidence of their effectiveness for preventing delinquency. This result is probably due to measurement difficulties, as well as to the many related influences and interactions among community, family, and individual factors in behavior.

There is a bit more information on violence prevention programs involving collaborations between schools and the community. Although once again the evaluations are incomplete, two programs are particularly promising.

One is an extension of the Violence Prevention Curriculum, described above, into surrounding neighborhoods via multiservice and health centers, boys and girls clubs, recreation programs, and other similar activities. These efforts were also promoted through media campaigns. The city of Boston supports this project which receives many requests for training and technical assistance.

The second promising program, the Paramount Plan in California, consists of a curriculum for fifth- and seventh-graders on alternatives to gang membership. It features meetings for parents and family counseling for teens at high risk for joining gangs. After participating in this program, 90 percent of the students responded negatively to the idea of joining a gang and still held that attitude a year later.

A program called SMART (School Management and Resource Teams), which coordinates schools and law enforcement agencies, has been introduced in over 20 cities. Reports and analyses of violent incidents are disseminated to local teams for action planning. The staff coordinates districtwide policies and procedures on student behavior, and develops cooperative relationships with police and other government agencies. In one district, those discipline problems receiving attention declined more than did other problems. Interagency cooperation was difficult to assess, however, and in an earlier 2-year three-city development phase, its implementation had barely begun.

Thus, many of the common strategies used to deal with school violence remain untested. Other approaches that involve coordinated efforts appear more promising, but still need to be fully evaluated.

CONCLUSION

Drug use, school misbehavior, and violence are sometimes the acts of the same students, and they often have common origins. Despite the similarities, each is usually handled separately, and no one strategy seems to work best for all students or all circumstances. It is unlikely that real benefits will come from limited changes in a single aspect of schooling. Instead, simultaneous attention to curriculum and instruction, school organization and governance, and relationships inside and outside the school is needed. Thus comprehensive approaches incorporating many strategies, involving parents, the community, and the school seem most promising. They must address the multiple risk factors and seek to build protections against them. Strategies will have to be adapted to local situations, and it will probably be necessary to make multiyear commitments to create and sustain change. Some of the most promising strategies are described below.

Conclusions on Disciplined Environments

Research on the elements that strengthen disciplined school environments is extensive and provides much guidance for program development. It indicates that whereas the mere adoption of a ''get tough'' policy seems ineffective, a combination of the following approaches is more likely to prove useful in the long run: a strong emphasis on the academic mission of the school; firm, fair, and consistently enforced discipline standards; and an ethic of caring that guides staff-student relationships.

This report has outlined how changes in curricular standards and organization, and school organization and management can affect learning environments. The following were found to be particularly significant:

- Tracking generally leads to discipline problems for students in low ability groups, and its elimination would help them greatly;
- Smaller schools, self-contained classes, and teacher involvement beyond the classroom all seem to contribute to the sense of caring;
- Alternative schools can also communicate a caring attitude and markedly improve student behavior;
- Suspension is not a very successful disciplinary measure, and in-school alternatives seem to be used for less serious offenses; and
- Principals who focus on instructional leadership and interpersonal relationships, and share planning with teachers are successful in reducing discipline problems in addition to increasing the level of student achievement.

These school strategies should also contribute in the long run to higher graduation rates (Goal 2) since they will help engage students more fully in learning.

Research on classroom management and organization is also well developed, but only at the elementary level. It shows that introducing rules at the beginning of the school year is essential for establishing and maintaining order, but the meaning of order varies by the task and situation. It does not necessarily mean silence and rigid compliance. Loosely structured settings, challenging assignments, and some efforts to stop misbehavior raise the risk of even more misbehavior unless the teacher has strong classroom management skills. Cooperative learning can improve achievement and interpersonal relations, and teachers' expectations influence student achievement. Low-achieving students do less well when teachers expect little from them than when they provide more assistance. There is little evidence, on the other hand, that many of the commercial classroom approaches to discipline are effective.

Conclusions on Drugs and Schools

There is some evidence of successful efforts to reduce students' use of drugs, but many specific approaches require further study before they can be prescribed as components of a successful program.

The most promising approaches are comprehensive, combining the teaching of resistance skills with correcting misperceptions about the prevalence of drug use. These, along with programs that teach personal and social skills (or ''life skills'') have consistently produced short-term reductions in substance use. There is some evidence that life skills/resistance skills programs project relatively well to a broad range of students as long as they are implemented in a culturally sensitive and relevant manner. Programs involving peer leaders often produce somewhat better results than those led by adults. Ongoing booster curricula are needed throughout the middle grades and senior high school to maintain positive impact on student behavior.

While more research is needed on these topics, the accomplishments of the past decade should nevertheless be recognized. Policymakers must (1) identify the nature and extent of the drug problem, and adopt the appropriate program which may require modifications to fit particular circumstances; (2) commit to continuous evaluation to ascertain program impact on student behavior, as well as on attitudes toward and knowledge about drug use; and (3) periodically assess the state of the art in drug use prevention to determine accurately what works and what doesn't.

Conclusions on Violence in Schools

Violence prevention curricula and training in conflict resolution have been studied extensively in terms of their aim to curtail student fights and assaults, and change attitudes toward solving problems with violence. While the results to date are encouraging, the research on this topic remains inconclusive.

A program to coordinate the efforts of schools and law enforcement agencies resulted in reduced discipline problems in a pilot school district. On the other hand, strategies to keep weapons and intruders out of schools are varied and largely untested. Nor is there much research on staff training or other actions schools might take to reduce violence. Other areas, such as gang activity and community coordination to reduce violence, are difficult to study because of their complexity. The most extensive research on gang problems suggests that a coordinated effort encompassing schools, job training programs, and other agencies may be needed.

RESOURCES

National Resources

The following U.S. Department of Education publications are available free of charge from the National Clearinghouse for Alcohol and Drug Information, P.O. Box 2345, Rockville, MD 20852, or by calling 301-468-2600 (toll free 1-800-SAY NO TO):

- *Success Stories from Drug-Free Schools: A Guide for Educators, Parents, and Policymakers*, 1991.
- *Growing Up Drug Free: A Parent's Guide to Prevention*, 1990.
- *Learning to Live Drug Free: A Curriculum Model for Prevention*, 1990.
- *What Works: Schools Without Drugs*, 1989.
- *Drug Prevention Curricula: A Guide to Selection and Implementation*, 1988.
- *National Commission on Drug-Free Schools. Toward a Drug-Free Generation: A Nation's Responsibility*, 1990.

The National Youth Gang Information Center sponsored by the U.S. Department of Justice provides free information on model designs for school-based programs, gang awareness curricula, and education-related bibliographies. They can be contacted at 4301 North Fairfax Dr., Suite 730, Arlington, VA 22203, or at 1-800-446-4264.

Suggested Readings

Baumrind, D. "The Influence of Parenting Style on Adolescent Competence and Substance Abuse." *Journal of Early Adolescence* 11[1](1991).

Benard, B. "Fostering Resiliency in Kids: Protective Factors in the Family, School, and Community." *Prevention Forum* 12[3](1992): 2–16.

Botvin, G. J., and E. M. Botvin. "School-based and Community-based Prevention Approaches." In *Comprehensive Textbook of Substance Abuse*, edited by J. Lowinson, P. Ruiz, and R. Millman, pp. 910–927. Baltimore: Williams & Wilkins, 1992.

Bryk, A., and Y. Thum. *The High School as Community: Contextual Influences, and Consequences for Students and Teachers*. Madison, WI: University of Wisconsin, Wisconsin Center for Educational Research, 1989.

Butterfield, G., and B. Turner. *Weapons in Schools: NSSC Resource Paper.* Malibu, CA: Pepperdine University, National School Safety Center, 1989.

Gaustad, J. *Schools Respond to Guns and Violence.* Eugene, OR: University of Oregon, Oregon School Study Council, 1991.

Gottfredson, D., G. Gottfredson, and L. Hybl. *Managing Adolescent Behavior: A Multi-year Multi-school Experiment,* Report No. 50. Baltimore: Johns Hopkins University, Center for Research on Elementary and Middle Schools, 1990.

Hansen, W. B., and J. W. Graham. ''Preventing Alcohol, Marijuana and Tobacco Use among Adolescents. Peer Pressure Resistance Teaming versus Establishing Conservative Norms.'' *Preventive Medicine* 20(1991): 414–430.

Hawkins, J. D., R. F. Catalano, and J. Y. Miller. ''Risk and Protective Factors for Early Alcohol and Other Drug Problems in Adolescence and Early Adulthood: Implications for Substance Abuse Prevention.'' *Psychological Bulletin* 112[l](1992): 64–105.

Jones, R. et al. ''Teacher Characteristics and Competencies Related to Substance Abuse Prevention.'' *Journal of Drug Education* 20[3](1990):179–189.

Mansfield, W., and E. Farris. *Public School Principal Survey on Safe, Disciplined, and Drug-Free Schools.* Washington, D.C.: U.S. Department of Education, National Center for Education Statistics, 1992.

McCaslin, M., and T. Good. ''Compliant Cognition: The Misalliance of Management and Instructional Goals in Current School Reform.'' *Educational Researcher* 21[3](1992):4–17.

Moles, O. *Student Discipline Strategies: Research and Practice.* Albany, NY. SUNY Press, 1990.

Oakes, J. ''Can Tracking Research Inform Practice? Technical, Normative, and Political Considerations.'' *Educational Researcher* 21(1992):12–21.

Office for Substance Abuse Prevention. *OSAP Prevention Monograph–1; Stopping Alcohol and Other Drug Use Before It Starts: The Future of Prevention.* Rockville, MD: U.S. Department of Health and Human Services, 1989.

U.S. Department of Education, Office of Policy and Planning. *Promising Drug Prevention Programs: An Interim Report to Congress.* Forthcoming.

Wilson-Brewer, R., S. Cohen, L. O'Donnell, and I. Goodman. *Violence Prevention for Young Adolescents: A Survey of the State of the Art.* Washington, D.C.: Carnegie Council on Adolescent Development, 1991.

CREATING COMPUTER-ASSISTED INSTRUCTION

We have developed Computer-Assisted Instruction (CAI) that makes it easy for a teacher to create software that will help at-risk and other students who respond well to interaction with a computer. We call the software Teaching Assistant (TA), and any teacher can learn to fill in the screens by typing them on their word processor. Guidelines for using CAI are included, such as activities that offer extrinsic rewards to students at risk who may place limited value on education. The guidelines include strategies such as creation of an active and thoughtful learning setting, visible recognition of various types, creation of curricula that interest these students, setting clear goals, using positive reinforcement, cooperative learning, inducing a readiness to learn, encouraging student responses in class, teacher efficacy, self-concept development, tutorial services, flexible scheduling, and alternative schooling options.

The software is available from Students-at-Risk, Inc., 1260 Brangwyn Way, Laguna Beach, CA 92651; Cost: $19.95.

CREATING CAI

The text for the TA program is developed using a standard word processor, for example, MicroSoft Word 5.1 for Macintosh or Word Perfect 5.1 for IBM compatibles. The file must be saved as standard ASCII text (in WP 5.1, it is called DOS text). It can also be created with Teach Text for the Macintosh or through the EDIT capability available on IBM compatible DOS.

TEACHING ASSISTANT USER MANUAL

The TA program is a computer-aided teaching assistant (computer-managed instruction program) that allows an instructor to create her/his own managed instruction software for each course. It can also be called an authoring program and probably would be by people who are familiar with authoring programs. If you have ever tried to use one and found it was more trouble than it was worth, this program will please you. We have consciously kept it very simple. It uses just five symbols (commands in computer talk). These are *, #, +,], and -.

The text for the TA program is developed using a standard word processor, for example Word Perfect 5.1. The file must be saved as standard ASCII text (in WP 5.1, it is called DOS text).

All of the symbols (commands) for the TA must be typed in as the first character of a line and may not be preceded by spaces. This means that the commands cannot be inserted into the middle of a line.

For example, here is the beginning line of a typical first screen (the page the reader will see when you open LUNG.CRS with the EDIT text editor on the disk):

*Screen 1 Lung Physiology?

The * indicates this is the beginning of a screen, so you always have to check to see that each screen begins with one. If you leave it out, that screen will not show when you run the program. It is an easy error to make and, the good news, to correct.

The 1 means that this is the first screen. We number them so we can have an easy way to keep track of the content on them. You may want to move the content around as you work on your first courseware (computer talk for what we are making).

Lung Physiology is the course title and it goes on Screen 1. Screens 2 and forward are the individual screen titles. These are the ones you may move around as you work.

The ? indicates this is an information page for the student and there is no correct response needed. The ? is a supplementary symbol or command and does not have to be the first character on a line of its own as the main commands do.

#Please press a key to continue

The # indicates you have reached the end of that section of text, usually the bottom of a page. It tells the program that it is time to go hunt and find out how to respond to the number the student typed in, if there was a question on the page. If there was no question, the student just moves on to the next page.

You have to keep track of the number of lines your screen will hold and see that there are not more than a screen full between the start of the screen where the * is and the end of the screen where the # is. Try to use no more than fifteen and see how that looks to you.

*Screen 2 Breathing 2

Note to reader: from here on explanatory text will be in parentheses.
(Breathing is the content on this screen and the first 2 tells us this is the second screen. The 2 after Breathing is the correct answer from the four possibilities you will see later, when you look at the screens for this course.)
What is the frequency of breathing in a normal, resting adult?

(*1*) 5 − 10 breaths per minute
(*2*) 11 − 14 breaths per minute
(*3*) 20 − 23 breaths per minute
(*4*) 50 − 70 breaths per minute

#Please enter your choice

+

Very good.

(The student indicated choice 2, the correct choice seen above as Breathing 2.)
(Now you write an explanatory note to the student who chose number 2.)
The average person breathes 11 − 14 times per minute under basal conditions. While this value is not useful in determining alveolar ventilation, it is an indicator of possible respiratory disorder.

]

(The] or right bracket causes the program to stop and wait for the student to hit the next key.)
(In the program now, we insert the responses to choices 1, 3, and 4, the incorrect responses. An incorrect response is signaled by a - so don't use the hyphen for anything else when you are typing the program.)

-

The correct answer is 11 − 14 breaths per minute. The breathing rate is discussed in Chapter 2, Pulmonary Ventilation. You should try to become familiar with this type of value because it is an easy value to observe. It will help you determine if the patient has possible respiratory distress.
Remember that if the patient is anxious or nervous, this value can change.

]

*Screen 3 Lung Function Tests 1

What is the basic reason for pulmonary function tests?

(*1*) Determine lung volume, air flow rates, and alveolar ventilation

(*2*) Determine how long a person can walk

(*3*) Determine if the patient smokes.

(*4*) Determine lung volume and blood pressure.

#Please enter your choice

+

Very good.

The basic purpose of pulmonary function tests is to determine the volume of air the lungs hold, how fast air can move in and out of the lungs, and how much oxygen can pass from the lungs into the bloodstream.

There are several supplementary texts on pulmonary function testing.

]

-

The basic purpose of pulmonary function tests is to determine the volume of air the lungs hold, how fast air can move in and out of the lungs, and how much oxygen can pass from the lungs into the blood stream.

This is the area you should understand. Try to read a chapter from one of the supplemental texts to develop your knowledge about the lungs and how you test for dysfunction.

]

*Screen 4 Tidal Volume 3

What does Tidal Volume mean?

(*1*) The amount of water in the lungs

(*2*) How much water moves in and out of the lungs

(*3*) The amount of air in one breath

(*4*) The total amount of air in the lungs

#Please enter your answer

+

Very good.

The Tidal Volume is the amount of air that is moved in and out of the lungs with each breath. This value is measured while the patient is breathing normally, requiring no exertion during the test.

]

-

The Tidal Volume is the amount of air contained in a single breath. This value is measured while the patient is at rest and breathing normally.
Some other values you should know are:
Total Lung Capacity
Vital Capacity
Functional Residual Capacity

]

*Screen 5 Final Screen?

This concludes the tutoring session on Pulmonary Physiology. The next session is on Renal Function.

#Thank you for working so hard. See you next session.

To review then, these are the commands and the subcommand:

*Screen title

The asterisk starts a screen title line. The screen title allows you to keep track of how the screens are organized.
? The question mark means that any response is appropriate and no correct response is expected. This is used with an informational screen that provides a message to the user but does not expect a correct answer.

'#' - displayed message

The command stops displaying the text file and waits for the user to enter a key. If a correct response was included in the '*' command, the program will branch to the correct response text if the entered character matches the correct response or to the incorrect response text if there is not a match.
All text between the '*' and '#' commands will be displayed as written with the text editor. Design your screens with this in mind.

'+' - correct response text

]'

The '-' command signals the start of correct response text.

When a correct response is entered after a '#' command, the program will search the text file until it finds a ' +'. The following text will be displayed on a clear screen until a right bracket (']') is found. The ']' causes the program to stop and wait for a key stroke. Any number of lines can be inserted between the ' +' and the ']'. The ']' must be on a line by itself and must be the first character on the line.

'-' - incorrect response text

]'

The '-' command identifies the start of the incorrect response text. When an incorrect response is entered after the '#' command, the program will search the text file until a '-' is found. The text following the '-' will display on a clear screen until the ']' is found. The program will then pause and wait for a keystroke.

Currently the command set is limited to only ' *', '#', ' +'/']', and '-'/']'. Using these simple commands, you should be able to build complicated tutoring examples.

Now, open EDIT and choose LUNG.CRS and start a new file. Make it five inches wide. Type in all the program material from the tutoring example beginning with

*Screen 1 Lung Physiology?

Type it exactly as we have.

Now save the program in EDIT or as a text file called LUNG2.CRS, not as a regular word processor file. For example, on MicroSoft Word for the Mac, you use the command Save As and then, at the bottom of the screen, under Save File As Type, you move the mouse up until you locate Text Only and save it in that format. That can be called ASCII, plain text, DOS Text (on an IBM with Word Perfect 5.1), and other names on other word processors.

Now, go to the Teaching Assistant subdirectory, which needs to have the following file copied into it:

TA.EXE for IBM
TA for Mac

When you have your file placed in the subdirectory, with TA.EXE (IBM) or TA (Mac) then type:

TA Lung2

Plain Lung is our original to use to check your work in case you made a mistake. Lung2 is your version of the program. Work on it until all the screen run Lung2 just like Lung runs.

You are ready to make a small program of your own material now.

Why don't you start keeping track to see if your students perform better when they have the tutoring supplement? Compare them with previous classes that did not use it. Nothing gives an instructor a morale boost like knowing you have improved your instruction and that your students are performing better than before your innovation.

ATTENTION DEFICIT DISORDER SUGGESTIONS

HEALTH SERVICES FOR EDUCATION

The following goals are taken from the report *Health/Education Connection* published in March 1990, indicating the recommendations of the American Association of Colleges of Teacher Education and the American Academy of Pediatrics.

Those most in need of health services are

- children with disabilities and handicapping conditions
- children with chronic illnesses or conditions
- children with health-related educational problems
- children with health-related behavioral problems
- children at risk of developing the foregoing problems

With regard to children with disabilities and handicapping conditions, Dr. Leo Schmidt, Chairman of the Department of Special Education at Cal State Fullerton, indicates that typical health services include the following:

- attention deficit disorder, which requires the help of a pediatric neurologist
- high-risk infants where the need is for proper parental training
- physical and occupational therapy
- communicative disorders, which require the help of a speech and language therapist

In general, the entire set of problems requires means for diagnosing the specific needs in each area, a formidable but doable task that would take time and long-term commitment. This would lead to confirmation or disconfirmation by a health specialist and then, as needed, treatment for the child and training for teachers and parents. Let's take the area most discussed in schools today and break down the sequence.

Attention Deficit Disorder, or ADD as it is called commonly, is a hot item in the schools. There are many approaches and many experts. One of the most complex models is that of Dr. Mel Levine of the Medical School at the University of North Carolina. His first book is titled *Keeping a Head in School,* published by Educators Publishing Service, Inc., Cambridge, Massachusetts, 1990. He focuses upon trouble concentrating, lack of interest in details, handing in schoolwork that is confusing to the teacher, being impulsive, trouble waking up and going to sleep, trouble controlling desires for what one wants, trouble controlling moods, and hyperactivity.

The University of California at Irvine Child Development Center uses a model that focuses upon these types of deficits, as well as disruptive behaviors. Dr. Nancy Colocino, Director of Guidance Services for Irvine Unified School District, is involved in training teachers and parents to use the UCI model. The steps in her approach are as follows:

(*1*) Teachers refer ADD suspected children using a district form.

(*2*) Parents are contacted, and a meeting is held to discuss the possibility that their child may be an ADD student. Great care is taken to see that the child is not identified as qualified for special education at this point. The costs are very high for special education services.

(*3*) The parents are given a checklist of attitudes and behaviors to look for to see if they are seeing some of the characteristics of the ADD child.

(*4*) They send the list back to the principal, and he or she gives the name of the child to the head of the student study team. This team consists of the student, a parent, teachers, an administrator, and district support personnel as needed. If there is a confirmation of the ADD possibility, the family is given the names of pediatricians who might help them if they don't already know one.

(*5*) The pediatrician may prescribe medication, and, if so, there needs to be followthrough in terms of the amount of medication. Sometimes the medication is changed, requiring further followthrough.

(*6*) The pediatrician may suggest no medication but, rather, a behavior management program. This can be carried out by a psychologist working in concert with the parents.

(*7*) It is also possible for the pediatrician to train a professor, who, in turn, trains mentor teachers to work with small groups of ADD children at school. They are basically working on teaching the children to manage their deficits and to reduce their distractibility.

Throughout this sequence, there are several places where the development of videos would be appropriate. The first is when the parents first learn that they may have an ADD child, and they need to be given guidance to move through the many steps and possibilities ahead. The second video might be developed around utilization of the medication and the many problems that can develop if the dosage is wrong or if the medication needs to be changed. The third video could be on the behavior management program with very specific suggestions for the parents. They need to learn how to reduce the many distractions they can control and, most of all, how to increase their patience in dealing with their ADD child. The fourth video might be directed to the mentor teachers who would need to work with teachers and small groups of ADD children in school.

USING EASYSTAT SOFTWARE AND THE TEACHING ASSISTANT: STATISTICS SOFTWARE AND MANUAL

EasyStat Software is designed to be used by individuals who are just beginning to use statistics or those who cannot remember much from previous exposure to statistics. The focus of the software and the *Teaching Assistant: Statistics Software and Manual* is not on learning formulas but, rather, on learning to identify nominal, ordinal, and interval variables and then use the variable types in a given project to select the right statistic. The software is especially useful for professional people who do not require an expensive statistics program that offers graphing and the capability to manipulate large numbers of subjects of 1,000 or more. It does, however, prepare the user to make use of expensive programs such as StatView for the Macintosh and the Statistical Package for the Social Sciences (SPSS) for IBM and Mac users.

Below you will find the documentation for using EasyStat. You can see at once how uncomplicated it is to use the standard statistics used in many studies in education and the social sciences. Following the EasyStat Documentation, we have included the Introduction to the *Teaching Assistant: Statistics Manual* to give you an idea of its level of difficulty and our notion of how it can be used.

Prices

EasyStat Software and Documentation	$25.00
Teaching Assistant: Statistics Software and Documentation	25.00
Teaching Assistant: Statistics Manual	10.00

Order from Students-at-Risk, Inc., 1260 Brangwyn Way, Laguna Beach, CA 92651.

EASYSTAT DOCUMENTATION FOR MACINTOSH

Program Design: William Callison; Programming: Jim Davis

1. To boot up EasyStat, put the disk in the Floppy Disk Drive, and it will appear as a little disk (icon) on the top right corner of your screen. Then double-click on the EasyStat Disk, and the EasyStat application program can be seen in the list. Double-click on it, and Screen 1 becomes the Main Menu. Click on Open, and Select the Database comes up. Double-click on Student Data Base. A menu with five boxes (fields) comes up. Number 1 is student names; 2−4 are reading test scores; and 5 is Gender where 1 = male and 2 = female.

2. To start, go to the Menu at the top, click on Window and, with the mouse button held down, move down to the EasyStat Main Menu. Click on Calculate, and you will go to the Analysis screen. Click on Statistics. Then Click on Test A and then double-click on Calculate.

3. The mean is the arithmetic average and is used when you have a normal distribution of students in the group. The median is the middle score and is used when you have a lot of high or low scores that weigh the distribution toward one end or the other. The Mode is the most common score and is used when you have two clusters of scores or a bimodal distribution.

4. The Standard Deviation (SD) is used to indicate how a group of students is spread out from the mean. There are three deviations above and three below the mean. If the students are all clustered in the middle, for example, the SD will be smaller than for another group where they are not clustered. This is handy when a teacher is trying to figure out how to give a test that will have a normal or spread out distribution.

5. Min and Max are the minimum and maximum scores, and one subtracts the low from the high to get the Range, a good tool for finding out if the student scores are clustered or spread out.

6. The Variance refers to the variance of scores around the mean. One finds the difference between each score and the mean, squares them, and divides by the number of cases.

7. The Total is the number of cases, usually referred to as the N.

8. In finding the SD, one Sums the deviations (X) times the Sum of the Squares of the deviations, divides by the number of students, and takes the square root to find the SD.

9. Now let's do a comparison of the means of Tests A, B, and C, a practical comparison to see if, for example, the students in the class showed improvement from the pretest (Test A) to the midyear post-test B and the post-test (Test C).

Step 1: Screen 1, which opens with a mean of 16.3 and a Standard Deviation of 2.04. Copy them on a sheet of paper so you can compare them with comparable data from Tests B and C.

Step 2: Now click on Continue and then click on Statistics. Go through the same steps for Test B. The mean is 17.36 (higher) and a Standard Deviation of 2.55. This means the students are more spread out than for Test A.

Repeat the procedure for Test C where the mean is 18.32 and the SD is 2.82. The mean is even higher than for Test B and the SD even more spread out.

This is probably the most common form of analysis, and teachers can understand how to use it. However, they may want to know if the boys did better than the girls, which they usually do in arithmetic, and these are arithmetic scores. To do this, we need to learn how to do Chi Square.

10. Arrow down to Chi-2 and press Enter. The word at the top of the screen is Category now.

Arrow down to Sex and press Enter. Note the word at the top of the little screen has changed to Observed now.

We will arrow down to Test A (the females) and press Enter. Now the word is Expected. (In Chi-2 analysis, we are trying to find out if one group, typically the Observed group or the experimental group, has outperformed the Expected or control group.)

Arrow down to Test B (the males) and press Enter. Zip we go through the comparison and get a Chi-2 result of 16.10. This difference is not great enough to be significant statistically. For it to be significant at the $p = .05$ level, the Chi-2 would have to be 36.4 as we see by looking at the Distribution of Chi-2 Table. There is an N of 25 and df (degrees of freedom), is $N - 1 = 24$. Moving across to .05, we see the minimum Chi-2 needed is 36.415.

11. Now we will carry out a "*t*" test. The *t* test is the most common statistic used in education by practitioners. Since you are very likely to want to really use this statistic, and use real data, you need to learn how to enter your own data (or for the moment, fake data).

12. Entering data: from the Analysis Screen Quit and go to the Main Menu. Click on New and name your file to be created Test 1. Click on Save and the Modify Structure Screen comes up. You are going to create a data base with fake data.

Type Name (for student name) in the box with the cursor at the left. Leave Character in the box under Type. Press Return, and you are in a new box on the left.

Type Test 1 and then hold down the mouse over Character and release it on Numeric. Press Return three times and go through the same steps to create Test 2.

Now let's practice deleting a field. Put the cursor at the left side of the Test 1 box and drag across until the box turns dark; then release the mouse button. Now click on the Delete button on the right side of the screen, and it is removed.

To insert a new field in an existing list, you select the box where you want the new field. In this case, Test 2 is already selected. Click on the Insert button on the right, and a new box says newfld0 (new field 0) comes up. Type Test 1 and make it a numeric field. You are ready now, so click on the OK button on the right. A new screen asks Input data records now? and you click on the Yes button. Type in the names and Test 1 and Test 2 scores for 10 imaginary students.

13. Now we will run a *t* test. Open your Test 1 file and when it comes up go to the Window Menu and release on EasyStat Main Menu.

Click on Calculate. Then click on *t* test and the *t* test Menu comes up. Click on Test 1 under Variable 1 and Test 2 under Variable 2. Then double-click on Calculate.

Now a screen comes up that says *t* test for variables: Test 1 minus Test 2. It will show the difference (in means) for Tests 1 and 2. That number is squared. *N* is the number of cases you have entered. If your *t* result is positive, your Test 2 scores were higher than those for Test 1. If the *t* result is negative, the scores for Test 1 were higher than those for Test 2.

For the *t* test, the *df* (degrees of freedom) is $N - 1$. A degree of freedom is technically the number of cases in a study minus the number of population parameters estimated. In a t test this would be $N - 1$. You need to know the *df* to find out if your *t* test result is statistically significant. To do so, turn to the rear of this documentation to the Tables and look up Distribution of *t* on Table 3.

Now you need to know if you are using a 1-tailed test or a 2-tailed test. If you are predicting in just one direction, where you believe the scores are very likely to go up, for example, you use the 1-tailed test. This might occur where you expect all reading scores to go up, if only because the students are a year more mature than they were a year ago when they last took the test.

Sometimes, however, scores might go up or down, as in attendance. Then you would use the 2-tailed part of Table 3 to find out if your *t* result is significant. It must be HIGHER than the score on the Table to be significant.

14. You can check to see if you were getting improvement, however. Escape back to your Statistics Table of the data you entered for Math.dat and press 15. You can check to see if you were getting improvement, however.

Escape back to your Statistics Table of the data you entered for Math.dat and press F4.

Stats is selected and you press Enter.

Now Math 1 is selected, and you press Enter and see a Mean of 27.0. Press Escape and press F4 again.

Stats is once again selected and you press Enter.

Arrow down to Math 2 and press Enter. The Mean is 31.4, which is definitely higher, just not high enough to be statistically significant.

15. Now let's do Analysis of Variance or ANOVA. Escape back to the opening menu and arrow down to *f*, so named because the result of our ANOVA analysis will be an *f* score or more accurately, the *f*-ratio of two variance estimates. For example, a teacher is interested in knowing whether she would like to use a whole-language approach to teaching reading or, perhaps, whole

language plus phonics. Think of these as Program 1 and Program 2. These are nominal variables, and reading scores are interval variables so we will be at the top right of our Type and Number of Independent Variables table for choosing the correct statistic. More precisely, we will be in the ''more than one'' part of that box since we have two ''experiments'' or programs that we want to compare. This calls for Analysis of Variance as our statistic.

16. Open the *f* file and you will see three groups of interval data. Group 1 is a phonics approach, Group 2 is whole language, and Group 3 is whole language, and phonics combined.

Press F4 and arrow down to Anova.

Press Enter and then press Enter again for 1-way.

We are using three groups, so enter 3 at the top of the page. The result is an *f* ratio of .42. We look at the Appendix for Table F and see that the numerator (top *df*) is 2, and the denominator *df* is 12. Looking at the Table F, we go to the column labeled 2 for the numerator and down the left to 12 for the denominator. Where they intersect, we see that, at the 5% level, the *f* ratio has to be 3.89 or more. Our *f* ratio is only 0.42, so it is not significant at the 5% or $p = .05$ level. What we have discovered, then, is the old, old story. There is no significant difference in using phonics, whole language, or whole language plus phonics in teaching reading, if we are dealing with just one class of less than twenty students whose scores we can use.

17. Now, let's press Escape and go back to the entry menu.

Press Enter and it will Close.

Press Open and arrow down to Student.

Press F4 and arrow down to Anova.

Press Enter for 1-way and indicate we will use three groups at the top of the page. Wow! Those bigger numbers give us an *f* score of 668.64, which is certainly going to be significant. Looking on the Table for *f* with a numerator of 2 and a denominator of 72 (let's use the figure for 120 on the right-hand side) anything above 3.07 is significant. We are off the chart with 668.64 and have groups where there is tremendous difference in the variance.

Press Escape and go back to the Student data page.

Press F4 and then press Enter for Stats. Choose Test A and we have a mean of 16.3.

Press Escape, press F4 and then Enter for Stats and arrow down to Test B where the mean is 17.4.

Press Escape, press F4 and Enter for Stats and go to Test C where the mean is 18.3, all big differences.

18. We can confirm this in yet another way by running a *t* test on the student data. Press Escape and go back to the Statistics Table for Student.

Press F4 and arrow down to *t* test.

Arrow down to Related mean and press Enter.

Arrow down to Tests A, B and C and press Enter after each one and we get a t result of -5.71 with a df of 24. Look on your Table 3, Distribution of t and go down to df for 24.

Go over two columns to .05 for a 2-tailed (scores can go either up or down) test and we get a figure of 2.064. Our -5.71 is significant beyond the .001 level. So we have checked our f result two ways (means and t tests). It was highly significant.

19. The Mann Whitney U test is an alternative to the t test to be used when you do not have a normal sample of students, for example, if you had a small sample of twenty-five students in a writing group and wanted to know if the girls did better than the boys. Instead of interval scores, as in a sample for use in a t test, we have ordinal scores ranging from 12 to 20, the high score. The program ranks the scores and then sorts them by gender. According to the Table for the Mann Whitney U, when $n1$, the smaller group and the males is 12, and $n2$, the larger group and the females is 13, the U is 35. This is not a significant difference. To be significant, as the table note says, the calculated U must be equal to or smaller than the tabled U of 35 to be significant.

20. Next, we will do the Spearman rank correlation coefficient. The Spearman test is a means of finding out whether two groups of scores correlate with each other. That's why its full name is the Spearman Rank Correlation Coefficient. It is the best known of the various tests of correlation. It may be referred to as Rho in some statistics texts because the table you look up Spearman results on is called Rho. The table we use is called Critical Values of the Rank-Order Correlation Coefficient. Ranked scores are ordinal variables and sometimes interval variables are converted to ranks so that a correlation can be computed.

A teacher thinks there is a correlation between writing ability, where she has ordinal scores, and leadership, where she can get several other teachers to rank a group of students to make her study possible. In this case ranking for leadership would also be an ordinal variable.

From the opening menu, press O for open and arrow down to Spearman. Press Enter and then F4.

Arrow down to Spearman.

Arrow down to Writing and press Enter.

Now Arrow down to Leadership and press Enter. Zoom. We have a positive correlation of the ranks of .84. To see if this is significant, we turn to Table 7 Critical Values of the Rank Order Correlation Coefficient. We enter the table with an N or number of students of 7. We should use the Level of Significance for a 2-tailed test since our correlation could have gone either way, high or low. To be significant at the standard .05 level we must have a correlation of higher than .786. We are in luck as our result is .94.

21. Now we move to Correlation of interval scores with interval scores. In this instance we are concerned with Prediction. If we wished to use one set of Reading scores at Grade 3 to predict Writing scores at Grade 4 we would use Correlation or Pearson Product-Moment Correlation to find our answer. To use

Correlation we need scores that are normally distributed and that seem like they will go together as, in this case, reading and writing skills.

At the opening screen, press O for open and arrow down to Correlation. Press Enter and when the data table opens press F4.

Now arrow down to Correlation and press Enter.

From our list of choices, arrow down to Reading and press Enter. Then arrow down to Writing and press Enter. Voila! We have the *r* level of +0.94. Turn to the Table 5 Values of r and enter the table with our *df* (degrees of freedom of $N - 2$ in this case) of 5. We should use the Level of Significance for a 2-tailed test since our correlation could have gone either way, high or low. To be significant at the standard .05 level we must have a correlation of higher than .754. We do in that our computed correlation is .94.

TEACHING ASSISTANT: STATISTICS

A Tutorial Manual to Help Beginning Students Learn to Use Statistics in a Meaningful Way

Introduction

This Manual has been written to guide students through an introduction to statistics. There are two ways to use the Manual. If you want a ''quick start'' in order to find out what statistic to run in order to carry out a study, turn to Chapter 7 right away. Chapters 7 and 8 are designed to help you select the appropriate statistics to run in whatever statistics software you have available. The program we have written to go with this Manual is called EasyStat. EasyStat is a low cost program designed for students who do not have a strong mathematics background, but who often have very significant job responsibilities that are best carried out by using statistical analysis. We have in mind teachers and other school staff who typically need statistics to quickly find out if the content they are teaching is being learned successfully by their students.

Our experience after twenty years of teaching educational administration is that educators often have poor math skills and have been turned off by the statistics courses they have taken in the past. These courses marched them through many complex formulas but when it came time to actually consider doing a study they had no idea how to select a particular statistic to carry out even a simple study. Even if they still had their statistics text and their course notes, they couldn't afford the time to try and look up what the various stat symbols meant so they could try to carry out the analysis of their data. So . . . they didn't do the needed study.

More recently another kind of problem is blocking the use of statistics. An educator may obtain a piece of statistical software or a spread sheet with various statistical functions available. All they have to do is enter their data . . . right? Sure, but when they run a t-test on a classroom math test someone comes out of the woodwork and attacks their results because the number of students (25), when divided in half for an experimental and a control group, is not large enough to be considered a "normal" population. The expert, probably a parent who is an engineer, at a PTA meeting, tells the principal that a Chi-Square should have been used. Since no one ever complained in previous reports to parents when no statistics were used, the principal makes an easy decision. Skip the statistics and just report the raw scores and the opinion of the teacher who taught the new program. She liked it, the kids liked it. Good enough.

But it isn't good enough, because Chapters 7 and 8 of *TA Statistics: A Manual* guide you to the right statistic without learning any formulas. A Chi-Square would show that there is no significant improvement with the new program and, worse, there will be a need for some expensive new materials and in-service training for many teachers in order to adopt the program. Tens of thousands of dollars will have been wasted when, two years later the state reports lower math scores for the schools using the "new" program. It really is more efficient for the principal to use a simple tutorial such as those in Chapters 7 and 8, select the right statistic (even if it takes an hour to choose the stat, enter the data and run the program) and to make an informed judgement about the new program.

What of the rest of the Manual? If you are in a hurry, just turn to the Index and look up the term you need to know. When time allows you can work your way through the Chapters from the beginning. This is, of course, the second way to use the Manual.

However you decide to use the Manual, you will find the correct answers at the end of each chapter. The problems identified are typical of the ones our students face each day in the schools.

Bibliography

Abrams, G. 1992. I love the kids. *Los Angeles Times* (Nov. 22):E1.

Adams, J. R. 1992. Medellin's new generation. *The American Spectator*, 24(12): 22−25.

Aguirre International. 1992. *Comprehensive school-based alcohol, tobacco, and other drug prevention programs: A handbook for implementation.* Report prepared for the U. S. Department of Education, Contract No. LC89049001, San Mateo, CA.

Aiello, Helene and Gatewood, Tom, 1989. The Glasgow mentor model: A program for at-risk middle grades students, in *Mentoring International*, Vol. 3, No. 3, Summer. Available from The International Centre for Mentoring, Suite 510, 1200 West Pender Street, Vancouver, British Columbia, Canada, V6E 2S9.

Alcohol, Health and Research World 1987, 3, (2).

Anchorage Alaska School District. 1991. Attention deficit disorders. CASP. *Today*, pp. 20−23.

Anglin, L. 1985. *Cocaine: A Selection of Annotated Papers from 1880−1984 Concerning Health Effects.* Toronto, Canada: Addiction Research Foundation.

Ashton, Patricia, and Rodman, Webb. 1986. *Making a Difference.* Longman. New York, New York.

Associated Press. 1992. Clara Hale: Worked with babies born to drug addicts. *Los Angeles Times* (Dec. 19):A 34.

Bandura, A. 1977. Self-efficacy: Toward a unifying theory of behavioral change. *Psychological Review*, 84:191−125.

Battjes, R. J. and Jones, C. L. 1985. Implications of etiological research for preventive interventions and future research. In C. L. Jones and R. J. Battjes (Eds.), *Etiology of Drug Abuse: Implications for Prevention*, NIDA Monograph Series 56 (pp. 269−276), Washington, DC: U.S. Government Printing Office.

Baumarind, D. 1985. Familial antecedents of adolescent drug use: A developmental perspective. In C. L. Jones and R. D. Battjes (Eds.), *Etiology of Drug Abuse: Implications for Prevention*, NIDA Monography Series 56, Washington DC: U.S. Government Printing Office.

Baumarind, D. 1991. The influence of parenting style on adolescent competence and substance abuse. *Journal of Early Adolescence*, 11(1).

Benesch, S. 1992. Messrs. clean. *The New Republic*, 207:10–13.

Bennett, William J. 1987. *What Works: Schools without Drugs*, Washington DC: U.S. Department of Education.

Benson, P. 1990. *The Troubled Journey: A Portrait of 6th–12th Grade Youth* A RepecTeen Resource Provided by Lutheran Brotherhood, a Fraternal Benefit Society, Minneapolis, MN.

Bernard, Bonnie, 1991. *Moving Toward a "Just and Vital Culture": Multiculturalism in Our Schools*. Portland, Oregon: Northwestern Regional Educational Laboratory.

Block, J., Block J. H. and Keyes, S. 1988. Longitudinally foretelling drug usage in adolescence: Early childhood personality and environmental precursors. *Child Development*, 59:336–355.

Bosworth, Kris. DIADS Project, Suite 253, Education Building, Bloomington, IN 47405.

Botvin, G. J. 1986. Substance abuse prevention research: Recent developments and future directions. *Journal of School Health*, 56(9):369–374.

Botvin, G. J. and E. M. Botvin. 1992. School based and community-based prevention approaches. In *Comprehensive Textbook of Substance Abuse*. J. Lowinson, P. Ruiz and R. Millman, pp. 910–927. Baltimore: Williams & Wilkins.

Boyd, M. Celeste, 1987. "A Survey of Currently Used Substance Abuse Prevention Materials in Los Angeles and Orange Counties," unpublished paper for the Educational Administration Program, California State University, Fullerton, CA.

Burkle, Frank. 1986. *hm Study Skills Program, Level B*. National Association of Elementary Schools, Alexandria, VA, 22314. This publication is for Grades 3–4; there are materials in print form for all grade levels, and Grades 8–12 have computer-assisted instruction, as well.

Butler, Kenneth, Gilmartin, Eve, and the Mt. Diablo Unified School District, Concord, California. 1986. The forms seen in this chapter were developed in the Mt. Diablo Unified School District.

Butterfield, G. and Turner, B. 1989. Weapons in schools: NSSC resource paper.

Callison, W., Crabtree, D., Ehlers, P., Evans, A., Richards, N., Sakanari, G., and Youngblood, D. 1990. Identifying characteristics of students at risk of substance abuse. Presentation of master's thesis and doctoral research at the meeting of the Partnership Academy Committee Substance Abuse Project, Orange, California.

Chatlos, C. 1987. *Crack: What You Should Know about the Cocaine Epidemic*. New York: Perigee Books.

Conservative norms. *Preventive Medicine*, 20:414–430.

Cowen, E. L., Zax, M., Izzo, L. D. and Trost, M. A. 1966. Prevention of emotional disorders in the school setting. *Journal of Consulting Psychology*, 30:381–387.

Delapenha, L. 1992. New challenges for changing times. *School Safety*, 24:11–13.

Drug abuse and dropouts. 1986. A Report of the Select Committee on Narcotics Abuse and Control, Ninety-Ninth Congress, Second Session, U. S. Government Printing Office.

Dryfoos, J. G. 1990. *Adolescents at Risk: Prevalence and Prevention*. New York: Oxford University Press.

Elliott, D. S., Haizinga, D., and Ageton, S. 1982. *Explaining Delinquency and Drug Use*. Boulder, CO: Behavioral Research Institute, Report 21.

Ezzell, C. 1991. Cocaine may piggy back on sperm into egg. *Science News*, 140:246.

Fackelmann, K. A. 1989. Cocaine mothers imperil babies brains. *Science News*, 135:198.

Fackelmann, K. A. 1991a. Smoking out cocaine's in utero impact. *Science News*, 140:302.

Fackelmann, K. A. 1991b. The maternal cocaine connection. *Science News*, 140:152 – 153.

Fisher, S., A. Raskin, and E. H. Uhlenhuth. 1987. *Cocaine: Clinical and Biobehavioral Aspects*. New York: Oxford University Press.

Friedman, Alfred S. 1985. Does drug and alcohol use lead to failure to graduate from high school? *Journal of Drug Education*, 15(4).

Gamson, William. 1968. *Power and Discontent*. Homewood, Illinois: Dorsey Press.

Gardner, R. A. 1970. *The Boys and Girls Book about Divorce*. New York: Bantam.

Gardner, S. 1992. Key issues in developing school-linked, integrated services. In *The Future of Children*, Vol. 2, No. 1, Behrman, R. (Ed) Los Altos, CA: Center for the Future of Children, the David and Lucille Packard Foundation, pp. 85 – 94.

Garfield, Emily F. 1981. *The Stanford D-E-C-I-D-E Drug Education Curricula*. Palo Alto, California: Project Pegasus.

Gaustad, J. 1991. Schools respond to guns and violence. *Oregon Study Council Bulletin*, 34(9).

Goodlad, J. 1983. *A Place Called School*. New York: McGraw-Hill.

Goodstadt, M. S. and Mitchell, E. 1990. Prevention theory and research related to high risk youth. In E. Goplerud (Ed.), *Breaking New Ground for Youth at Risk: Program Summaries*, pp. 7 – 23 (DHHS publication No. ADM 89 – 1658), Washington, DC: U. S. Government Printing Office.

Goplerud, Eric N. 1990. *Breaking New Ground for Youth at Risk: Program Summaries*, Office for Substance Abuse Prevention, Washingtron, DC: U.S. Government Printing Office.

Gottfredson, D. Gottfredson, G. and Hybl, L. 1990. Managing adolescent behavior: A multi-year multi-school experiment, report no. 50. Johns Hopkins University, Center for Research on Elementary and Middle Schools.

Gray, Kenneth. 1991. Vocational education in high school: A modern phoenix? *Phi Delta Kappan* (February).

Griffith, D. R. 1992. Prenatal exposure to cocaine and other drugs: Developmental and educational prognoses. *Phi Delta Kappan*, 74:30 – 34.

Guidelines for School Based Alcohol and Drug Abuse Prevention Programs. 1982. *Research in Education* (March).

Guild, P. and McKinney, L. n.d. *Using Learning Styles to Help Students Be Successful: A Synthesis of a Study of the Learning Styles of Low Achievers in Seattle Public Schools, 1989 – 1990*. Seattle: Pat Guild Associates.

Haberman, Martin. 1991. The pedagogy of good teaching. *Phi Delta Kappan* (December):290 – 294.

Harrell, A. V. 1985. Validation of self-report: The research record. In B.A. Rouse, N. J. Kozel, and L. G. Richards (Eds.), *Self-report Methods of Estimating Drug Use: Meeting Current Challenges to Validity*, NIDA Manuscript Series 57, pp. 12 – 21, Washington, DC: U.S. Government Printing Office.

Hawkins, J. D. and Catalano, R. F. 1989. Risk and protective factors for alcohol and other drug problems in adolescence and early adulthood: Implications for substance abuse prevention. Revised paper presented October 1986 at the *Symposium on the*

Prevention of Alcohol and Other Drug Problems, Center of Alcohol Studies, Rutgers University, NJ.

Hawkins, J. D., Lishner, D. M., and Catalano, R. F. 1985. Childhood predictors and the prevention of adolescent substance abuse. In C. L. Jones and R. D. Battjes (Eds.), *Etiology of Drug Abuse: Implications for Prevention*, NIDA Monograph Series 56, pp. 117–131, Washington, DC: U.S. Government Printing Office.

Hawkins, J. D. et al. 1985. Childhood predictors and the prevention of adolescent substance abuse. In C. L. Jones and R. J. Battjes (Eds.), *Etiology of Drug Abuse: Implications for Prevention*, NIDA Research Monograph 56, DHHS Pub. No. (DAM) 85–1335, Washington, DC, U.S. Government Printing Office, pp. 75–126.

Hirschi, T. 1969. *Causes of Delinquency*. Berkeley: U of C Press.

Hyland, Timothy F. and J. Robert Schrenker, 1982. The evolution of a community drug abuse program. *Research in Education* (February).

Implications for substance abuse prevention. *Psychological Bulletin*, 112(1):64–105.

IOX Assessment Associates, 1988. *Program Evaluation Handbook: Drug Abuse Education*. Los Angeles, CA.

Irvine Unified School District. 1987a. *GOAL* (Guidance Opportunities for Affective Learning) Program; *STAR* (Social Thinking And Reasoning) Program; *PLUS* (Promoting Learning and Understanding Self) Program; and *STAGES: Skills to Manage Stressful Changes* Program, Irvine, CA: Irvine Unified School District.

Irvine Unified School District, 1987b. STAR (Social Thinking And Reasoning) Program and *STAGES: Skills to Manage Stressful Changes* Program, Irvine, CA: Irvine Unified School District.

Irvine Unified School District. 1990. *The Guidance Assistants' Survival Manual* (elementary and secondary). Irvine, CA: Irvine Unified School District.

Jessor, R. J. and Jessor, S. L. 1977. *Problem Behavior and Psychological Development: A Longitudinal Study of Youth*. New York: Academic Press.

Johnson, L. L. 1992. Crack in the family. *Essence*, 23(4):38.

Johnson, L. D., O'Malley, P. M. and Bachman, J. G. 1987. *National Trends in Drug Use and Related Factors among American High School Students and Young Adults*, National Institute of Drug Abuse, Rockville, Maryland.

Johnson, L. D., O'Malley, P. M. and Bachman, J. G. 1989. *Drug Use, Drinking, and Smoking: National Survey Results from High School, College, and Young Adult Populations 1975–1988* (DHHS Publication No. ADM 89-1638). Washington, DC. U.S. Government Printing Office.

Jones, C. L. and Battjes, R. J. 1985. The context and caveats of prevention research on drug abuse. *Etiology of Drug Abuse: Implications for Prevention*. NIDA Monograph Series 56 (1-12). Washington, DC: U. S. Government Printing Office.

Jones, R. et al. 1990. Teacher characteristics and competencies related to substance abuse prevention. *Journal of Drug Education*, 20(3):179–189.

Kandel, D. B. 1978. *Longitudinal Research on Drug Use: Empirical Findings and Methodological Issues*, New York: Wiley and Sons.

Kandel, D. B. 1992. Epidemiological and psychosocial perspectives on adolescent drug use. *Journal of American Academic Clinical Psychiatry*, 21(4):328–345.

Kaplan, H. B., Martin S. S., and Robins, C. 1982. Applications of a general theory of deviant behavior: Self-degradation and adolescent drug use. *Journal of Health and Social Behavior*, 23(4):274–294.

Kappel, Jerold. 2003 Upper Lake Drive., VA 22091, (703) 620-2760. As cited in Substance Abuse Funding News, October 15, 1993. CD Publications, Silver Springs, MD.

Kasarda, J. D. 1989. Drugs and the dream deferred. *New Perspective Quarterly*, 6:16−20.

Kiersey, D. and Bates, M. 1978. *Please Understand Me: An Essay on Temperament Styles*. Del Mar, California: Promethean Books, Inc.

Kovach, J. A. and Glickman, N. W. 1986. Levels and psychosocial correlates of adolescent drug use. *Journal of Youth and Adolescence*, 15(1):61−77. LaCroix, S. 1989. Jailing mothers for drug abuse. *The Nation*, 248(17):585−588.

Linquanti, R. 1992. *Using Community-wide Collaboration to Foster Resiliency in Kids: A Conceptual Framework*. Western Regional Center for Drug-Free Schools and Communities, Northwest Regional Educational Laboratory, Portland, Oregon.

Lofquist, W. 1989. The spectrum of attitudes: Building a theory of youth development. In *New Designs for Youth Development*, 9(4):3−6.

Lorion, R. 1990. Substance Use by School Age Children. Figure demonstrating compilation of use levels, Department of Psychology, University of Maryland. College Park, Maryland.

Los Angeles County Office of Education. 1993. *Perinatal Substance-Exposed Children: The Schools Respond*. Downey, CA: Los Angeles County Office of Education, Classroom Interventions and Family Issues.

Malibu, CA: Pepperdine University, National School Safety Center.

Mansfield, W., and E. Farris, 1992. Public school principal survey on safe, disciplined, and drug-free schools, U.S. Department of Education, 45 pp.

Marcus, Sheila. 1990. Project nods. Papers presented at *Fourth Annual Drug Free Schools and Community Conference*, Falls Church, Virginia, June 17−22.

Maspero, B. J. 1989. *Differences in the characteristics of dropouts and graduates of a continuation high school*. Unpublished doctoral dissertation, United States International University, San Diego, California.

McCaslin, M. and Good, T. 1992. Compliant cognition: The misalliance of management and instructional goals in current school reform. *Educational Researcher*, 21(3):4−17.

McPartland, J. and Slavin, Robert E. 1990. *Policy Perspectives: Increasing Achievement of At-Risk Students at Each Grade Level*, Superintendent of Documents, Washington, DC: U.S. Government Printing Office.

Moles, O. 1990. *Student Discipline Strategies: Research and Practice*. Albany, NY.

Moskowitz, J. M. 1989. The primary prevention of alcohol problems: A critical review of the research literature. *Journal of Studies on Alcohol*, 50(1):54−88.

Multi-year multi-school experiment, Report No. 50. Baltimore: Johns Hopkins University.

National Institute on Drug Abuse. 1987. *National Household Survey on Drug Abuse: Population Estimates 1988* (DHHS Publication No. ADM 89−1636). Washington, DC. U.S. Government Printing Office.

Neighborhoods in Action. 1990. *Mobilizing Your Community to Raise Drug-Free Kids*. Los Angeles, California: Scott Newman Center.

Newcomb, M. D., Maddahian, E., and Bentler, P. M. 1986. Risk factors for drug use among adolescents: Concurrent and longitudinal analyses. *American Journal of Public Health*, 76:525−531.

Nobles, Wade. 1984. Alienation, human transformation and adolescent drug use: toward a real conceptualization of the problem. *Journal of Drug Issues* (Spring):243 – 253.

Novak, J. and B. Dougherty. 1980. *Staying In . . . A Dropout Prevention Handbook K – 12*, Madison, WI: University of Wisconsin.

Novak, J. and Hammerstrom, W. 1976. *Desk Reference: Facilitating Career Counseling and Placement*, Wisconsin Vocational Studies Center, Madison, Wisconsin: University of Wisconsin.

Oakes, J. 1992. Can tracking research inform practice? Technical, normative, and political considerations. *Educational Researcher*, 21:12 – 21.

Oetting, E. R. and Beauvals, F. 1987. Common Elements in Youth Drug Abuse: Peer Clusters and Other Psychosocial Factors. *Journal of Drug Issues*, 22, (2), 133 – 151.

Office for Substance Abuse Prevention (OSAP). 1989. OSAP Prevention Monograph-1;

Office of Substance Abuse Prevention (OSAP). 1991. *The Future by Design*. Department of Health and Human Services, No. (ADM)91-1760. Rockville, Maryland.

Office of Substance Abuse Prevention. 1991. *Prevention Plus III*. U.S. Department of Health and Human Services No. (ADM)91-1817, Washington, DC.

Orandi, Mario, Weston, Raymond, and Epstein, Leonard (Eds.). 1992. *Cultural Competence for Evaluators: A Guide for Alcohol and Other Drug Abuse Prevention Practitioners Working with Ethnic/Racial Communities*. U.S. Department of Health and Human Services, OSAP, No. (ADM)92-1884, Rockville, Maryland.

Parker, J. G. and Asher, S. R. 1987. Peer relations and later personal adjustment: Are low-accepted children at risk? *Psychological Bulletin*, 102 (3), 357 – 398.

Patterson, G. R., B. D. DeBaryshe, and E. Ramsey. 1989. A Developmental Perspective on Antisocial Behavior, *American Psychologist*, 44, (2), 329 – 335.

Pentz, M. A. 1986. Community Organization and School Liaisons: How to Get Programs Started, *Journal of School Health*, 56, (9), 382 – 388.

Peterson, R. 1992. *A Taxonomy of Common Teaching Methods, 2nd Revised Edition*. Laguna Beach, CA: Pelican Press of Laguna.

Pittman, K. 1992. *Promoting Youth Development: Strengthening the Role of Youth Serving and Community Organizations*. From ''Partners in People Conference: A Day to Build Coalitions for Children and Youth. Berkeley, CA: January.

Political considerations. *Educational Researcher*, 21:12 – 21.

Popkin, M. 1983. *Active Parenting Handbook*. Marietta, Georgia: Active Parenting Publishers.

Popkin, M. 1990. *Active Parenting of Teens*. Marietta, Georgia: Active Parenting Publishers.

Prevention Programs: An Interim Report to Congress. Forthcoming.

Rachal, J. V., Guess, L. L., Hubbard, R. L., Maisto, S. A., Cavanaugh, E. R., Waddell, R., and Benrud, C. H. 1980. *Adolescent Drinking Behavior, 1*, Sample Studies. Research Triangle Institute, Research Triangle Park.

Rachal, J. V., Guess, L. L., Hubbard, R. L., Maisto, S. A., Cavanaugh, E. R., Waddell, R., and Benrud, C. H. 1982. Alcohol misuse by adolescents. *Alcohol health and research world* (spring).

Radius, Marcie and Lesniak, Pat. 1986. *Student Study Teams: A Resource Manual for Trainers*. Sacramento, CA: California State Department of Education, Special Education Division and the Special Education Resource Network.

Reeves, Sandra. 1988. Self interest and the common weal: Focusing on the bottom half. *Education Week* (April 27):14—21.

Report of the Superintendent's Middle Grade Task Force. 1987. *Caught in the Middle, Educational Reform for Young Adolescents in California Public Schools*, Sacramento, California: California State Department of Education.

Researcher, 21[3]:4—17.

Revkin, A. C. 1989. Crack in the cradle. *Discover*, 10:62—69.

Richards, N. and Smith, M. J. 1985. The long term effects of social skills training in elevating overall academic grade point average, school attendance, health level, and resistance to drug use and peer pressure. Paper presented at the *Annual Convention of the American Psychological Association*, Los Angeles.

Richards-Colocino, N. 1990. Risk Assessment Survey. Assessment Instrument used for dissertation, United States International University, San Diego, California.

Richards-Colocino, N. 1991. School-based assessment of students at risk for drug abuse. Dissertation, United States International University, San Diego, California.

Rist, M. C. 1990. The shadow children. *The American School Board Journal*, 177(1): 19—24.

Robins, L. N. 1980. The natural history of drug use. Evaluation of treatment of drug abusers, *ACTA Psychiat. Scand.*, 62(284).

Robinson, T. N., Killen, J. D., Taylor, C. B., Telch, M. J., Bryson, S. W., Saylor, K. E., Maron, D. J., Maccoby, N., and Farquhar, J. W. 1987. Perspectives on adolescent substance abuse: A defined population study. *Journal of American Medical Association*, 258(15):2072—2076.

Rosemond, J. 1989. Is your child hyperactive? *Better Homes and Gardens*, 22:38.

Rosenbaum, James E. 1992. Apprenticeship learning: Principles for connecting schools and workplace, in *Youth Apprenticeships in America: Guidelines for Building an Effective System*, Washington, DC: W. T. Grant Foundation.

Rubin, R. A. and Balow, B. 1978. Prevalence of teacher-identified behavior problems. *Exceptional Children*, 45:102—111.

Sachs, A. 1989. Here come the pregnancy police. *Time*, 133:104—105.

Sappington, Jack P. 1979. *The Predictive Strength of Nine School Related Indicators for Distinguishing Potential Dropouts*, San Diego, California: United States International University.

Schaps, E., et al. 1978. *Primary Prevention Evaluation Research: A Review of 127 Program Evaluations*, Walnut Creek, CA: Pacific Institute for Research and Evaluation.

Schmoke, K. 1989. A war for the surgeon general, not the attorney general. *New Perspective Quarterly*, 6:12—15.

School and community. *Prevention Forum*, 12(3):2—16.

Schulte, Janet L. 1985. Resource guide to 15 available drug and alcohol prevention education curricula. Oregon Traffic Safety Commission, State Library Building, Salem, OR 97310-0290, June.

Shaffer, J. J. and Jones, S. B. 1989. *Quitting Cocaine*. Lexington, MA: Lexington Books.

Simcha-Fagan, O., Gersten, J. C., and Langner, T. S. 1986. Early precursors and concurrent correlates of patterns of illicit drug use in adolescence. *Journal of Drug Issues*, 16(1):7—28.

Bibliography

Simpson, Bert K. 1987. Peer Assistance Leadership Program, Orange County Department of Education, 200 Kalmus Drive, Costa Mesa, CA.

Skager, R. 1990. What to consider when selecting or designing instruments for assessing adolescent substance use. Paper presented at *Fourth Annual Drug Free Schools and Community Conference*, Falls Church, Virginia, June 17–22.

Skager, R. and Frith, S. L. 1989. Identifying high risk substance users in grades 9 and 11: A report based on the 1987/88 California substance use survey. Report to the Attorney General John K. Van De Kamp, Sacramento, California.

Skager, R., Frith, S. L. and Maddahian, E. 1989. Biennial survey of drug and alcohol use among California students in grades 7, 9, and 11: Winter 1987–88. Report to the Attorney General John K. Van De Kamp, Sacramento, California.

Smith, M. J. 1975. *When I Say No, I Feel Guilty*. New York: Bantam.

Smith, M. J. 1986. *Yes, I Can Say No*. New York: Arbor House.

Spitz, H. I. and Rosecan, J. S. 1987. *Cocaine Abuse New Directions in Treatment Research*. New York: Brunner/Masel Publishers.

Spivack, G. 1983. *High Risk Early Behaviors Indicating Vulnerability to Delinquency in the Community and School*, Washington, DC: National Institute of Juvenile Justice and Delinquency Prevention, Law Enforcement Assistance Administration.

Staff, 1983. *A Study of Children's Attitudes and Perceptions about Drugs and Alcohol*. Middeltown, Connecticut: Weekly Reader Publications.

Stasz, Cathleen, McArthur, David, Lewis, Mathew, and Ramsey, Kimberly. 1990. Teaching and learning generic skills for the workplace. R-4004-NCRVE/UCB. University of California, Berkeley: National Center for Research in Vocational Education.

Substance abuse prevention. *Journal of Drug Education*, 20(3):179–189.

Swaim, R. C., Oetting, E. R., Edwards, R. W., and Beauvais, F. 1989. Links from emotional distress to adolescent drug use: A path model. *Journal of Consulting and Clinical Psychology*, 57(2):227–231.

Towers, Richard L. 1987. *Student Drug and Alcohol Abuse*. Washington, DC: National Education Association.

U.S. Department of Education. 1991. Cocaine Kindergartners: Preparing for the first wave. Hearing before the committee on the judiciary United States Senate. J-102-16:1–64.

Villarreal, S. F., McKinney, L. and Quackenbush, M. 1991. *Handle with Care: Helping Children Prenatally Exposed to Drugs and Alcohol*. Santa Cruz, CA: ETR Associates.

Waller, M. B. 1993. Helping crack-affected children succeed. *Educational Leadership*, 6:57–60.

Washton, A. M. 1989. *Cocaine Addiction*. New York: W. W. Norton and Company Inc.

Weiss, R. D. and Mirin, S. M. 1987. *Cocaine*. Washington, DC: American Psychiatric Press.

Werner, E. E. and Smith, R. S. 1982. *Vulnerable but Invincible*. New York: McGraw-Hill.

Western Center Drug Free Schools and Communities. 1992. *Confidentiality of Student Records: A Guide for School Districts Establishing Policies and Procedures for Alcohol and Other Drug Use Student Assistance Programs*. Portland, Oregon: Northwest Regional Educational Laboratory.

Williams, T. 1989. Cocaine kids: The underground American dream. *New Perspective Quarterly*, 6:21–25.

Wilson-Brewer, R., Cohen, S., O'Donnell, L., and Goodman, I. 1991. *Violence Prevention for Young Adolescents: A Survey of the State of the Art.* Washington, D.C.: Carnegie Council on Adolescent Development..

Wolin, S. J. and Wolin, S. 1993. *The Resilient Self: How Survivors of Troubled Families Rise above Adversity.* New York: Villard/Random House.

Young, Jeffery. 1987. Proposal for a western regional substance abuse prevention and education center. California State University, Fullerton, CA.

Index